READING THE BIBLE

Intention, Text, Interpretation

Robert D. Lane
Malaspina College
Nanaimo, British Columbia

UNIVERSITY
PRESS OF
AMERICA

Lanham • New York • London

Copyright © **1994** by
University Press of America,® Inc.
4720 Boston Way
Lanham, Maryland 20706

3 Henrietta Street
London WC2E 8LU England

Library of Congress Cataloging-in-Publication Data

Lane, Robert D. (Robert Delan).
Reading the Bible : intention, text, interpretation / Robert D. Lane.
p.   cm.
Includes bibliographical references and index.
1. Bible—Reading.   I. Title.
BS617.L24   1993   220.6'1—dc20   93–15271 CIP

ISBN 0–8191–9114–0 (pbk. : alk. paper)

This book is dedicated to all of my grandchildren - with love.

Robert D. Lane

3/94

ACKNOWLEDGEMENTS

First of all I want to thank the Malaspina College Board for providing me with the time necessary to complete this book. Being able to concentrate on one topic for an extended time is extremely beneficial.

Secondly, I want to thank John Marshall, who read the manuscript with care and gave me many useful suggestions. John kept reminding me to find and keep my own voice and not to try for some "academic" style that is not me. Much of what is good about the book is because of John.

Thanks also to Steve Lane and Margaret Lane Riley, who read the manuscript with care and who also made many useful suggestions. And thanks to Karen Lane, who talked about the manuscript with me whenever I felt the need to do so. She too contributed to what is good in the book.

I owe Professor Douwe Stuurman and Professor Hobart Sorensen a great debt - they inspired me when I was their student and taught me to care about texts. My colleague, Dr. Charles VanAntwerp, has argued with me for many hours about religion, philosophy, and Kierkegaard - and I wish to acknowledge the stimulation, inspiration, and exasperation he has provided.

I want to hand the book on to Erik Michael Lane, Alexander DeLan Lane, Nicholas Brandstaetter, Kyle Brandstaetter, and Andrew Lane Marshall, all of whom will, I hope, soon be readers of the Bible stories.

TABLE OF CONTENTS

FOREWORD

The Bible. It has for centuries loomed very large indeed in our society, our culture. So, you have no doubt thought about it, wondered about it from time to time. If you were brought up in a tradition that celebrates the Bible, you may, out of curiosity, have tried occasionally to read it, and each time found it to be a strange, exotic, and baffling work. Impenetrable. Opaque.

As indeed it is for those who encounter it without some preparation. The Bible was written centuries ago, in an ancient culture, with a world view radically different from our own. As a result, there are things you need to be aware of before you can penetrate the veil of time that is draped over it.

In addition, most of us find it difficult to approach the Bible dispassionately, without prejudice. We read it through a haze of culturally induced preconceptions (whether positive or negative). The mist that clouds the Bible has been, for both believers and non-believers, a serious obstacle to their reading the text with clear understanding and appreciation of its contents. When we approach it with open minds, with awareness of its historical and cultural context, it emerges as a work with remarkable properties.

It is helpful to have a guide to enable you to find your way to the rich rewards the book can make available to you. Robert Lane, the author of this book you are now holding, is an eminently qualified and gifted guide.

First of all, he has a deep affection for and long acquaintance with the stories of the Bible: he has for many years taught courses (among many others) in the Bible as a literary work, one that he himself found richly provocative to reflect upon, has found to be stimulating in his thinking about the problems and possibilities of human existence.

Second, the author approaches the Bible free of any dogmatic assumptions. He is not a believer in the Bible, but rather a lover of its riches. Third, he has a profound knowledge of the cultural context out of which the Old and New Testaments emerged. fourth, he is a trained, practiced, and sensitive literary critic, since he taught English and American literature for many years.

Fifth, he has studied and taught philosophy, including logic, for years, and this is reflected in the quality of his thinking. It is at once precise, disciplined, and sensitive. It repeatedly reflects strength in logical thought, in philosophical insight, as well as a high level of literary sensibility.

Lane is a unique combination of philosopher, artist, scholar, and literary critic, moved by passion as well as by precision of thought. Even all this, however, does not give a full inventory of his talents. He also taught mathematics to pilots in the US Marine Corps. He is competent at repairing automobiles, at building houses, and is entirely at home in the new world of computers. He is without doubt a fully alive and creative human being.

What you have here, in this book, is an author, a guide with an extraordinary range of gifts who will open your eyes to the meaning and beauty caught up in the stories of the Bible, will enable you to use them as an endless source of reflection and insight, not only into the human adventure but also into yourself, your own person, set down in the context of this larger adventure.

Consider, as an example, the provocative distinction Lane makes between *official line* and *story line,* that is, between the accepted world view of the writers of the Bible, the set of generally accepted assumptions from which they worked, and, on the other hand, the lasting contents of the stories themselves, their literary and philosophical merits.

This pair of ideas (among a great many others in the book) is likely to open up congenial pathways for you in the thicket of biblical narrative, and traveling along these paths will undoubtedly enrich your awareness of the world and yourself set down in it.

Lex Crane
Santa Barbara, California
January, 1993

PREFACE

In the following pages you will find a few facts and much interpretation. I do not apologize for that, for it is impossible to read the bible without interpreting - after all, a reader has to stand somewhere in order to see the text. Mine is a secular approach, for I am not driven by religious belief of any particular kind, although I do share with the religious the awe of creation and the occasional fear of the unknown.

I have used the King James translation of the bible for all of the long quotations that are needed for a reasonable discussion of the stories, and I have used the New English Bible for several of the shorter quotations. I do this in part to give the reader a flavour for the different translations and in part because of copyright limitations. I use the New English Bible in my classes because of its superb footnotes, introductory essays, and other scholarly material. Whichever translation the reader is using the main thing to remember is that the stories in the bible are important and exciting while much of the commentary and criticism (including, of course, my own) is secondary.

My students have found reading the bible is enriched by a companion who can point to various aspects of the text and bring to life the characters and stories presented therein. They say that the essays contained here have helped them to understand the stories and to appreciate them more deeply. Many other useful materials are to be found in the library, public or institutional. PBS has produced a fine introductory series called *Testament* and a show on the Dead Sea Scrolls which is a "must see". The magazine *Biblical Archaeology Review* is a beautiful, helpful, and well-balanced periodical with fascinating reviews, stories and pictures that help to bring to life the Near Middle East and the biblical texts. It is scholarly and general, and a joy to read. The current issue (January/February 1993) has complete information on some two dozen digs that are looking for volunteers. Its publisher also produces some interesting and useful slide sets and video tapes.

Those of you with a computer, a modem and access to the Internet will want to investigate the Ioudaios (Greek for "Jew") forum to find some 550 scholars actively discussing first century life, Judaism and Christianity. To find out more or to subscribe send an e-mail message to "listserv@vm1.yorku.ca" with the single line (no subject) "info ioudaios". The forum provides lively discussion (over one recent two day period I received 24 messages), book reviews, articles, course outlines for religious studies courses, and many other services.

For teachers who will be using this book for classes in religious studies, civilization, humanities, or Bible as literature courses, additional information for assignments, class projects, papers, examinations, and the like can be obtained by sending me an e-mail message at "laneb@mala.bc.ca" with your specific request. I will send you material if possible to deal with your specific requests.

As for reading what follows: just dive right in ... and enjoy.

Bob Lane
Nanaimo, B. C.
January, 1993

CHAPTER 1: INTRODUCTION

First the inevitable question: Why another book on the bible? Answer: (1) teaching a class in which I use the Bible as a text has taught me that many liberal arts students have no familiarity with the book, and have difficulty approaching the Bible for a number of reasons. Most have never read it, yet some find it irrelevant, and some find it too "sacred" ever to read it. This book is intended as a secular Midrash and students' companion to the Bible. I treat the Bible as comprised of stories, human stories, to be approached with curiosity, not religious awe. I treat the texts of the Bible with the respect due to any great literature. I try to show that the Bible is not irrelevant, but has an importance to the contemporary consciousness. (2) Many colleagues in the liberal arts report a lack of Biblical knowledge on the part of their students. This lack of familiarity with the stories of the Bible makes it difficult to understand and respond to many of the literary texts of our culture which often assume a familiarity with the basic stories of the Bible. (3) I love these stories, and I love writing and thinking about them. (4) I am on sabbatical leave and I have to do something.

I employ no particular literary theory. I deconstruct when doing so helps to understand what the story means. I mention literary forms when that is useful, and I point to features of the texts that may have been overlooked. I have certain beliefs which will manifest themselves in the readings I offer. I do not pretend to be a Bible scholar; I too, like most readers, know the work in translation. If this approach is eclectic I offer no apology. The critic's task is always to point - to point to aspects of the work that may have been overlooked or under-emphasized. I want to de-mystify the texts and make them accessible to readers as important literary texts. My general notion of literature includes these claims: literature is about the world, interpretation is a creative act, intention is a necessary condition for writing of any kind, there are four focal points for any work of literature: poet, text, world, and reader. In what follows, if I emphasize one of these over the others it will be text. The biblical text is complex and sophisticated narrative exhibiting many layers of intention in its final form. In the second book of Samuel, for example, we read the exciting love story of David and Bathsheba, and learn how David, driven by desire for the beautiful Bathsheba, brings her to his bed and makes her pregnant while her husband Uriah is in David's army fighting the enemies of Israel. David eliminates Uriah by sending a letter (carried by Uriah) to the commander telling him to place Uriah in the fiercest fighting and then to fall back leaving him alone to be killed. After Uriah is killed Bathsheba mourns for him for the appropriate time and then David brings her into his house and takes her as his wife. (2 Sam. 11,12)

Shortly after this we are told that "what David had done was wrong in the eyes of the Lord." And then, as we read in the King James version:

> And the Lord sent Nathan unto David. And he came unto him, and said unto him, There were two men in one city; the one rich and the other poor.
> 2. The rich man had exceeding many flocks and herds:
> 3. But the poor man had nothing, save one little ewe lamb, which he had bought and nourished up; and it grew up together with him, and with his children; it did eat of his own meat, and drank of his own cup, and lay in his bosom, and was unto him as a daughter.
> 4. And there came a traveller unto the rich man, and he spared to take of his own flock and his own herd, to dress for the wayfaring man that was come unto him; but took the poor man's lamb, and dressed it for the man that was come to him.
> 5. And David's anger was greatly kindled against the man; and he said to Nathan, As the Lord liveth, the man that hath done this thing shall surely die:
> 6. And he shall restore the lamb fourfold, because he did this thing, and because he had no pity.
> 7. And Nathan said to David, Thou art the man. Thus saith the Lord God of Israel, I anointed thee king over Israel, and I delivered thee out of the hand of Saul;

8. And I gave thee thy master's house, and thy master's wives unto thy bosom, and gave thee the house of Israel and Judah; and if that had been too little, I would moreover have given unto thee such and such things.

David will pay for his lust; the child he conceived will die and the other threats will also come to pass. The punishment will fit the crime: the child conceived in sin will die; the man who could not control his sexual appetites will be punished by having his wives taken in front of everyone. Note the layers of narrative here. Nathan tells David a parable. David is moved by the story. He sentences the fictional man to die. Nathan tells David that he is the man. The story is used to get the king to see himself and to judge his own acts. Just as Uriah carries his own death warrant to Joab in the form of a letter of execution, David comes to issue a death sentence on himself through Nathan's story. When Joab opens the letter carried by Uriah he will see David's intention; when David "opens" the story carried by Nathan he will see the Lord's intention.

Nathan relates a fictional narrative in order to get the king to see the truth about his own situation. Nathan's intention is clear - he uses story to reveal truth. Once he gets David to see that the rich man in the story has done wrong then all he has to do is get him to see that he is like the rich man in the appropriate moral way. Self delusion, though powerful in human affairs, can be broken by story. David has then judged himself. But there is another layer of intentional meaning here also. "The Lord sent Nathan..." adds a layer to the narrative which reveals another story of alleged divine intervention in the understanding of the events. And this story in turn is related by a writer or editor who is shaping the larger story of the books of Samuel for his audience. We get the sense that David would never have admitted guilt for killing Uriah in order to have Bathsheba, but he is able to see and respond to characters in stories. As readers we too are to respond to the stories and to that end have been given narrative access to the larger story pointed to by phrases like "The Lord sent Nathan...."

The Old Testament version of Esther begins:

Now it came to pass in the days of Ahasuerus, (this is the Ahasuerus which reigned, from India even unto Ethiopia, over an hundred and seven and twenty provinces:) (King James, Esther 1)

Not only does this sentence signal that the reader is to accept the story as a report but it also establishes time and place. "The events here related" functions like "and it came to pass" except that "the events here related" stands between a past "lived" event and the report of the event while "and it came to pass" is most often used to suggest an inevitable and divinely ordered string of events manifesting themselves in time. While Nathan used fictional narrative in order to get the king to see the truth, the writer of Esther uses the truth, or at least what we might call "factoids" to establish a fictional narrative. That is, we are given a list of events which are placed in time and space by markers that sound decidedly like those of factual reports or historical documents. The story unfolds quickly: the king is giving one enormous party for the people, to show off his majesty, and after several days of drinking and feasting he decides to order his queen to dress up in something pretty and come forward to display her beauty and at the same time make the king feel even more mighty and splendid. She refuses to come in answer to the royal command, and the king, not used to being disobeyed, is incensed by her disobedience. He confers with his wise men, who are versed in law and religion, and they advise him that in order to keep order and not have women getting "uppity" he must punish the queen by banning her from his sight and replace her with a queen who is more able to conform to the rules of the kingdom. He does ban Queen Vashti, and he begins the search for a new queen. This plot device is necessary in order to get Esther into the king's bed. After trying out many young and beautiful virgins the king chooses Esther as his new queen. We just do not know if there really was an Esther who was a Jewish queen at this time, but the story uses every device to make the events appear to be actual. Real or fictional matters not for the story goes on to show how Esther under the direction of her kinsman, Mordecai, is able to save the Jewish people from an execution order by outsmarting Haman who, as the king's second in command, has gotten the king to order the destruction of the Jewish people in all the provinces. Esther, at threat of death, pursues a plan to overturn Haman and to topple him from power while at the same time preventing the destruction of her Jewish people.

At a crucial point Haman misreads the king's intentions, for when the king asks Haman "What should be done for the man whom the king wishes to honour?" Haman believes that the king is speaking of him. Misreading intentions can be dangerous and Haman misreads not only the king's intentions but also Esther's intentions and in a complete reversal of fortunes he ends up hanged on the very gallows he had built to hang Mordecai. The letters from the king to the provinces are changed to allow the Jews to defend themselves and they end up killing 75,000 of their enemies instead of being destroyed themselves. The story is one that is read by rabbis on Purim, one of the great festivals celebrated by the Jews every year.

After reading the book of Esther in the Old Testament then you should read the version which appears in the apocrypha. The second version differs from the first in having about 140 more lines and all of those additional lines tell of God's involvement in the plot. Dreams and portents are suddenly present and the intention of the author is clear in the additional lines. God, who does not appear in the Hebrew version, is suddenly omnipresent in the Greek version, *and we can read the intentions of the Greek author in those added lines.* Now God is the author of human events and is directly involved through dreams and intervention in the unfolding of events. We readers are to see that God is directly responsible for the outcome of stories and is controlling the events from afar.

Much of the great writing of our Western tradition comes from a Judeo-Christian culture. It is difficult to read Dante, Spinoza, Milton, Goethe, Shakespeare, Descartes, Newton, Kant and hundreds of others without some knowledge of the stories and the ideas of the Bible. Contemporary artists continue to draw on the images and forms of the biblical stories to create their stories, and whether they are believers or not the basic patterns of the Bible are still present to be considered, incorporated or dismissed. The biblical stories, of course, have special meaning for Jews and Christians because they are believed to be a record of God's covenant with a chosen people. In the Old Testament this covenant is in the form of a promise of land in return for obedience to a set of rules. In the New Testament the covenant is in the form of a promise for salvation in return for obedience and belief. The "promised land" of the Old Testament is land on this earth; the "promised land" of the New Testament, as described by Paul and other early Christians, is not of this earth.

It seems obligatory in a book like this to state where I "am coming from." I am not a Jew. I am not a Christian. I was raised in a Christian family. We attended an Episcopal church when I was a small boy; after my mother remarried we attended a Lutheran church where I was confirmed at a young age. Shortly after that we started to attend a Methodist church, but none of these changes was, to my knowledge, based on any matters of doctrine, but rather on social reasons. I remember getting in trouble with the Lutheran pastor as a child because in Bible class I would ask real questions. "Thou shalt have no other Gods before me," it said in the catechism. Why? The canned answer was: "The Lord, thy God, is a jealous God." "Why is he jealous?" I would ask, "what would God have to be jealous of?" "Don't ask questions," the pastor would say, "just memorize the material." That was the lesson of the church: do not ask questions; just memorize the stuff. There really was no life in the church. People came in, sat down, listened quietly, put some money in the collection plate, and then left to carry on with their lives as before. After hearing a sermon on the evils of "drink" and card playing, in which the punishments for disobedience were extremely uncomfortable, we would all get in our car and go to one of my step-uncle's for an afternoon of drinking beer and playing pinochle. I learned to hate Jews (for they were somehow responsible for killing Jesus), Catholics (for they had all the riches), and Methodists (I cannot remember why). I learned hypocrisy, racism, and sexism (now called the "traditional" values by nostalgic writers who find the word "traditional" all fuzzy and warm). I read the Bible frequently because the stories were full of violence, sex, and mystery. I remember asking my mother what 'womb' means and she was very nervous and asked me where I had heard that word. When I told her I found it in the Bible she did not seem to know what to say. I had her! She arranged for my step-father to teach me about the "birds and the bees." He in turn sub-contracted to a teen-aged farm hand who gave me a brief but descriptive lecture about things that I already knew. (The lecture, I remember, started like this: "So, you want to know about fucking...," my teacher at least exhibiting a sense of audience.)

After a few years in public schools and four years in the United States Marine Corps, I learned about sex and violence in more direct ways, and stopped reading the Bible until I was in university. At the University of California in Santa Barbara I was assigned as a teaching assistant to Professor Douwe Stuurman, who taught a course on the Bible. His classes were always full of interesting people. In the front row were the nuns, who, he said, were there to spy on him. Then came the middle-aged students looking for therapy, the literature and philosophy students, and the atheists who sat in the back. I tried to sit in a different part of the room each time. Stuurman had a Freudian, Eastern, Calvinist, Proustian background and the ability to mesmerize an audience. Above all he opened up the text for me. I read it with fresh eyes. These stories were marvellous works of art! Stuurman's lectures were inspiring (I used to call them "Stuurman on the mount") and unlike my Lutheran pastor, he asked questions all the time. When not at the university I spent my time cleaning the Unitarian Church in Santa Barbara which meant that I had the op- portunity to talk with Lex Crane, who was ministering there then. His background in literature was extensive and we used to have long talks about "meaning" while I should have been cleaning the toilets. I flirted with the idea of becoming a Unitarian minister, but never got the "call." Because of this and more, I believe the Bible is worth reading and studying, not as moribund scripture but as living literature.

The first few stories in the Old Testament develop a recurring pattern in human affairs:

- the creation   creation (innocence)
- the fall and the   conflict (sin)
  first murder
- the flood   suffering (purification)
- the rainbow   resolution (salvation)
- the tower of Babel   beginnings

This pattern is familiar to us because we do in fact find ourselves in a world that we cannot explain the origin of, even in our most thorough going scientific descriptions. "Why is there anything at all?" is a basic question that defies answers. We can easily understand how that question leads to religious answers, to answers that defy verification, for it is difficult to imagine an answer to that question that would be verifiable in the strict scientific sense. The answer we are given is a story which begins: "In the beginning of creation, when God made heaven and earth...." The story tells us how not why. It does not presume to know why but takes as "evidence" for what might have been a clear notion of what is: we find ourselves walking on the earth, surrounded by the sky, nurtured by sunshine and water, sharing our world with many other species of animals, fish and birds. Plants, trees, flowers abound. Where did they come from? In this story we are told that they come form the creative command of a powerful spirit-god who creates by fiat. "Let there be light" - and there was light begins the whole chain of events. Other stories tell of the beginnings of life in different ways. For example, the Hopi Indians have a creation myth which tells the story this way:

> In a remote time Spider Grandmother thought outward into space. She thought and breathed and sang and spun the world into existence. So threads and stories, spinning and spirals all began

with Spider Grandmother.[1]

"Thought," "breathed," "sang," are the operative verbs in this story. They suggest a certain kind of creation: mental, intangible, structured. Diction, which is merely *choice of words, reveals intent*. A particular recipe lies behind a description which employs just these words, a recipe which includes a pattern for building "reality" as well as a description of a given "reality." Reading stories always entails paying close attention to the writer's diction, for in the selection of a vocabulary a writer chooses a value system. Look at these lines by Wordsworth:[2]

> No motion has she now, no force;
> She neither feels nor sees;
> Rolled round in earth's diurnal course,
> With rocks, and stones, and trees.

What a simple vocabulary Wordsworth uses to tell us of a motionless young woman who has died. The words "force," "motion," and "diurnal" come from the vocabulary of science and are used here to contrast life and death with the scientific vocabulary of Newtonian physics. "Diurnal" is the only word in the stanza likely to send a reader to the dictionary. And what does this word mean? "Daily." Wordsworth could have used "daily" in the line; it is a word he would have had in his vocabulary. But he chooses "diurnal." What does he gain by this choice? "Diurnal" hints at "die," "urn," "eternal" - all words, and through them images, which cluster around the chosen word and reveal a complex of emotional and intellectual concerns that "daily" just does not. It is in the choice of diction that the poet negotiates the meaning transfer from intention to interpretation.

The poet who wrote the creation story in Genesis also reveals intention through diction. One repeated phrase that in its repetition is highlighted as surely as is the light which results form the first command is the phrase "God saw that it was good" repeated after each creative act. From the very beginning we are told of a world that has value and goodness built right into it by the act

---

[1] Quoted here from "Hopi" a Corporation of Public Broadcasting film produced by New Day Films in New York.
[2] William Wordsworth "A Slumber Did My Spirit Seal," *The Norton Anthology of English Literature*, W.W. Norton and Company, Third Edition, page 142.

of the creator-god. Good is not added like a cosmetic but is shown through the language to be a fundamental part of the cosmos. As the myth of our beginnings unfolds in the thoughts and spinnings of the Genesis poet we see that into this place of perfect good enters chaos as a result of disobedience and jealousy. Good is followed immediately by its opposite and God drives Adam from the garden.

One way of approaching these early stories is to think of them as maps. They were constructed after the fact as ways of explaining and charting the unknown past of how and why. In that respect they are backwards looking. But they also contain a perspective from the present projecting into the future. They contain within them a story about how we ought to be. And the language of these stories is often the language of dream - symbolic language - a language that means more than it says, a language that is found in poetry and in children. When our immediate family experienced the first death in the family which our kids experienced it happened like this: the phone call came saying that Grandpa Jim had died and that his funeral would be in a military cemetery in a few days. Margaret, our daughter, was about three years old. She heard her mother on the phone and guessed that something was wrong. She asked her older brothers (seven and eight) what was going on. "Grandpa Jim is dead." "What does that mean?" "They will put him in a hole in the ground." "And put dirt over top of him." "And you will never see him again."

She was puzzled. Later she went off to bed without saying much of anything. In the middle of the night I heard her weeping quietly in her crib. I went to pick her up and held her against my chest. She was in that state between sleeping and waking and was sobbing over and over again: "I don't want to go down in that hole; I don't want to go down in that hole." That is symbolic language. What heart knew head guessed. The stories of the Bible are written in that kind of language. At the level where the human cry of mortality and mystery emerges is to be found the story line of the best of the stories from the Bible collection. At another level, of course, is the official line, which offers an explanation, a reading of the stories, proclaims an interpretation, an ordering conceptual map.

The Bible stories can be seen as maps - maps of concepts constructed in language which trace psychological or social processes. But do they *record* or *construct* the facts? In what follows I will argue that, like all literature, they do both. A recent literary critic puts the distinction this way:

The recognition that our concepts are constructions of language systems...tells us nothing about their relation or lack of relation to reality. It follows that the antithesis between "constructing" and "recording" is unreal, for it opposes a genetic category to a logical one; it confuses the process by which formulations come into being (constructing) and the logical status of these formulations ("recording"). The opposition becomes unreal as soon as we recognize how much constructing is required in the process of recording. The fact that a reader's interpretation of a text is, in a sense, his construction is no argument against (or for) its adequacy to the text. Similarly, the fact that a literary work is constituted by the imagination, or by a system of literary conventions, does not prevent it from qualifying as a record or representation of reality.[3]

A valuable approach as reader is to consider that reading a text is a performing art. I do not mean by this that one needs to learn to be an oral interpreter, although that is a good skill to develop. I mean that in reading a text one must engage every bit of creativity, of sensitivity, of intellect and feeling that one possesses. The story is in the text, but its full experience is in the mind of the reader. The story provides form and directs responses, and the reader completes the communicative act. Think of the text as a musical score and yourself as a performing musician. The notes are there - are in the score - and you must be able to perform them on your musical instrument. You need to bring technical skill, sensitivity to nuance, and a knowledge of the language of musical notation to the task.

I believe that most of us at some time or other confuse items from one logical category with items from another, and, as a result end up believing and stating silly or nonsensical things. Sometimes we confuse the menu with the meal, or the map with the landscape, or our theory with reality; in short we sometimes make category mistakes. We sometimes confuse our favorite theories about the world with the way the world is. Stories often contain theories of a kind (or *official lines* as I will call them) - these are

---

[3] Gerald Graff, *Literature Against Itself,* University of Chicago press, Chicago and London, 1979, page 199.

combinations of presuppositions, conventions, assumptions, assumed value judgements. And these official lines are evident in the verbal structure of a compound narrative. In what follows I will try to show that separating the official line from the story line is a necessary aspect of reading the Bible. Stories provide maps of a culture's deepest hopes and fears, of its value system and its "take" on reality. Maps, of course, like language, select certain features and ignore others; and like language, maps are cultural expressions of elements significant to a society.

Look at a reproduction of the Roman Peutinger Table, a ribbon map originally some twenty-five feet long by one foot wide showing the Roman world from Britain to India. A complex strip map, it was apparently constructed to aid generals and merchants to find their way around the empire. It is a map with Roman efficiency: great chunks of recalcitrant land are forced into a narrow highway from Rome to the ends of the world. Physical space is distorted to fit the utility of the enterprise. In another marvellous map of the thirteenth century, the Ebstorf map, which is some nine feet in diameter, Jerusalem is shown in the very center of the map with Christ's head at the top, feet at the bottom and hands to the east and west. The mapmaker projects certain features from the *world view* into the view of the world. "Maps are by nature distortions of physical space." And interpretations are by nature distortions of stories.

We can say that a map is distorting physical space only if we know what would count as non-distorted physical space. Just as there can be no counterfeit money unless there is some genuine money, there can be no distortion unless there is some way of knowing about it. Stories too are like that. A general model for map making and story telling looks like this:

Scientists, story tellers, and map makers

1. select certain features from the physical world based upon complex considerations of beliefs, function, and reality;

2. make guesses about the way the world works, and put these guesses in the form of hypothesis, map, painting or story;

3. these guesses are improved upon, amended, corrected, or thrown away.

The stories in the Bible grow out of a certain place and a certain people. By now they are overlaid with centuries of interpretation and have become presented as Repositories for Truth instead of vehicles for truth. The god of the Old Testament, for example, is a complex projection based in part on the needs of a nomadic people: above all this god had to be a portable god, not one assigned to a particular valley or mountain, but one that moved with his people. Place dictates image. We can expect to find in these stories a concern with survival in a near-desert climate - a desire and hope for the oasis with its life giving water, shelter and comfort. Is it any wonder that the garden of Eden appears as the perfect place for human life? Later ages will describe this metaphoric place not as "a palm at the end of the mind" but as a place with streets paved with gold. And that change in image tells us something about the story tellers.

The Bible is sometimes referred to as a "transparent" text or a "laminated" text. The images here suggest an important aspect of the biblical texts. If the text is transparent what is it we readers are supposed to see through the text? And if laminated what makes up the layers? The transparent text is supposed to reveal the Truth of God. Readers, says this approach, are to look through the text to see the hand of the divine at work behind the scenes. Reading in this way requires the reader to have a point of view to begin with, to start with an official line which is used as a template for the stories' meaning. In this way the text is not so much transparent as it is a mirror. One tends to see one's own preconceptions when looking through this "transparent" text. To think of the biblical text as laminated is to become aware of the layers of textual accretions that have built up over the years and through the translations. Stories, legends, poems, oral materials, chronicles, letters, have all been folded into the final product, with frames and transitions added, and with direct commentary from time to time.

In what follows I want to point to the excellence of the Hebrew texts in translation, suggest a way of reading those texts which depends upon the creative involvement of the reader, and provide you with some sense of the excitement of reading these stories with fresh eyes and an open mind. Reading these stories is a way of reading yourself.

THE HOLY LAND

The stage for the Biblical drama is the world of the ancient Near East, the meeting place of three continents: Asia, Africa, and Europe. This territory today is made up of the modern states of Turkey, Syria, Lebanon, Israel, Jordan, Egypt, Saudi Arabia, Iraq, and Iran. Now (1990) the area is well known to North Americans from daily maps on television used as backdrops for news reports about the United Nations action against Iraq in the area. Once more the winds of war are blowing in the Middle East, an area of the world buffeted by those winds for centuries. It is an area of conflict between peoples looking for a home. It is an area of conflict because for centuries other countries have dominated various parts of the land for military strategy, for religious strategy, or for commerce. Today oil brings the armies to the desert. In the past it has been land, water, agriculture, trade routes and other religious concerns of the day.

The Middle East is an area of widely contrasting terrain, climate and culture. It includes the rugged mountains of Armenia, the great Arabian Desert, and, in between, the long, crescent-shaped strip of land known as the Fertile Crescent, which stretches from Egypt on the southwest, up the Mediterranean coast through Israel and Syria, and down the Tigris-Euphrates Valley to the Persian Gulf. It has always been an exciting and romantic setting for the magnificent characters who have walked on its stage. The patriarchs walked the desert sands with their flocks. Pharaohs built pyramids for their long sleep. Legendary heroes like Moses and Jesus are to be found here in the desert, conversing with their God, teaching their flocks. Here Alexander the Great stretched out his arm of conquest. Here too the Roman armies fought the local peoples. Caesars walked the earth here. David and Solomon reigned briefly over a united kingdom of Israel. In Egypt Antony and Cleopatra loved and lost. Deborah, Rebekah, Jael, Mary and Elizabeth, Sarah: these powerful and strong women people the stories set in this landscape. Today tanks are strewn across the landscape; a reminder in sculptured and bullet pocked iron of the continuing conflict in this desert of despair.

At stage centre, as far as Hebrew history is concerned, is the land of Palestine, a narrow corridor between the Mediterranean Sea and the Arabian Desert with Syria and Lebanon on the north, and Egypt on the south. Pushed up against the Mediterranean on the west and with Jordan on the east, the modern state of Israel is impressive first of all because of its size. It is very small. Measuring about 150 miles "from Dan to Beersheba," the Biblical idiom for its north-south extremities (Judges 20:1), it has nevertheless always played a significant role in the political, economic, and cultural life of the ancient world. Situated astride the major highways joining Egypt and Mesopotamia, Palestine commanded a strategic location for military and commercial affairs. Trade between Assyria, Babylon, Persia and Egypt often moved through the lands of Palestine. Too often the larger neighbours were also moving soldiers, chariots and war machines into the area as the power struggles between larger nations waxed and waned. At times in her history, for example, during the unified reigns of David and Solomon, Israel was able to capitalize on her strategic location and gather income from the trade caravans travelling north and south. But more often than not, one of the larger nations was on her soil as an invading army or as a landlord exacting tribute and taxes from the people.

In such a small country one does not expect the vast topographical differences that one finds. Southern Israel (the Judean Wilderness) is dry rocky land that looks like places on the moon. Rough, rocky terrain gives life to a few thistle-like plants, small trees, and tough grass wherever there is any moisture at all. This is the land of the Dead Sea, a large land-locked body of water so filled with salts as to make sinking in it impossible. Around the Dead Sea are the hills and valleys in which Qumran and Masada were built over 2000 years ago. Here the Dead Sea Scrolls were found in the caves around Qumran, and here Herod the Great built a magnificent castle for his family and for protection should he ever need it. Summer temperatures climb to 48 degrees Celsius as the brilliant sunshine is reflected off the rocky terrain much like a reflecting oven. With a stark beauty of its own the Judean Wilderness figures prominently in many of the bible stories from both the Old and New Testaments. Even here some rain falls in the winter months and provided water for the hardy settlers who stored it in deep underground cisterns for use during the dry summer months. There are really just two seasons in Israel: summer and winter, the first running from May to October. The moisture laden winds from the Mediterranean and the long season of winter rains nourish olive, fig, orange and date trees on many of the hill slopes of the Judean Wilderness. Fields of grain and vineyards are spread across the intervening valleys.

The Central Highlands have been divided historically into three regions of Galilee, Samaria (Ephraim) and Judah (or Judea). Galilee, in the north, is separated from the central heartland of Samaria by the important east-west Valley of Jezreel, through which passed the major trade route linking the Palestinian coast and Syria. The Valley of Jezreel is a fertile plain drained by the Kishon River and across from which Mount Tabor (1,843 ft.) and Mount Gilboa (1,6987 ft.) face each other. It was at Mt. Tabor that Deborah gathered her armies to defeat Sisera as we are told in the book of Judges.

North of Jerusalem one finds vegetation and a hospitable landscape, and though no well-defined geographical feature separates Samaria from Judah one has to travel but a few miles south or east of Jerusalem or Bethlehem before entering upon the forbidding Judean Wilderness mentioned above. Here the stony, gray hills support no vegetation throughout most of the year. South of Beersheba the Judean Hills flatten out into the barren southern steppe, the Negeb, which merges with the Sinai Desert.

The Jordan valley is the most characteristic geographical feature in Israel. A part of the great geological rift which extends through Syria and continues southward as the Wadi Arabaly it parts the country lengthwise from north to south, and through it the Jordan River descends in its serpentine course. The Jordan's waters are supplied by springs at the foot of Mount Hebron and empty finally into the Dead Sea. The Jordan supplies three lakes, and one gets a sense of the rapid descent of its waters by contrasting the surface level of the three. Lake Huleh is 223 feet above sea level; the Sea of Galilee is 695 feet below sea level, and to the south, the Dead Sea is 1,285 feet below sea level. From the Sea of Galilee to the Dead Sea is, as the crane flies, only about 65 miles but three times that distance as the river meanders from north to south.

Claims and counter claims to the lands in the Near East have been an integral part of the history of the area and continue to be a source of conflict. Prime Minister Begin of Israel has argued since 1967 that Israel should hold the Golan Heights and the West Bank of the Jordan because the country is so defined in the Bible. So far Israeli tanks have been able to provide backing for the Biblical argument.

Abraham and Sarah, Isaac and Rebekah, Jacob, Samson, Deborah, and all the other characters from the Old Testament stories live their lives here in this land where water is so precious and where the sand and the stars meet at the horizon on endless clear nights. The Judean Wilderness is just that: a wilderness. To cross it took a wily, tough and hardy people who knew how to survive in an inhospitable land without easy access to food and water. Where rocks are everywhere in the landscape it is no surprise that they play an important and recurring part in the imagery of the stories. When water is so scarce it is not surprising that wells and rivers become central meeting places for bringing together the people and the flocks. Every betrothal scene in the Old Testament is set by a well. Moses' main concern while leading the tribes through the wilderness is to find water.

For one raised in North America with its vast distances, miles and miles of countryside, forests that go on for miles and miles, it comes as a shock to discover that Bethlehem is but three miles from Jerusalem. In my Sunday School memory the journey from Bethlehem to Jerusalem was a long journey indeed especially when travelling on a donkey. But then my Sunday School memory was filled with all sorts of falsehoods.

One of the most interesting sites is the marvelous Caesarea on the Mediterranean Sea. Built about 2000 years ago, Caesarea still exhibits evidence of the Roman influence, with its baths, its wide streets, and its arena for sporting events. Herod the Great, who figures prominently in the Jesus story, was a rich and powerful king who has to be one of the world's greatest opportunists. As powerful men struggled for ascendancy in Rome and one "Caesar" after another crossed the Tiber to seek the highest office on earth, Herod was able, by quick maneuvering and clever "politicking" to stay always on the side of the person in power. He snuggled up to the right general time after time and hence was able to keep the power and influence required to rule and exploit the country. He was also interested in architecture, was influenced by the Romans in all things, and built many of the lasting monuments in Jerusalem, Jericho, Masada, and Caesarea.

As Martin Noth puts it:[4]

> About 22 miles south of the Carmel solient there was a fairly old, quite small place called "Strato's Tower". This place had been made over to Herod in the year 30 B.C. with a whole coastal area. On its site Herod had a magnificent city built at great expense over a period of twelve years, with artificial harbour installations and with all the public buildings such as theatre, ampitheatre, and hippo-drome which formed part of a complete Hellenistic-Roman city. In

---

[4] *The History of Israel,* Martin Noth, Harper and Row, New York, 1958, page 415.

the year 10 B.C. it was ceremoniously opened with magnificent games for which Augustus and Livia gave a considerable sum. ...Herod called the city "Caesarea"....

Caesarea, Bethlehem, Jericho, Nazareth: all are cities we have heard of from Sunday School days on. But the most famous, the most beloved, the most complex and mysterious of cities is Jerusalem. Even before David's time Jerusalem was an important city, but from David on its place in history was assured. To go there today is to go back in time at least 3,000 years, and it is to visit the holy site for three of the world's largest religions. Divided into four quarters (the Jewish Quarter, the Armenian Quarter, the Christian Quarter, and the Arab (Moslem) Quarter), old Jerusalem thrives behind its ancient walls with some of its inhabitants waiting for the Messiah to arrive through the Golden Gate, others waiting for the Second Coming of Christ, and others waiting for Mohammed to reappear. This is the city of Godot. Everyone is waiting. Waiting for Godot. Waiting for God. It contains more temples, mosques, and churches per square foot than any other city in the world. Bullet pocked stone walls are silent testimony to the fact that the religious conflicts of thousands of years are still very much alive. Evidence from the first temple period abounds and one feels while walking in the Old Jerusalem that there are several layers of city below one's feet. It is here that David chose to build his capital: "In view of the jealousy and bad feeling between the two Kingdoms of Judah and Israel...with the sure instinct of the wise statesman he chose a city on neutral soil between the territories of the two kingdoms. This was Jerusalem..." Later Solomon would fortify the city and still later battle after battle would be fought there as it became the holy place for Jews, Moslems, and Christians, and the temporal place to capture if one wanted to control the area. Babylonians, Romans, Crusaders, each motivated by different urges fought and died there to gain control of the city - this magic and bloody city of Jerusalem. The three religions: Judaism, Christianity, and Islam share few things: these are one God, the patriarchs, especially Abraham, and Jerusalem.

To Jews and Moslems one belief is central: "Hear, O Israel, the Lord of our God, the Lord is one" or as Moslems put it, "There is no God but God."

Both religions demand submission to the will of God - "Islam" means "submission" - and regard fulfillment of his commands as the main road to salvation. Both separately, have a large body of law, a regimen of rite and custom. Jews derive theirs from the Hebrew Bible and the rabbinical traditions of the Mishneh and Talmud. And more, because Judaism is ready to develop and to disagree: it has several strands today, conservatism of belief going, usually, with strictness of observance. But all agree that a covenant with God, sealed at Sinai, selects the people of Israel for special favour - including the "land of milk and honey" - in return for special devotion.

Moslems draw their beliefs from the Koran , the word of God revealed through Mohammed; and from the quite distinct Hadith, traditions of what the Prophet himself said or did. An Arab trader, he received his first "revelation" about 610 A.D. (the start of the Moslem era). Moslems are not free to develop their tradition just because times have changed: "the messenger of God" was the last of the prophets (of whom Jesus was one), and the revelation he received final and complete. Belief in God, prayer, fasting, pilgrimage and charity are the pillars of Islam.

Christianity is the odd religion out. Central to it is not the oneness of God, but his incarnation in the person of His son, Jesus Christ; who, we are told "was crucified, dead and buried. The third day he rose again...he ascended into heaven." Why? For the redemption of humankind, from the sin it had in-herited from Adam and Eve. In the Christian story it is God's grace expressed through His only son which promises redemption and victory over death.

The common denominator: Jerusalem. Hence, it is not strange that Jerusalem is, to continue the theatrical image, at the very heart of stage centre, bustling today with Jews, Christians, and Arabs who live, work, pray, and fight together focussed by their beliefs and sharing a complex, violent, and passionate history.

The Bible gives us a particular, a prejudiced, look at this history; though, of course, it is not a history book in the modern sense of history. As Auerbach says, "the Old Testament presents universal history: it begins with the beginning of time, with the creation of the world, and will end with the Last Days, the fulfilling of the Covenant, with which the world will come to an end." Throughout this "history" some sense of place is essential in understanding the feelings of the characters who are working out their destinies on this particular human stage.

CHAPTER 2: WHAT IS THE BIBLE?

Most of us use the words "the bible" confidently, sure that they refer clearly to some text, some specific book. They do not. Often we hear someone say, "It's in the Bible," or "but the Bible says...," and for the most part we understand what they mean, though it is important to notice that there is no unambiguous "thing" the words "the Bible" refer to. In some sense, of course, the same may be said about any book: when we say, for example, *The Great Gatsby*, do we know exactly what object in the world has that name? Fitzgerald's novel existed first in manuscript form, then was printed, and was a set of galley proofs; they in turn were corrected and reset for printing. In spite of the care taken there may have been errors (in spelling, punctuation, a word changed here or there) that were not found and corrected until the second edition or later. Which is the unique object picked out by the words "The Great Gatsby"? Is it the manuscript? the galley proofs? the first edition? or is it the "critical" edition published later which includes all of the amendments and variants over the history of the edition? Many of us would argue that it is the latter edition, the critical edition, combining as it does all of the changes, authorial emendations, printer's errors, and editorial corrections that is *The Great Gatsby,* and we would use any such edition in doing any critical analysis of Fitzgerald. Fitzgerald wrote about fifty-five years ago and he wrote in English. We have the manuscript and all of the editions of *The Great Gatsby.* Furthermore, Fitzgerald was alive when it was published and could go over the text after printing to insure its accuracy.

Or, think of a somewhat earlier book, T. S. Eliot's *The Waste Land.* When we use the words "The Waste Land" to refer or pick out some item in the world, what exactly do we refer to? Is it the handwritten manuscript? the corrected copy with Pound's changes? the typescript? the fair copy? the first edition? If we look at *T. S. Eliot The Wasteland: A Facsimile And Transcript Of The Original Drafts Including The Annotations Of Ezra Pound* we find all of these drafts and changes and can see how much influence Ezra Pound had on the final poem. Pound made hundreds of corrections and suggestions to the handwritten manuscript, many of which were incorporated by Eliot. Studying that facsimile gives the reader an idea of the organic nature of a text. Pound's editorial pen wipes out whole stanzas as he prunes the manuscript, or adds as he makes suggestions about changes and alternatives. Part of the initial excitement of the discovery of the Dead Sea Scrolls was that we hoped to have something like the Eliot book to give us a better idea of the history and development of the Biblical texts.[1]

The text of a creative work, like stories which are related orally, is a constantly changing, almost living, thing. The arrival of the printing press made for more textual stability since there is something fixed about the printed word which is not present in the spoken word. Legends and sayings of cultural heroes related as part of a culture's oral tradition would obviously have had less stability than those texts which were written down and later printed. In the examples of Fitzgerald and Eliot we have two writers who were alive while their work was maturing and who were able to follow it through the maturation process from initial intent to final production.

Imagine a somewhat more difficult problem with an older literary text. Let's say you are editing a new edition of "Hamlet" by Shakespeare. You want to get the text as accurate as possible, as close to what Shakespeare actually wrote as is humanly possible. You start by trying to find the manuscript (so called foul papers). But after some four hundred years no one has been able to find any of the foul papers. We just do not have one original manuscript for Shakespeare's plays. We do have the *First Folio*, an edition published in 1623, some half-dozen years after the author's death. But we also have two quarto editions of "Hamlet". Which is the "real" play? There are three early texts of "Hamlet": the first quarto (Q1) of 1603, a pirated, garbled version; the second quarto (Q2) of 1604-05, probably set up by the printer from

---

[1] The discovery of the Dead Sea Scrolls and the controversy over their publication is an excellent seminar topic for students. There is as well an excellent PBS show on the scrolls.

Shakespeare's own manuscript; and the text of the play as it appears in the first folio (F1) of 1623. A typical example of the differences between the three versions occurs in III, iv; towards the end of the closet scene:

Q1 reads:

Ham.: Why doe you nothing heare?
Queene: Not I.
Ham.: Nor do you nothing see?
Queene: No neither.
Ham.: No, why see the King my father, my father
        in the habite
  As he lived, looke you how pale he lookes,
  See how he steales away out of the Portall,
  Looke, there he goes. (Exit Ghost)

In Q2 the text reads:

Ham.: Doe you see nothing there?
Ger.: Nothing at all, yet all that is I see.
Ham.: Nor did you nothing heare?
Ger.: No, nothing but our selves.
Ham.: Why looke you there, looke how it steales
        away:
  My Father in his habite, as he lived,
  Looke where he goes even now out at the
        Portall.
        (Exit)

In the First Folio we find:
Ham.: Do you see nothing there?
Qu. : Nothing at all, yet all that is I see.
Ham.: Nor did you nothing heare?
Qu. : Nothing but ourselves.

Comparing these three versions we find many differences in spelling, in syntax, in utterances. In Q2 the Queen's line in response to Hamlet's question about seeing is changed strikingly by the addition of "yet all that is I see" which is a much different claim than the simple "no, I see nothing" of Q1. If we looked at the complete scene we would find even more striking differences: in

Q1 the Queen swears she will help Hamlet in whatever he devises. There is nothing of this in the other versions. When F1 is compared with Q2, it will be seen that Hamlet's speeches have been considerably altered; F1 omits nineteen lines that occur in Q2. Further the version in Q2 is so lightly punctuated that at times it is difficult to determine the sense of the passages. F1 is a more carefully prepared version, but probably not a direct printing from Shakespeare's manuscript. There is a discrepancy also between the two versions at the end of the scene. In Q2, the scene ends at "Exit" and the next scene begins with: "Enter King, and Queene, with Rosencrans and Guyldensterne," as if the Queen had gone out and come in again. In F1, Gertrude is left alone at the end of the scene for a few moments, and then the King enters alone. Rosencrantz and Guildenstern do not enter until the King calls for them, at line 32.

Which version should you as a modern editor choose? Which is the "real" text of "Hamlet"?

Shakespeare, of course, wrote in English; at a time when printing, libraries, scholars, and universities were all around. Imagine now the problems in selecting what will go into the Bible. Here is material going back some *three thousand* years, and written in languages quite strange to us today. The Old Testament was written in Hebrew, which was an ancient Semitic language spoken in the territory of present day Syria. Beginning in about 500 B.C. Aramaic began to supplant the Hebrew language in Palestine, where in the days of Jesus a dialect of the Aramaic was the language commonly spoken. The New Testament was written in Greek with a few words and expressions in Aramaic. In short, "the Bible" is always a work in translation, in addition to being an edited text. We call the editor (or editors) who put together the books of the Bible a redactor from the Latin *redactus*, which means "to write out or draw up, to arrange for publication." Many parts of the two testaments were undoubtedly part of an oral tradition for years before ever being written down in the language of the day. To read the texts today in translation is to read the end result of a complicated human process of selection, translation, and judgement which necessarily removes us from the "original" texts. Some of the apparent contradictions and oversights in the stories come from the various sources being brought together in the final draft by a redactor who could not change things consciously without great trouble of spirit because these books were believed to have been written by God. It would be the height of blasphemy to edit God's words. The Bible then is a compilation of texts put together around 100 A.D.[2] and established as canon by editorial (theological) committees of Catholics, Protestants, and Jews. Look, for example, at the differences between the Hebrew and Christian Bibles:

TORAH	HEBREW BIBLE	CHRISTIAN BIBLE
Genesis, Exodus, Leviticus, *Numbers, Deuteronomy*	5	5

NEBI'IM (PROPHETS)

Former prophets: *Joshua, Judges,* *Samuel, Kings*	4	6
Major prophets: *Isaiah, Jeremiah,* *Ezekiel*	3	3
Minor prophets: *Hosea, Joel, Amos,* *Obadiah, Jonah, Micah, Nahum, Habakkuk,* *Zechariah, Zephaniah, Haggai, Malachi 1*		12

KETHUBIM (WRITINGS)

Psalms, Proverbs, Job, Song of Songs, *Ruth, Lamentations, Ecclesiastes,* *Esther, Daniel, Ezra-Nehemiah,* *Chronicles*	<u>11</u>	<u>13</u>
Total	24	39

As I mentioned in Chapter one "Esther" appears in the Old Testament and in the Apocrypha in the Christian Bible, and is worth looking at to see the differences between the two renditions of the same story. In the Old Testament version there is no mention of God or His influence on events in the world of the story. In the Apocrypha version divine influence is seen throughout the story. The Greek version found in the Apocrypha, provides an

---

[2] The oldest extant Hebrew manuscript of the entire Old Testament is the Leningrad bible which dates from 1008 A.D.

explicit religious element to the story, while in the Hebrew version God is not mentioned. Both versions provide a foundation for the Feast of Purim, but the Greek version becomes a cosmic story of God's intervention into Hebrew history. Not only do we find different books in different compilations, but we also find the same book writ twice.

As a current book on the Old Testament puts it:[3]

> Modern editions of the Bible are the end products of a long and complex textual history. Since none of the authors' original manuscripts (autographs) of Biblical books has survived, the oldest manuscripts in our possession are copies, which in turn were copied by hand from yet other copies, and so on back to the originals. From the time of Ezra the task of copying Biblical manuscripts and thus keeping the books in circulation fell to the lot of professional scribes known as Sopherim ("men of the book").
>
> They originally wrote in a consonantal Hebrew on scrolls of papyrus or leather (the codex or book form did not appear until the third century A. D.) with no system of punctuation, versification, or chapter divisions. Notwithstanding the reverence in which these copyists held the Biblical text, the primitive conditions under which they worked made common errors of the eye and ear unavoidable.

We have to be careful when we use "the Bible" to refer to "a text" since there are so many different collections of texts which we might be referring to. Usually when we say "the Bible" we mean to use the words to refer to the collection of works we are familiar with or which has been a part of our religious training. The important English versions of the Bible are:

> 1384 Wyclif's first translation of the entire
>   Bible.
> 1525 Tyndale, translated from Hebrew and Greek.
> 1535 Coverdale.
> 1537 Thomas Matthew.

---

[3] *Introduction to the Old Testament*, James King West, The MacMillan Company, New York, 1971, p. 5.

1539 The Great Bible.
1560 The Geneva Bible.
1568 The Bishop's Bible.
1611 King James.
1881 English Revised.
1901 American Standard.
1952 Revised Standard Version.
1976 The New English Bible.
1981 The New King James Version.

Most of us who know the bible at all know the King James version, a version which has caught the imagination of millions of readers with its Shakespearean language and its rich and vivid images. Complete with chapters and verse numbers, the King James runs to 1,189 chapters with 929 Old Testament and 260 New Testament chapters.

COMPARING DIFFERENT TRANSLATIONS

What difference does any of this make? Yes, there are many translations, and yes, there are various readings among the translations, and , yes, there have been errors in the text from time to time.[4] Just as with Shakespeare's plays, or any other literary text, we want to make sure that we have the best text when attempting to discover or uncover meaning. The differences can be more than "mere style," and at times change the meaning. Compare these four versions of Psalm 100:

King James Version:

1. Make a joyful noise unto the Lord, all ye lands.
2. Serve the Lord with gladness; come before his
   presence with singing.

---

[4] The first Bible printed in North America was not in English, Latin, Hebrew, of Greek - but in the Algonquin Indian language, published in 1663, by John Eliot, a dissenter who emigrated to North America and became known as the"Apostle of the Indians."
As to errors, the so-called "printers" Bible was a King James Version printed in 1702 with this error: "Printers (princes) have persecuted me without cause."

3. Know ye that the Lord is God: it is he that
   hath made us, and not we ourselves: we are his
   people, and the sheep of his pasture.
4. Enter into his gates with thanksgiving, and into
   his courts with praise: be thankful unto him,
   and bless his name.
5. For the Lord is good, his mercy is everlasting;
   and his truth endureth to all generations.

Revised Standard Version:

1. Make a joyful noise to the Lord, all the lands!
2. Serve the Lord with gladness!
   Come into His presence with singing!
3. Know that the lord is God!
   It is he that made us, and we are his;
   We are his people, and the sheep of his pasture.
4. Enter his gates with thanksgiving,
   And his courts with praise!
   Give thanks to him, bless his name!
5. For the Lord is good;
   his steadfast love endures for ever,
   and his faithfulness to all generations.

The New King James Version

1. Make a joyful shout to the lord,
       all you lands!
2. Serve the Lord with gladness;
   Come before His presence with singing.
3. Know that the Lord, He is God;
   It is He who has made us,
       and not we ourselves;
   We are His people
       and the sheep of His pasture.
4. Enter into His courts with praise.
   Be thankful to him,
       and bless His name.
   For the Lord is good;
   And His truth endures to all

generations.

<u>The New English Bible</u>

1. Acclaim the Lord, all men on earth,
   worship the Lord in gladness;
   enter his presence with songs of
      exultation.
2. Know that the Lord is God;
   he has made us and we are his own,
      his people, the flock which he
      shepherds.
3. Enter his gates with thanksgiving
   and his courts with praise.
4. Give thanks to him and bless his
      name;
   for the Lord is good and his love is
      everlasting,
   his constancy endures to all
      generations.

Are we to acclaim the Lord by shouting or by making a joyful noise, or by singing his praise? Or are the lands supposed to make the joyful noise (RSV) while the people are to sing? Are the lands and the people the same or different? One translation says we are his while another says we are his people. Is there a difference? Does "his people" suggest a coherence, an identity, a unity that is missing in just "his"? Are we his individually or collectively? Are we to go into or before his presence? One says "into his presence" which is much more embracing and inclusive than "before his presence" and suggests a quite different relationship between worshipped and worshipper. And yet another says "enter his presence with songs of exultation" which again has a different connotation. If one either enters his presence or goes into his presence that suggests a kind of merging with God that is not in the phrase "before his presence" which suggests a complete difference between the subject and the object of the gladness and thanksgiving. That is a significant difference. How are we to relate to this God? Are we to be supplicants who stand before him or are we to be taken into his presence to know first hand the mercy, truth and love that are predicated in the poem as eternal attributes of god? And, which is it: his steadfast love or his mercy which endures "to all generations"? These kinds of differences abound in the various translations, but above all it seems important to remember that, as Northrop Frye puts it: "...Christianity...from the beginning has been dependent on translation."[5]

Each time a new translation of the Bible is published there is a hue and cry about the passages that are "ruined" by the new translation. Familiarity in this case does not lead to contempt but to a conventional response: the translation most familiar to us must be the "right" one. Some of the best known stories are subtly different in different translations. In the New Testament, for example, Luke 2.14 has caused a great deal of critical comment because the newer translations of the passage restrict the peace declared by the heavenly hosts to a subset of mankind. The King James version has, 'Glory to God in the highest, and on earth peace, good will toward men.' The blessing of peace is clearly one to be given to all peoples, and is unconditional in its distribution. Many people, Christian and non-Christian, respond to that famous passage at least once a year. It expresses a hope for the future, a possible world in which peace and good will extend beyond our tribal concerns to include the entire family of human beings.

The Revised Standard Version, however, translates the passage differently. Here we find: "Glory to God in the highest, and on earth peace among men with whom he is pleased." There is an obvious and severe restriction on the blessing delivered by the multitudes of heavenly hosts in this rendition. "Among men with whom he is pleased," sounds much more like the Old Testament God who has chosen a certain people to bless and cares nothing about the rest of humankind. Here there is a *quid pro quo*.

In the New English Bible the translators give the passage as, 'Glory to God in highest heaven, and on earth his peace for men on whom his favour rests.' Now instead of the highest glory being bestowed on God, it is God in the "highest heaven" as if there are many layers of heaven, with possible gods in each layer, for if there is a highest heaven there must be a lowest heaven. Again, as with the Revised Standard Version, peace is to be distributed only to those men who are favoured. Once again this rendition seems to suggest an arbitrary God - arbitrary as long as we are not aware of what the criteria are

---

[5] *The Great Code: The Bible and Literature, Northrop* Frye, Harcourt, Brace, Jovanovich, New York and London, 1982, p. 3.

for being favoured - who favours some and not others. And unlike the cases of Fitzgerald or Eliot we have no author to check with to determine what is intended. Indeed we have no "foul papers" either, but are constantly making copies of copies of the text. Cut off from the author's original intention, and without any of the original manuscripts, we are in a position that requires extreme caution and creative reading.

These differences are understandable. Every generation needs to translate its literary classics, to try to bring to bear on the old texts the new knowledge of language and a new vocabulary of life. Greek classics also are newly translated by each generation, and as we learn more about the syntax and semantics of the texts, our translators do their best to bring us texts which are close to the intention contained in the original. But translators are also people with certain assumptions and beliefs, people who work out of an official line, stated or not. Most of us are always reading the Bible through the eyes of a committee of translators. Sometimes, as in the example from Luke, a completely different meaning is evident in different translations. Other times the differences are more subtle, are found in the particular diction chosen by the translator, or in the metaphor chosen as vehicle of meaning. Compare these three versions of the same early story:

RSV (Genesis 3.20-22)

The man called his wife's name Eve, because she was the mother of all living. And the Lord God made for Adam and for his wife garments of skins, and clothed them.
Then the Lord God said, "Behold, the man has become like one of us, knowing good and evil; and now, lest he put forth his hand and take also of the tree of life, and eat, and live for ever" - therefore the Lord God sent him forth from the garden of Eden, to till the ground from which he was taken. He drove out the man; and at the east of the garden of Eden he placed the cherubim, and a flaming sword which turned every way, to guard the way to the tree of life.

NEB (Genesis 3.20-22)

The man called his wife Eve because she was the mother of all who live. The Lord God made tunics of skins for Adam and his wife and clothed them. He said, "The man has become like one of us, knowing good and evil; what if he now reaches out his hand and takes fruit from the tree of life also, eats it and lives for ever?" So the Lord God drove him out of the garden of Eden to till the ground from which he had been taken. He cast him out, and to the east of the garden he stationed the cherubim and a sword whirling and flashing to guard the way to the tree of life.

KJ (Genesis 3.20-22)

And Adam called his wife's name Eve; because she was the mother of all living.
Unto Adam also and to his wife did the Lord God make coats of skins, and clothed them.
And the Lord God said, Behold, the man is become as one of us, to know good and evil: and now, lest he put forth his hand, and take also of the tree of life, and eat, and live for ever:
Therefore the Lord God sent him forth from the garden of Eden, to till the ground from whence he was taken.
So he drove out the man; and he placed at the east of the garden of Eden Cherubims, and a flaming sword which turned every way, to keep the way of the tree of life.

Two of the three have a "flaming sword" while the third has a "sword whirling and flashing." One sees a flaming sword as on fire while the flashing sword is reflecting the light from some other source like the sun. The visual image is different even if the meaning is not: in all cases the way to eternal life is blocked by cherubims and a sword. The Lord God character in the RSV passage speaks in sentence fragments while in NEB he is given a complete sentence in the form of a rhetorical question. King James handles that difficulty by not using quotation marks at all and by a judicious use of the colon. The colon plus the "therefore" give the King James version a stronger and more formal sounding causal relationship between the actions in the story. Whether the clothes were garments or tunics or coats seems to tell us more about the time and place of the translation than about how to visualize these two characters after they learn about good and evil, and suddenly for the first time feel guilty about their nakedness.

A bit later in Genesis we are told about the relationship between the women of the earth and the sons of God or the sons of the gods:

RSV (Genesis 6.1-2)

When men began to multiply on the face of the ground, and daughters were born to them, the sons of God saw that the daughters of men were fair; and they took to wife such of them as they chose.

NEB (Genesis 6.1-2)

When mankind began to increase and to spread all over the earth and daughters were born to them, the sons of the gods saw that the daughters of men were beautiful; so they took for themselves such women as they chose.

KJ (Genesis 6.1-2)

And it came to pass, when man began to multiply on the face of the earth, and daughters were born unto them,
That the sons of God saw the daughters of men that they *were* fair; and they took them wives of all which they chose.

RSV and KJ have the sons of God taking the women as wives while NEB has the sons of the gods taking the women. How many gods are there? How many sons of gods are there? Heaven, or whatever the name of the home of the gods is, seems to be a place populated with several randy sons. The picture we get from the beginning is a confused one as to the heavenly population. This story sounds like so many stories from the Greeks and other middle eastern tribes, who tell of gods with god like sexual appetites who visit the earth from time to time for strikingly non-spiritual sports. KJ uses a recurrent phrase, "and it came to pass," which suggests an inevitability about the events depicted in the story - the sense one gets is that the story is already there in all of its details just waiting for the next paragraph of narration to reveal it. The suggestion is that there is an eternal text already written with a beginning, middle and end. In all cases the offspring of the union of woman and son of god will be giants.

One of the oddest, and possibly oldest, stories is found in the early part of Exodus after Moses has been chosen by Yahweh to lead his people out of Egypt. Moses and Zipporah, with their young son, are traveling toward Egypt to begin the task of convincing the Pharaoh to release the Hebrews from slavery and oppression. On the way they stop for the night. Moses is attacked by Yahweh. First he is chosen then he is attacked. Here is the story:

RSV (Exodus 4.24-26)

At a lodging place on the way the Lord met him and sought to kill him. Then Zipporah took a flint and cut off her son's foreskin, and touched Moses' feet with it, and said, "Surely you are a bridegroom of blood to me!" So he let him alone. Then it was that she said, "You are a bridegroom of blood," because of the circumcision.

NEB (Exodus 4.24-26)

During the journey, while they were encamped for the night, the Lord met Moses, meaning to kill him, but Zipporah picked up a sharp flint, cut off her son's foreskin, and touched him with it, saying, 'You are my blood-bridegroom.' So the Lord let Moses alone. Then she said, 'Blood-bridegroom by circumcision.'

KJ (Exodus 4.24-26)

And it came to pass by the way in the inn, that the Lord met him, and sought to kill him.
Then Zipporah took a sharp stone, and cut off the foreskin of her son, and cast it at his feet, and said, Surely a bloody husband *art* thou to me.
So he let him go: then she said, A bloody husband *thou art,* because of the circumcision. [emphasis God's]

RSV's rendition has the clearest pronoun reference to indicate who gets touched with the foreskin, and KJ is the only translation that has the party staying in an inn. A "lodging place" is not at all specific while "encamped" suggests a tent pitched on the sands of the desert, but the Elizabethan "inn" seems completely out of place for the time and place of the journey. What seems to be reported here is an ancient ritual which sounds like it includes a magical incantation chanted to protect the bride-groom from the local god-power. In the Moses story this attack can indicate the danger of the quest, but other than that it points out the nature of this Yahweh that Moses is dealing with: irrational and unpredictable.

The famous beginning of the Book of John is another example of the subtle differences that translations can make in the text and hence in our understanding of it.

RSV John 1.1-5

In the beginning was the Word, and the Word was with God, and the Word was God. He was in the beginning with God; all things were made through him, and without him was not anything made that was made. In him was life, and the life was the light of men. The light shines in the darkness, and the darkness has not overcome it.

NEB John 1.1-5

When all things began, the Word already was. The Word dwelt with God, and what God was the Word was. The Word, then, was with God at the beginning, and through him all things came to be; no single thing was created without him. All that came to be was alive with his life, and that life was the light of men. The light shines on in the dark, and the darkness has never mastered it.

KJ John 1.1-5

In the beginning was the Word, and the Word was with God, and the Word was God.
The same was in the beginning with God.
All things were made by him; and without him was not any thing made that was made.
In him was life; and the life was the light of man.
And the light shineth in darkness; and the darkness comprehended it not.

KJ is the only translation to announce unequivocally that "in him was life" - which is the theological point or proclamation of the story that John tells us in his gospel. The other translations emphasize the conflict between light and darkness in a struggle for mastery. In all the translations the idea of special creation is presented and the divine is seen as the Word or spirit and not as the material. This idea is consistent with the Genesis creation story and the

"In the beginning..." opening harks back to the Genesis opening reminding us that John is telling a story about the beginning of things just as surely as is the writer of Genesis. Here the story is about the beginning of Christianity and the opening line proclaims that Christ was present with God from the beginning of time. This is obviously a re-reading of the Genesis story from a particular official line - John reads back into the story the proclamation of his own story.

Most of us read the Bible in translation and should remember that translations change over time because of additional knowledge and can be influenced by certain assumptions and beliefs. Language is a living, growing, organic sort of symbolic system, and as such is never frozen in time with its meaning locked up forever. No matter how we approach this complex set of texts - as myth, as literature, as history, or as revealed "truth" - we are aided in our task with some knowledge of where it came from, how it came together as one "book," and how it grew into the collection of living literature which we know today.

Armed with some critical sense of the complex nature of the question, "What is the Bible?" we are better able to discover its meaning or meanings in a close reading of the text we have today.

With Fitzgerald's *The Great Gatsby* or Eliot's *The Wasteland* we deal with a text by a single author, written in English. With Shakespeare's "Hamlet" we have a further comlexity - no original manuscript exists, and three different texts compete for our attention. The Bible poses an even more complex set of problems. Written in ancient Hebrew and New Testament Greek, languages which are no longer living; compiled over the years in various "packages;" written by who knows who - we have to be careful making claims about this collection of books.

IS THE BIBLE TRUE?

People who claim the bible is literally true, if they are to retain a rational stance, have to explain (1) which "bible" they have in mind; (2) the several contradictions[6] which occur in all versions; (3) what it means for a text to be literally true. When Yahweh says "my bow I set in the sky..." aren't we to take "bow" as a metaphor for rainbow? Metaphor plays an important part in the Biblical texts and literal interpretation seems to block the possibility of reading these texts as we read other texts - with an eye and ear to figures of speech and to the many levels of meaning such figures can bring to a reading of a text. Mistakes in fact and inconsistencies in account are also stumbling blocks for the literalists. For example, everyone knows that pi is equal to 3.1416...and that the relationship between the circumference and diameter of a circle has not changed its value significantly over time. As we have improved our method of calculation we have seen it change from 3 1/7 to a computer generated number with billions of places, but it has always been known to be more than three. And yet we find:

> He then made the Sea of cast metal; it was round in shape, the diameter from rim to rim being ten cubits; it stood five cubits high, and it took a line thirty cubits long to go round it. All around the Sea on the outside under its rim, completely surrounding the thirty cubits of its circumference, were two rows of gourds, cast in one piece with the sea itself. (1 Kings 7, v.23)

A simple deduction here yields a value of 3 for *pi*. How can the literalist explain this? If by saying, "Well, it's just a human mistake," are we then justified in asking how do you know this is the only "human mistake"? What criteria are to be used to determine what counts as a "human mistake"? The hypothesis (if it is one) that everything in the Bible is true is not justified because of this one counter example. Someone making the "truth of the Bible" claim must have some other sense of "truth" in mind than "corresponding to the facts."

---

[6] Compare, for example, II Samuel 24:1 and I Chronicles 21:1. Or think about Genesis I and how its possible to have days and nights before the sun exists.

DIFFERENT VERSIONS OF THE SAME STORY

There are a large number of "doublets" in the Old Testament. For example 2 Samuel 24.1 tells us that "the anger of the Lord was kindled against Israel, and he incited David against them, saying, 'Go, number Israel and Judah.'" But in Chronicles (1 Chron. 21.1) the same event is given in this way: "Satan stood up against Israel, and incited David to number Israel." Not only are the causal forces different in the two versions but also the results are different, for in the first case, Israel, we are told, has 800,000 men and Judah has 500,000 men; while in the second version the count is Israel 1,100,000 men and Judah 470,000 men. Israel in the Chronicles census has become a much larger nation than its neighbour to the south. We are given the decalogue in both Exodus 24.4 and also in Exodus 34.28, and there are differences in the parallel stories. Hagar is ejected from Abraham's household in Genesis 16 and again in Genesis 21. In the first telling of the story Sarai mistreats Hagar because she is jealous of her ability to conceive, and Hagar runs away. In the second version of the story Sarai asks Abraham to drive Hagar away from the camp and after checking with Yahweh Abraham does so.

The ten commandments are reported twice. In Exodus 20 we read:

God spoke, and these were his words:
I am the Lord your God who brought you out of Egypt, out of the land of slavery.
You shall have no other god to set against me.
You shall not make a carved image for yourself nor the likeness of anything in the heavens above, or on the earth below, or in the waters under the earth.
You shall not bow down to them or worship them; for I, the Lord your God am a jealous god. I punish the children for the sins of the fathers to the third and fourth generations of those who hate me. But I keep faith with thousands, with those who love me and keep my commandments.
You shall not make wrong use of the name of the Lord your God: the Lord will not leave unpunished the man who misuses his name.
Remember to keep the sabbath day holy. You have six days to labour and do all your work. But the seventh day is a sabbath of the Lord your God; that day you shall not do any work...

Honour your father and your mother, that you may live long in the
land which the Lord your God is giving you.
You shall not commit murder.
You shall not commit adultery.
You shall not steal.
You shall not give false evidence against your neighbour.
You shall not covet your neighbour's house...wife, ...slave...ox...or
anything that belongs to him.

Later in the book of Deuteronomy we are told the same story over
again. This time Moses reports on the giving of the law and tells what the Lord
said with only very slight changes. In the Sinai episode of Exodus 24 verses
9-11; 12-15a; and 15b-18a seem to be reporting three different versions of the
same event. We read of three different summons to ascend Sinai: the first fo-
cuses on the covenant between Israel and its God in the context of a covenant
rite, climaxing in a covenant meal, and a vision of the God of Israel. The
second concentrates on Yahweh's personal role in writing and handing over
his law on two stone tablets, while the third revolves around the unique mode
of Yahweh's appearance on the mountain as a mysterious presence that looks
like a fire behind a cloud.

Doublets are important in the New Testament as well. In the synoptic
gospels we read of Jesus' birth in two of the three gospels and the two versions
differ on some important points. Mark gives us no birth narrative at all, and
Paul never mentions either the miraculous birth or any of Jesus' miracles. The
crucifixion story in the gospels also differ in some interesting ways which we
will consider in a later chapter.

THE IMPORTANCE OF THE BIBLE

"The Bible," as Frye says, "is clearly a major element in our own
imaginative tradition, whatever we may think we believe about it. It insistently
raises the question: Why does this huge, sprawling, tactless book sit there
inscrutably in the middle of our cultural heritage like the "great Bogg" or

"Sphinx" in *Peer Gynt*, frustrating all our efforts to walk around it?"[7]

Standing at the centre of our own cultural heritage, the Bible has meant different things to different people over the years - at one time believed to be the answer to all human questions, at another thought to be a tissue of fabrications meant to keep people in line and to promote a certain kind of power structure. The importance of the book will depend upon whether its human stories touch us as readers - depends upon the stories living within us, moving us to contemplation and to action in the real world. To the extent that the concerns, characters and events of this book can engage your mind and heart - to that extent the Bible is a living and important work.

MYTHOLOGY AND THE BIBLE

In Leviticus (18:9) we read: "The nakedness of your sister, the daughter of your father, or the daughter of your mother, whether born at home or elsewhere, their nakedness you shall not uncover," (NKJV, p. 119). This same passage, in *The Living Torah,* is translated less euphemistically as: "Do not commit incest with your sister, even if she is legitimate or illegitimate, you must not commit incest with her," (*TLT,* p. 346). The message, in either translation, is clear enough: even a half-sister is taboo as a sexual partner. And yet, of course, Abraham, the sacred hero-ancestor of the Old Testament, does marry his half-sister and even denies she is his wife on two occasions, passing her off as only his sister.

The Leviticus discussion of "nakedness" in which "uncover the nakedness of" becomes a way of talking about incest or the act of sexual intercourse in general is useful in understanding the story of Ham's curse. First a few words about interpretation in general. Are all readings of a text equally valid? What counts as evidence for a given reading? When is the instructor "reading into the text" and when is s/he reading the text?

Look again at the first murder story, the Cain and Abel story. We are told that Abel's sacrifice is acceptable to Yahweh and that Cain's is not. We are not told why one is acceptable and the other is not. We can read back into

---

[7] Frye, *op.cit.,* p. xviii, xix.

the story and say that Yahweh knew already that Cain was a bad piece of work since Yahweh knows all, but this doesn't really help us to follow the story or learn what makes a sacrifice acceptable, because to take this approach is to give up on reading stories entirely and to accept a kind of fatalism. We could also look for further information about the story in another story, for example, we could point to the allusion to Cain and Abel in the book of Hebrews: "By faith Abel offered unto God a more excellent sacrifice than Cain, by which he obtained witness that he was righteous, God testifying of his gifts: and by it he being dead yet speaketh." (Heb. 11.4) This passage occurs in the famous discussion of what faith is, and the writer uses several examples from the Old Testament to make the point that faith is "the substance of things hoped for, the evidence of things not seen." It is a good idea as a reader to search out further examples of the use of a word like "faith," or a phrase like "uncover the nakedness" to see how the writers used the word or phrase. But notice that the use of "faith" In Hebrews is not just a report of how the word is used it is an interpretation of the earlier story. In Hebrews several examples form the book of Genesis are used to provide examples for how a Christian should have faith - all of the heroes of the Genesis stories are heroes therefore they must have had faith - but that is to read back into the stories from a particular point of view.

Ham's story is also instructive as an example of a way of reading the texts. Here is how I read the story and why:

> "And he drank of the wine, and was drunken; and he was uncovered within his tent.
> And Ham, the father of Canaan, saw the nakedness of his father, and told his two brethren without. ...
> And Noah awoke from his wine, and knew what his younger son had done unto him.
> And he said, Cursed be Canaan; a servant of servants shall he be unto his brethren."

There are clues in the story that are intriguing: if all Ham did was see his father naked then why is the punishment so great? The curse of Ham is passed on to his son Canaan and to his son's sons - and the curse is that their offspring will be servants (read slaves) to the others. Also, we read "and he knew what his younger son had done unto him" which suggests more than merely seeing him naked, for how could one know that another had seen him? These bits of evidence are not conclusive but they are sufficient to make one wonder what is going on. Now we do want to know how the phrase "saw the nakedness of" is used in the books - not how it is interpreted but what it means. And so we look for the phrase in other parts of the collection. It shows up in Leviticus in a long discussion of what sexual practices are to be prohibited.

"And if a man shall take his sister, his father's daughter, or his mother's daughter, and see her nakedness, and she see his nakedness; it is a wicked thing; and they shall be cut off in the sight of their people: he hath uncovered his sister's nakedness: he shall bear his iniquity." (Lev. 20.17)

This passage is translated "Do not commit incest with your sister, even if she is the daughter of only your father or mother. Whether she is legitimate or illegitimate, you must not commit incest with her," in THE LIVING TORAH by Rabbi Aryeh Kaplan. ["see her nakedness" = "uncover her nakedness" = "commit incest with her"]. The phrases "see his nakedness" or "uncover her nakedness" are translated "commit incest" as can be seen above. So what was Ham's crime? Homosexual incest. And that is in the story.

Here is Robert Alter, Professor of Hebrew and Comparative Literature at the University of California at Berkeley, and the author of *The Art Of Biblical Narrative:*

> All the other biblical occurrences of the common idiom "to see the nakedness of" or "to uncover the nakedness of" are explicitly sexual, usually referring to incest (it is precisely the phrase used for the act Ham perpetrates on his father Noah), and perhaps Joseph feels a kind of incestuous violence in what the brothers have done to him and through him to his father. Reuben, ... the first born of the ten, actually lay with Bilhah, Jacob's concubine and Rachel's maid and conjugal surrogate, not long after Rachel's death, when Joseph was still a boy. (p.164)

What about the application of the Leviticus rules of sexual conduct to the Genesis heroes? Is Abraham exempt from this sexual taboo? Was he not subject to the laws because he came much earlier and in that earlier time there were no such laws yet revealed to men and women? Or is this just an example of an inconsistency in the Bible, which we hear of all the time?

What one says about this kind of problem will depend upon what one knows about the dynamics of the Old Testament - the literary, historical, and philosophical ingredients which make up these books. Myth is one of these constituents, and an important one. "Myth" is not used here to mean merely "fictional," or "not real," but in its full sense. As the German theologian, Bartsch, has said, "Myth is the expression of unobservable realities in terms of observable phenomena." Myth then is always used to interpret reality, to *read* the physical and psychological world. Myth is metaphor. It is story. It explains the complex in terms of the simple. It may be non-rational, but it is not *false*. Myth is true to not true of the world. The non-rationality of myth is its very essence, for religion requires a demonstration of faith by the suspension of critical doubt. "In this sense," as Edmund Leach puts it, "all stories which occur in The Bible are myths for the devout Christian whether they correspond to historical fact or not."[8]

REDUNDANCY AND INFORMATION

One of the common characteristics of all mythological systems is that of *redundancy*. Important stories are told in several different versions. A second characteristic is *information*. Myths are information "packages" delivered in several forms (redundancy) in order that we may get the "message" (information). For example, man/woman is created twice in Genesis; then, as if the first two men/women were not enough, we also have the story of Noah, in which God starts anew once more. Edmund Leach, commenting on this characteristic of redundancy, writes: "Now in the mind of the believer, myth does indeed convey messages which are the Word of God. To such a reader the redundancy of myth is a very reassuring fact. Any particular myth in isolation is like a coded message - badly snarled up with noisy interference. Even the most confident devotee might feel a little uncertain as to what precisely is being said. But, as a result of the redundancy, the believer can feel that, even when the details vary, each alternative version of the myth confirms his understanding and reinforces the essential meaning of all others."[9]

---

[8] Leach, Edmund, *Genesis as Myth and Other Essays*, Jonathan Cape, 1969, London, page 5.

[9] *Ibid*. page 9.

Another characteristic of myth is its binary aspect: seeming opposites as heaven and earth, male and female, living and dead, good and evil, first and last, gods and people. In an attempt to bridge these binaries, a new element, "mediation," is introduced into the story. "Mediation" is achieved by introducing a third category which is "abnormal" or "anomalous." Thus myths are full of fabulous monsters, incarnate gods, virgin mothers, and the like. This middle ground of half-gods and super-humans is abnormal, non-natural, holy. It is typically the focus of all taboo and ritual observance. Leach, commenting on the tales of the patriarchs, says, "this long series of repetitive and inverted tales asserts: (a) the overriding virtue of close kin endogamy, (b) that...Abraham can carry this so far that he marries his paternal half-sister..., (c)that a rank order is established which places the tribal neighbours of the Israelites in varying degrees of inferior status...the myth requires that the Israelites be descended unambiguously from Terah, the father of Abraham."[10]

Notice that in the Noah story Noah becomes a unique ancestor without the implication of incest. (And yet the theme of homosexual incest recurs when drunken Noah is "seduced" by his own son Ham). Myth can be seen as a way of establishing certain basic taboos or rituals in a culture. In this sense myths are repositories for human beliefs about what ought to be the case. In order, for example, to discourage certain sexual practices we might invent stories showing the terrible consequences of participating in those practices. These stories can be used to suggest what behaviour is prohibited and what behaviour is commanded. We are what we read, and the simplest way to teach ethics to a people is to recite stories.   Stories are vessels for the official line - the prescribed way of behaving within a culture.

TRUTH AND STORIES

Northrop Frye in *The Great Code: The Bible and Literature*[11] says that "the Bible tells a story" and "the Bible is a myth" are essentially the same statement. Frye argues (p. 31, ff) that myth means, first of

---

[10] *Ibid*. pages 21, 22.

[11] Northrop Frye, *The Great Code: The Bible as Literature*, Harcourt Brace Jovanovich, New York and London, 1982.

all, *mythos* or plot - the sequential ordering of words, and in this sense all verbal structures are mythical. Hence, he says (p. 30) "to demythologize any part of the Bible would be the same thing as to obliterate it." If one stretches the meaning of the word "myth" in this way then one has the problem of universalizing: if every verbal structure is a myth then calling a given story a myth tells us very little. But, there is a second sense of mythical that Frye develops here (and in his earlier works). He says, "mythical...means the opposite of "not really true": it means charged with a special seriousness and importance." (p. 33) "Mythology," he writes, "is not a *datum* but a *factum* of human existence: it belongs to the world of culture and civilization that man has made and still inhabits." (p. 37) In this second sense myth is not merely a mistaken explanation of natural phenomena but is rather a form of imaginative and creative thinking that helps to produce the world we occupy. And that world includes our stories just as it includes the objects of the physical world. Again Frye: "...the real interest of myth is to draw a circumference around a human community and look inward toward that community, not to inquire into the operations of nature." (p. 37)

If we ask questions about the truth value of the statements in the Bible then we work within a correspondence theory of truth, asking "is this statement true OF the world?"; better to ask "is this story true TO the world?" Many statements are true in both senses: "there came a famine in the land" is true of the world and true to the world of the story in which it occurs as a device for moving characters around.

Some see myth as primitive science, in which sense we are to think of myths as limited methods for explaining the phenomena we discover in the world. For example, one might think of the end of the flood story in Genesis as a putative explanation for why we have rainbows in the world. Or, as some have argued, the creation story (only one of them, remember), which has Eve made from Adam's rib, is there to "explain" why women are subordinate to males. Offering the "justification" for a social convention in the form of a story is a part of the larger human story. Although conventions change, there is something that does not change - the human need to tell stories.

Mythology's themes are of perennial interest, and more than this, possess a value that is real. Mythology is also document and record - existing not merely in the dim past, but in the living present - of peoples' thought, of their attempt to attain that happiness which Virgil tells us, arises from "knowledge of the causes of things."

Myth has these characteristics:

1. form: primarily narrative (but may be pictorial)
2. time: set in the past or the universal present -
   the same thing said in a different way at the same
   time - or, more simply, the past is universally
   present.
3. subject-matter: themes are drawn from the realm of
   the non-verifiable, or at least from that which was
   incapable of demonstration at the time of the
   creation of the myth.

There are these kinds of myth:

1. myths of the gods
2. nature myths
3. myths of origins
4. philosophical myths
5. myths of the "hereafter" or the other world

they function as:

6. allegories
7. explanations of the beginnings of something
8. para-scientific explanations
9. expressions of the collective story of an age.

A myth is living or dead not true or false. We cannot refute a myth because as soon as we treat it as refutable it is no longer a myth but has become hypothesis or history. We need not believe everything we read in the Bible as literally true (because it is not), but it can be read as pointing toward a truth, or truths, about the human story. Sometimes we may smile at the naivete of the stories but we should never sneer at them. Often the seeming naivete is indeed just that, seeming. A myth is a story about something that never happened but is always true.

CHAPTER 3: BROTHERS, TOKENS AND TYPES.

The book of Genesis is a collection of stories woven together by some unknown redactor. The work contains legend, poetry, fantasy, genealogy, short story, and other literary forms which are blended together to form a more or less coherent whole. Genesis is a kind of universal history; like other myths, it presents a story about what the beginning of time may have been like. It opens with *two* distinct creation myths: one emphasizing the transcendental nature of the creator god and the other emphasizing the human-like properties of the same creator god. The first god creates by fiat, by giving verbal commands, the second creates by breathing air into a lump of clay. The two may be different versions of the story by different poets, or they may be contrary projections of the complex human creation called god. The "third," if the projection is read as a psychological ground, would be this: the *verbal* is the lump of clay. God speaks and the world begins. God speaks and life begins. The creative power of speech is celebrated in the beginning. Language with its formal aspects - its rules of syntax and semantics - is the perfect analog for creation itself, since language gives us the power to create order and meaning out of the chaos of experience.

The creation myth can be read as a description of any act of creation: first the intention, then the translation from mind to matter, and then the evaluation: "and it was good." Professor Douwe Stuurman, who taught The Bible as Literature at the University of California in the nineteen sixties, pointed out in lectures that the creation myth, when read aloud, will be heard to be an accurate description of the completion of any creative act. He told us the story of his first wife, a blind poet, who had asked him to read Genesis 1 and 2 aloud to her and who when he finished said "that is precisely the feeling of creating a poem." In writing a poem one starts with an idea and a blank and formless page. The creative act of beginning to "blow" life into that page and after some time (and with some luck) giving form to the stuff of the mind, transforming it into a new medium has formed a completed work. Human creation, like Eliot's *The Wasteland*, is often a multi-staged affair with false starts, revisions, crumpled failed attempts tossed away, and a complex of discovery and creation. The poet does not know the poem until it is finished. And when finished the feeling is there to be expressed: "And it is good."

Read this way 'good' is an aesthetic term, as in "*Shane* is a good movie" or "*King Lear* is Shakespeare's best play." Value terms are ambiguous in that sense, for we use many of the same to describe both aesthetic and moral judgments, 'good' doing service in both categories of judgments. "And it was good" as used in Genesis is evaluative, but not in the moral sense. The story itself is silent on the moral status of the creation and therefore the puzzle of how evil can arise in a perfect creation arises only because of the confusion between aesthetic and moral uses of the word 'good.' 'Is the universe and everything in it good?' is the wrong question to ask when 'good' is used in the moral sense. Such a question gets currency only if one presupposes that the logically prior assertion 'God is good' is true, and that there is a perfect transfer from creator to creation. But in the creation myths in Genesis we have no argument to establish the truth of that claim, in fact, Genesis actually tells us very little about God. "In the beginning of creation, when God made heaven and earth..." presupposes the existence and nature of God and the reader has the task of creating God from the narrative stuff provided. From the first line of the book the main character is a given, yet a mystery, a term looking for a referent. Here again confusion arises when we fail to see that the particular kind of verbal act the writer uses in the story is not one to be evaluated by some correspondence theory of truth, but is rather a proclamation or statement in the sense that the Canadian Constitution is a proclamation or set of statements. If one says of a country's constitution, 'It is true' what exactly is one saying? Constitutions constitute the rules of the game, and are, as we all know, subject to interpretation throughout time. The logical status of many statements in the Bible is similar to the logical status of rules of a game: 'three strikes and you are out' not only regulates the game of baseball, it also constitutes the game. "And it was good" is thus proclamation and aesthetic judgment. God, as an objective being, is presupposed by the priests who compose the account of the creation. God, as a character in a narrative, is yet to be discovered.

After the creation stories come a series of "beginnings" stories. We are given a story which "explains" the multiplicity of languages in the world. We are told why pain and death enter the world. We are told of the first murder and of god's method of dealing with the first murderer. He does not use capital punishment but instead marks Cain as a stranger, someone cut off from society and from the earth itself. The jealousy that motivates the act of murder is the second indication (the first had been the disobedience of Eve and Adam) we have of the source of conflict and that conflict comes from the human creatures' inner thoughts and feelings. A seed of conflict, of internal disruption grows in the psyches of the humans and proves to be the narrative source of the evil that enters the story in opposition to the expected goodness transferred from creator to created. Cain, unable to accept God's rejection of his gift, strikes out against his brother instead of addressing his own psychic problems of insensitivity and jealousy, and is punished by complete and awful rejection. We are shown in this story of the first murder that the results of murder are to make the murderer non-human: God removes Cain from life, from human society, and even from the fruits of the garden. Isolated, Cain must walk the earth alone and friendless marked so that no one will kill him to relieve him from his life sentence. Cain's mark is a visible sign of God's absence and punishment as well as a symbol of the burden Cain must carry to his grave as a result of the inner turmoil that led him to commit fratricide.

As human-like characters enter the narrative, they are presented as nomadic mideastern tribesman who wander the semi-arid country of Canaan and Egypt and who learn the importance of dreams and of a belief in the future. Abraham, who is a hero to three religions, walks onto the stage as the father of countries who has, above all, the virtues of loyalty and obedience. In the most powerful and disturbing narrative in the collection, Abraham is commanded by Yahweh (the Hebrew name for the creator-god) to sacrifice his young son. This, Abraham agrees to do, but is stopped at the last moment by Yahweh, who it seems, is only testing Abraham's obedience. A ram is substituted for the boy and the end of human sacrifice is signalled. This story has haunted the twentieth century imagination - Kirkegaard wrote a book based on the questions raised by this 300 word story - because it raises so many profound questions. If a voice orders you to do something how do you know the voice is the voice of god and not of the devil? If god demands complete and unthinking obedience is god worthy of worship? Can we worship a being willing to murder to make a point? Is an action good because god says so or does god say so because it is good?

The other key idea in the book of Genesis is nationality. Yahweh and his chosen people join in the covenental stories that image the agreement and promise between Yahweh and the Patriarchs. If you will follow me, says Yahweh, I will provide you and your offspring with land. The narrative that follows traces the covenant from generation to generation through a number of deceitful, lustful, conflict-ridden, loving, loyal, ordinary people.

But the overriding theme developed in this set of stories is this: how can human beings learn to resolve conflicts without committing fratricide? The first murder, of brother by brother, is a description of the worst failure: homicide. The relationship of brotherhood is expanded and developed to metaphorically include our relationship with each other within the human tribal family, and in the triumphant meeting of Jacob and Esau hatred and conflict melt away into a very human embrace that suggests a way for all of us to behave. Esau, who had lost his birthright to Jacob his younger brother, had said to himself, "The time for mourning for my father will soon be here; then I will kill my brother Jacob." Esau's threat is real, his injury greater than Cain's, and the expectation of yet another murder of brother by brother is acute. When finally the two brothers are reunited we are prepared for the worst.

> Jacob raised his eyes and saw Esau coming towards him with four hundred men; so he divided the children between Leah and Rachel and the two slave girls. He put the slave girls with their children in front, Leah with her children next, and Rachel with Joseph last. He then went on ahead of them, bowing low to the ground seven times as he approached his brother. Esau ran to meet him and embraced him; he threw his arms round him and kissed him, and they wept. (Gen. 33 1-5)

Instead of arms raised in anger we get arms that embrace. Anticipating a weapon we get a kiss. Conflicts between brothers need not end in murder. The word "brother" is given to us just at the moment of recognition to remind us that these two are brothers. Reconciliation occurs in the midst of danger as we are reminded by the mention of an army of men and by the prudent way that Jacob arranges his people, using the slave girls and their children to protect the inner circles of Leah and his favorite Rachel. And who is in the centre of the protective shields? Joseph. Joseph of the many coloured coat; Joseph the special.

LITERARY DEVICES

Robert Alter, in his excellent book *The Art of Biblical Narrative* (upon which I draw heavily in the following), writes:

> The God of Israel, as so often has been observed, is above all the God of history: the working out of His purposes in history is a process that compels the attention of the Hebrew imagination, which is thus led to the most vital interest in the concrete and differential character of historical events. *The point is that fiction was the principal means which the biblical authors had at their disposal for realizing history.*[1] (emphasis mine)

Fiction is the key to understanding the many biblical stories. "Fiction" comes from the Latin, "fictio," which means "a making, counterfeiting." It is a form of "fingere", "to make, to form, to devise." Think of "fiction" in the sense of making or forming and not in its sense of "false". When I say the bible is fiction I am not saying that the Bible is false. What I am saying is that the Bible is a creation, a making, a story which is formed and molded to certain ends; it is a formed and molded story in the same way that *The Great Gatsby* is a novel. Obviously, there are many differences between the stories presented in the Bible and the stories presented in twentieth century novels. The techniques of narration have evolved and the conventions that stand behind a literary work have also changed over the last 2,500 years. But the basic enterprise of story telling has not changed significantly. And, what we need to realize is that the religious vision of the Bible is given depth and subtlety by being conveyed through the sophisticated resources of prose fiction. Like the Greeks, the Hebrews learned to tell their story in a unique way, to glorify their God in songs, poems, and anthems. Unlike the Greeks, they chose a different genre.

> The ancient Hebrew writers purposefully nurtured and developed prose narration to take the place of the epic genre which by its content was intimately bound up with the world of paganism, and appears to have had a special standing in the polytheistic cults. The

---

[1] Robert Alter, *The Art of Biblical Narrative,* Basic Books Inc., New York, 1981, page 32.

recitation of the epics was tantamount to an enactment of cosmic events in the manner of sympathetic magic. In the process of total rejection of the polytheistic religions and their ritual expressions in the cult, epic songs and also the epic genre were purged from the repertoire of the Hebrew authors.[2]

Any comparison of the Homeric gods with the god of the Old Testament reveals the essential difference between the two cultures. Although the Homeric poems played the same role in Greece that the Old Testament stories did in Palestine, in the subsequent development of the civilization from which they grew, the differences are dramatic. The Olympian gods, as conceptual representations of the power which governs the universe, are totally irreconcilable with the one god of Abraham. The Greek conception of the nature of the gods and their relation to humans is so alien to us that it is difficult for the modern reader to take it seriously. The Hebrew basis of European Christianity has made it almost impossible for us to imagine a god who can be feared and laughed at, blamed and admired and still worshipped with sincerity--yet these are all proper attitudes toward the gods on Olympus.

The Hebrew conception of god is clearly an expression of the emphasis on those aspects of the universe which imply a harmonious order. Any disorder in the universe is blamed on man and woman, not on God. Thus we have a story to explain why there is death and pain in this otherwise perfect world. Human errors bring about the advent of pain, sin, and death. Interestingly, there can be no sin without God since "sin" is a thoroughly religious word. Those ancient Hebrews expressed their feelings and awe when faced with the wonder and miracle of life; yet, they also had to make sense of the world they found themselves a part of - a world with life and joy but also death and suffering.

In all the stories in the Bible the Hebrew writers struggle to reconcile evil with an *a priori* assumption of one all-powerful, all-knowing and just God. Greek poets and philosophers conceived their gods as an expression of the disorder of the world they inhabited: the Olympian gods, like the sea and the wind, follow their own will even to the extreme of conflict with each other,

---

[2] "The 'Comparative Method' in Biblical Interpretation--Principles and Problems" *Gottingen Congress Volume,* Leiden, 1978, page 354.

and always with a sublime disregard for the human beings who may be affected by the results of their actions. They are not concerned with morality and leave it for human beings to talk about. The Old Testament God, on the other hand, is presented most of the time[3] as one who is intimately involved in morality to the extent of providing in the decalogue the covenant between him and his people and following (cf. Numbers) with hundred of rules and regulations to be followed by the people.[4]

The epic poems of Homer provide a much different conceptual scheme than do the prose narratives of the Hebrew writers. The difference between the Greek and Hebrew hero, between Achilles and Joseph, for example, is remarkable, and has led many to claim that there are no heroes in the Old Testament. These Hebrew heroes are all tentative, all flawed in spirit or in body and seem too common to be *real* heroes. Homer's poetry depends largely on image and other poetic devices for its marvellous effect while the Hebrews use the devices of a newly developed prose narrative to convey an equally marvellous subtlety. The subtle interplay of Homeric lines is not often found in the Bible, not because the Hebrews were inferior artists but because they were writing in a different genre and hence employing different techniques.

As Alter puts it:[5]

> The Bible presents a kind of literature in which the primary impulse would often seem to be to provide instruction or at least necessary information, not merely to delight. If, however, we fail to see that the creators of biblical narrative were writers who, like writers elsewhere, took pleasure in exploring the formal and imaginative resources of their fictional medium, perhaps sometimes unexpectedly capturing the fullness of their subject in the very play of exploration, we shall miss much that the biblical stories are meant to convey.

---

[3] The Book of Job deals directly and differently with the problem of god and morality based upon theism. We will consider its contribution to the philosophical discussion in a later chapter.

[4] I am not suggesting here that morality is merely following the rules. Rule compliance is, however, a big part of the Old Testament approach to morality.

[5] *Op. Cit.*, Alter, page 46.

In the next few pages we shall consider some of these "formal and imaginative resources" in an attempt to see how a knowledge of them can help us to understand the complex stories we are told in the Bible. While discussing these formal attributes of the literary style we will also want to know more about the informal attitudes, the conventions, that the writers and readers shared and which, as in all literature, provided the soil for the growth of the formal structures which we call narratives. To stay with the plant metaphor for a moment, one can say that the conventions extant at a given time provide the "root system" for the literature which grows above ground as a formal production of the human mind. Let us look at a few of the key literary devices employed by the Hebrew writers:

1. verbal repetition
2. thematic key words
3. delayed exposition
4. reiteration of motifs
5. dialogue
6. narration
7. type-scene

The very famous opening passages of the King James Genesis will serve to show several of these devices at work.

In the beginning God created the heaven and the earth.

2. And the earth was without form, and void; and darkness was upon the face of the deep. And the Spirit of God moved upon the face of the waters.

3. And God said, Let there be light; and there was light.

4. And God saw the light, that it was good: and God divided the light from the darkness.

5. And God called the light Day, and the darkness he called Night. And the evening and the morning were the first day.

6. And God said, Let there be a firmament in the midst of the waters, and let it divide the waters from the waters.

7. And God made the firmament, and divided the waters which were under the firmament from the waters which were above the firmament: and it was so.

8. And God called the firmament Heaven. And the evening and the morning were the second day.

9. And God said, Let the waters under the heaven be gathered together unto one place, and let the dry land appear: and it was so.

10. And God called the dry land Earth; and the gathering together of the waters called he Seas: And God saw that it was good.

11. And God said, Let the earth bring forth grass, the herb yielding seed, and the fruit tree yielding fruit after his kind, whose seed is in itself, upon the earth: and it was so.

12. And the earth brought forth grass, and herb yielding seed after his kind, and the tree yielding fruit, whose seed was in itself, after his kind: and God saw that it was good.

13. And the evening and the morning were the third day.

14. And God said, Let there be lights in the firmament of the heaven to divide the day from the night; and let them be for signs, and for seasons, and for days, and years:

15. And let them be for lights in the firmament of the heaven to give light upon the earth: and it was so.

16. And God made two great lights; the greater light to rule the day, and the lesser light to rule the night: he made the stars also.

17. And God set them in the firmament of the heaven to give light upon the earth,

18. And to rule over the day and over the night, and to divide the light from the darkness: and God saw that it was good.

19. And the evening and the morning were the fourth day.

20. And God said, Let the waters bring forth abundantly the moving creature that hath life, and fowl that may fly above the earth in the open firmament of heaven.

21. And God created great whales, and every living creature that moveth, which the waters brought forth abundantly, after their kind, and every winged fowl after his kind: and God saw that it was good.

22. And God blessed them, saying, Be fruitful, and multiply, and fill the waters in the seas, and let fowl multiply in the earth.

23. And the evening and the morning were the fifth day.

24. And God said, Let the earth bring forth the living creature after his kind, cattle and creeping things, and beast of the earth after his kind: and it was so.

> 26. And God said, Let us make man in our image... in the image
> of God created he him; male and female created he them...and He
> rested on the seventh day from all his work which he had made.

Perhaps the first thing we notice about this creation story is that we are
confronted with a very talkative God. The writer chooses to present the story
(and uses the word "story" to describe it) in a kind of permanent present tense
with the commands of God clearly presented as verbal performances. This is a
God who creates by verbal fiat. And stories are verbal constructs, which also
create by verbal fiat: there is no character, no action, no place until some words
are spoken or written; until we name the objects of the world we have no way
of linguistically referring to them: no words, no world. The repetition of the
imperative 'Let there be...' shows us that we are confronted here with one god,
with one God for whom language is important: after creating something he
immediately names it, and then evaluates it. Everything is brought into being
by the verbal order of God; then named by him (later Adam will be given the
task of naming the animals) as if the creation of an entity is not complete until
it is given a name. The repetition of the imperative 'Let there be...'is an
obvious literary device which draws our attention to the verbal power of this
unique god. A comparison with other creation myths is instructive.[6] Nowhere
else is this verbal quality so dramatically presented.

A pattern emerges: on the first day light enters the world for the first
time and then each day's creative work produces more complex components of
the world and its inventory. By the sixth day mammals and complex fruits and
trees are present. These created things are not part of a logical progression of
ever more complex structures; for example, how can there be day and night
before there is a sun? They are more an expanding circle of consciousness.

---

[6] In the Vedic Indian *Brhadaranyaka Upanisad* we read: "...in the beginning this universe
was but the Self in the form of a man. He looked around and saw nothing but himself.
Thereupon, his first shout was, "It is I!"; whence the concept "I" arose....Then he was afraid. -
And that is why anyone alone is afraid. - He considered: "Since there is nothing here but myself,
what is there to fear?" Whereupon the fear departed; for what should have been feared? it is
only to a second that fear refers. However, he still lacked delight. - Therefore, one lacks delight
when alone. - He desired a second. He was just as large as a man and woman embracing. This
Self then divided himself in two parts; and with that there were a master and a mistress....He
united with her, and from that mankind arose." Quoted here from Joseph Campbell's *The
Masks of god: Primitive Mythology,* 1968, The MacMillan company of Canada.

From the instant of conscious awareness (light) the child's world expands until it finally includes a sense of the cycles of day and night, a realization of something outside the individual ego, and a powerful acquaintance with the external world with all of the stuff which it contains. A psychological, not a logical pattern develops.

KEY WORDS IN THE STORIES

"And God saw that it was good" appears after each creative act, after each day's work. One way of reading the Hebrew creation story is as a description of any creative act. Write a poem, make a pot, or build a bird house - if all goes well the feeling of "and it was good" comes after completing the day's work. Further, the description is accurate in that first comes the idea ("Let there be...) and then that idea is given reality ("and it was so"), and then the reality is blessed ("and it was good"). From concept to concrete being is a good description of a creative act - and with the act comes the sense of making something out of formlessness by acting on raw material with a consciousness that can then see that it has form, and can value the new creation. The voice of God in this creation myth is a voice which imparts value to the universe ("And it was good"), gives form to an earth that was without form ("Let there be"), and fills up that which was void ("and it was so").

Does that mean that value is in the universe? That is certainly the position presented here in this story, presented in the narrative, but not argued for. The value claim is asserted, is given form in the repetition of the evaluative utterance of the only character in the story, but it is presupposed, not offered as the conclusion to an argument. At this point we are given a god who is different from his creation, a god who acts verbally on the stuff of the universe to give it form and announces the aesthetic value of the creation. Unlike other mid-eastern creation stories where the god-creator is the stuff of the creation here we have a distinct verbal character who commands the things of experience into being. This god does not make things from parts of his body, does not give birth to his creation, but, instead, commands the mental to produce the physical.

Thematic key words in this narrative include: "let", "God", "and", "good". To reiterate: "let" serves as an imperative, a command on each of the days of the creation and tells us of a god who creates by fiat and who infuses matter with concept and name. "God" is the name of the author of this creation and we are made to feel that he is one, that he is all powerful, and that he is a god who speaks in a human tongue. "And" functions to introduce each day and each part of the total creative effort. It gives each sentence equal weight, hence equal importance. Coordinating conjunctions tend to do that, especially "and", which refuses to attach more weight to one main clause over another leaving each conjoined clause separate and equal. There is also the sense of a huge enterprise which the series of "and" introduced sentences provides: and ..., and..., and..., filling up the void with earth and stars, sun and moon, plants and animals, oceans and dry lands.

Using this passage as a model as one reads the stories can provide a key for several of the literary devices used by the Hebrew writers to relate their accounts of god, man and woman, and their relationships. Anytime one notices verbal repetition it brings about an effect which influences meaning. Sometimes repetition changes from verbatim repetition to near repetition with slight changes that subtly introduce a new level of meaning. For example, at the end of the sixth day, for the first time, an adverb ("very") is used in the value assessment: "And god saw every thing that he had made, and , behold, it was very good." Also, we get "behold" for the first time. It is as if we were present to review all of the week's work, to look back at the creative activity of those first six days with a cumulative feeling of the celebration of creativity urged on by "beholding" the fruits of the creative spirit which now flourish in what was before a formless void. Land, sky, sun, moon, plants and animals are all celebrated in this short creation myth. That feeling of celebration, of creativity, is what is true about this story. Those who insist that it is a literal explanation of the beginnings of species reduce its meaning by failing to recognize the literary subtleties of the piece that raise it above mere literal prose. What we find in the creation account is not a psuedo-scientific description of the origin of the species but a fully conceived and richly presented *story* about creativity.

Creation as described in this story is a process and not a series of events. The question of how there can be days before there is a sun disappears when one realizes that the acts of creation are presented as process and are of a whole. Critics who argue that these kinds of inconsistencies are evidence that the story is not to be taken literally because to do so leads to inconsistency have not realized that they too are depending on a literal model as their stalking horse. But this is not a newspaper account of the creation of the universe, full of brute facts to be checked against what is, nor is it theory to base predictions on; it is a poem celebrating creativity and worth.

DELAYED EXPOSITION

Later in Genesis we are told of Joseph and his many brothers; brothers who are jealous of him and of his special treatment by their father Israel (Jacob). The brothers decide to kill him, are talked out of it by Reuben, and then they decide to throw Joseph into a pit:

> When Joseph came up to his brothers, they stripped him of the long, sleeved robe which he was wearing, took him and threw him into the pit. The pit was empty and had no water in it....Meanwhile some Midianite merchants passed by and drew Joseph up out of the pit. They sold him for twenty pieces of silver to the Ishmaelites, and they brought Joseph to Egypt. (Gen, 37, 23 ff.)

What is important in this passage is what we are *not* told. We are not told anything about Joseph's feelings or whether he was afraid that he would be killed by his brothers (fratricide again) or sold into slavery. The author delays telling us anything about Joseph's response to the attack by his brothers until much later in the story when the brothers are sent to Egypt to get food. There, in a brilliant scene where Joseph knows his brothers but they know him not, we are told of the feelings Joseph had when his brothers sold him to the Ishmaelites.[7] We are told that when his brothers sold him he pleaded with them but they turned a deaf ear to his pleas. Now they are in a position where they must plead for food from this same brother (although they do not yet know it is Joseph, we do) and hope that he will not turn a deaf ear to their importuning. Joseph, who had his coat of many colours stolen by his brothers, now provides each brother with a new suit of clothes. By delaying this information until later in the story the writer is able to create an ironic scene where we know more than the characters and can see the relationship between the attack on Joseph and the request to Joseph.

---

[7] Early in the story we are told that the Midianites sold him; later it seems the brothers sold him. This inconsistency probably comes from different strands of the story being woven together by a redactor.

Joseph could no longer control his feelings in front of his attendants, and he called out, 'Let everyone leave my presence.' So there was nobody present when Joseph made himself known to his brothers, but so loudly did he weep that the Egyptians and Pharaoh's household heard him. Joseph said to his brothers, *'I am Joseph; can my father be still alive?'* (Gen. 45, 1-3, emphasis added)

Joseph is alone with his brothers, and he must announce himself in Hebrew: 'I am Joseph...'! There in a strange land, surrounded by people speaking a strange language, the sound of Hebrew would surprise, and the announcement 'I am Joseph' would be like hearing a person returned from the dead. "His brothers were so dumfounded at finding themselves face to face with Joseph that they could not answer." We heard nothing from Joseph in the pit; now we hear nothing from the surprised brothers responsible, albeit it unknowingly, for Joseph's dreams coming true. Delayed exposition plays a key part in producing the complex of feelings that we go through in the recognition scene.

MOTIFS

A motif is a concrete image, sensory quality, action, or object that occurs in the narrative and that takes its meaning from the defining context of the narrative (water in the Moses cycle, stones in the Jacob story). When a motif is reiterated throughout the story, take note, for it may carry a shifting meaning from context to context. In the story of Samson we are introduced to the motif of flame or fire from the beginning. "And while Manoah and his wife were watching, the flame went up from the altar towards heaven..." (Judges 13, 20 ff.)...and there are torches and burnt tow, and the destructive force of fire. Samson's father makes a burnt offering after hearing that he was to have a brave son. As the flame goes up toward heaven from the altar, an angel of the lord ascends in the flame. Later Samson catches three hundred foxes, ties firebrands between them and turns them loose in the corn fields and vineyards of the Philistines. Imagine the foxes running desperately, wildly, and spreading destruction wherever they run. Destruction comes in a blind rage of fire, and the Philistines answer with fire torture for Samson's wife and her father. Fire becomes a defining characteristic of Samson; not a metaphor for him, but a metonym for his destructive rage at the end of the story, a rage, which is, like fire, blind.

DIALOGUE

When King David is "old and stricken in years" the process of maneuvering for the crown begins as the various sons of David prepare to make a claim for the throne. Adonijah, believing he has a right to his father's position, declares himself next in line and gathers a group of loyal followers, priests and soldiers. Bath-sheba, the mother of Solomon, has an interest in the outcome of this struggle for power, and wants very much for her son to be the one who gets David's blessing and David's crown. In the King James translation of the First Book of Kings we hear:

> 11. Wherefore Nathan spake unto Bathsheba the mother of Solomon, saying, Hast though not heard that Adonijah the son of Haggith doth reign, and David our Lord knoweth it not?
>
> 12. Now therefore come, let me, I pray thee, give thee counsel, that thou mayest save thine own life, and the life of thy son Solomon.
>
> 13. Go and get thee in unto king David, and say unto him, Didst thou not, my lord, O king, sear unto thine handmaid, saying, Assuredly Solomon thy son shall reign after me, and he shall sit upon my throne? why then doth Adonijah reign?
>
> 14. Behold, while thou yet talkest there with the king, I also will come in after thee, and confirm thy words.
>
> 15. And Bathsheba went in unto the king into the chamber: and the king was very old; and Abishag the Shunammite ministered unto the king.
>
> 16. And Bathsheba bowed, and did obeisance unto the king. And the king said, What wouldest thou?
>
> 17. And she said unto him, My lord, thou swarest by the Lord thy God unto thine handmaiden, saying, Assuredly Solomon thy son shall reign after me and he shall sit upon my throne....
>
> 20. And thou, my lord, O king, the eyes of all Israel are upon thee, that thou shouldest tell them who shall sit on the throne of my lord the king after him.

We can be sure what Nathan the prophet will say. Bath-sheba addresses her husband with honorifics while remembering all the time to repeat his name and to repeat the name of Solomon. David the king must pass on the kingship to Solomon. But, an even more magnificent use of dialogue comes when

Bath-sheba changes the rehearsed script crafted by Nathan to an even more effective rhetoric. She reminds the king of his vow to his God. The promise to make Solomon king is not just a promise to her but also to God. Bath-sheba, by adding the oath to god and the idea that all of Israel is watching David to see that he does right by Solomon, is very convincing and we see she knows how to talk to her husband. She knows of his need for public ego massage. She knows of his susceptibility to clever flattery. The artist here is presenting us with a complex and subtle change in dialogue which reveals, in the context of the scene, the character of the speaker, as well as the relationship between Bath-sheba and King David. Nathan's entrance completes the task as David is overwhelmed by the two of them, and of course, Solomon will get the job.

SPOKEN LANGUAGE

Spoken language is the substratum of everything that is human and divine in the Bible, and the Hebrew tendency to present stories by giving us speech is testimony to this belief that the spoken word will lead us to the essence of things. Dialogue can also be effective when used in a contrastive way. In the Second Book of Samuel Amnon pretends to be sick so that he can ask his sister Tamar to come into his tent to nurse him. Amnon lusts after his sister and finally after sending all the servants away, rapes her. Their exchange:

> ...he caught hold of her and said, 'Come to bed with me, sister.' But she answered, 'No, brother, do not dishonour me, we do not do such things in Israel; do not behave like a beast. Where could I go and hide my disgrace? - and you would sink as low as any beast in Israel. Why not speak to the king for me? He will not refuse you leave to marry me.' He would not listen, but overpowered her, dishonoured her and raped her. (2 Sam. 13.12-15)

Tamar's eloquent refusal, couched in a long speech is dismissed by Amnon, whose response to her plea is the brutal act of rape followed by his only words - the three words, 'Arise, be gone,' by which he dismisses her after the incestuous rape. The contrast between Tamar and Amnon is heightened by this skillful use of dialogue in this scene. It is important to realize that these stories are not primitive, but are presented with a set of literary conventions as complex and valid as any of our current ones. Dialogue is one of those literary conventions which, when we pay attention to its use, can enhance the meaning and enjoyment of biblical stories. As Alter says:[8]

> In any given narrative event, and especially, at the beginning of any new story, the point at which the dialogue first emerges will be worthy of special attention, and in most instances, the initial words spoken by a personage will be revelatory, perhaps more in manner than in matter, constituting an important moment in the exposition of character.

Biblical narration is the subject of many critics[9] and in this matter it is instructive to compare the Greek with the Hebrew writers. The differences are easy to spot. As Auerbach puts it, "...the basic impulse of the Homeric style: to represent phenomena in a fully externalized form, visible and palpable in all their parts, and completely fixed in their spatial and temporal relations"[10] while the Hebrews externalize only so much of the phenomena as is necessary for the purpose of the story, leaving in the background time and place, feeling and thought unless such expression is crucial to the narrative. As he puts it:[11]

> It will at once be said that this is to be explained by the particular concept of God which the Jews held and which was wholly different from that of the Greeks. True enough - but this constitutes no objection. For how is the Jewish concept of God to be explained? Even their earlier God of the desert was not fixed in form and content, and was alone; his lack of form, his lack of local habitation, his singleness, was in the end not only maintained but developed even further in competition with the comparatively far more manifest gods of the surrounding Near Eastern World. The concept of God held by the Jews is less a cause than a symptom of their manner of comprehending and representing things.

---

[8] *Op. Cit.*, Alter, page 6.
[9] See, for example, in addition to Alter's *The Art of Biblical Narrative, The Bible and the Narrative Tradition,* edited by Frank McConnell, Oxford University Press, 1986.
[10] Erich Auerbach, *Mimesis*, Doubleday Anchor Books, New York, 1957, page 4.
[11] *Ibid.* page 6.

While Homer is celebrated for his precise detail and descriptive power, the biblical writers can be celebrated for their superb economy - economy to the point of sparseness at times. But, as Auerbach says, "in Homer, the complexity of the psychological life is shown only in the succession and alternation of emotions; whereas the Jewish writers are able to express the simultaneous existence of various layers of consciousness and the conflict between them."[12] It is different with biblical stories partly because the aim of the Jewish writers is not to bewitch the senses but to provide the"necessary" narrative that makes up and expresses their   claim to absolute historico-religious truth.

In Homer's famous opening to the *Odyssey:*

> Sing, Muse, of that versatile man, who wandered far, after sacking Troy's holy citadel. He saw the cities of many men, and knew their mind; he suffered much on the deep sea, and in his heart, struggling for a prize, to save his life...

we notice the invocation to the muse, the placing of the story in time, and a preview of the events, the travels that will be sung about. His story of wandering is to follow the Trojan War and the time and place are explicit. Compare that opening with the opening of the Book of Ruth:

> Long ago, in the time of the judges, there was a famine in the land, and a man from Bethlehem in Judah went to live in the Moabite country with his wife and his two sons. The man's name was Elimelech, his wife's name was Naomi, and the names of his two sons Mahlon and Chilion. They were Ephrathites from Bethlehem in Judah. They arrived in the Moabite country and there they stayed.
>
> Elimelech Naomi's husband died, so that she was left with her two sons. These sons married Moabite women, one of whom was called Orpah and the other Ruth. They had lived there about ten years, when both Mahlon and Chilion died, so that the woman was bereaved of her two sons as well as of her husband.

---

[12] *Ibid.*, page 10.

The stacking up of information, sentence atop sentence is typical of the Old Testament. Compression of time, economy of narrative, speed of narration all are a part of the biblical style. In this compressed narrative we are given a tremendous amount of information and absolutely no description, we are given motivation for action but no feeling by the characters. Deaths are recorded but reactions to them are not. All of this allows for concentration on Ruth alone as this short story unfolds. Her eventual marriage to Boaz will make her the great grandmother of King David; hence cleverly suggesting that racial intermarriage is to be tolerated since Ruth, as we are told, is a Moabite, and is the mother of Ohed: the father of Jesse, the father of David. The theme of the story is beautiful and simple: we must show hospitality to strange or new ideas or persons. And, the writer presents this bit of didacticism by a simple narrative style that gains power from the context of the entire Jewish story - from Ruth to David to Jesus with the mention of Bethlehem. Biblical writers seem motivated not by a desire to be accurate poets of the senses but rather to fit their stories into a predetermined "Story". The purpose or intention of this official "story" is always accessible; from the Christian point of view Ruth is an important reminder of the universality and Old Testament authority of the Christian story. The human story is the more important one: the love and openness to the new, of a loyal and steadfast woman, can give birth to new nations.

Form and content have long been recognized as two distinct aspects of literature. Many have argued that the two can not be meaningfully separated - that form is content or content is form. Though interesting, those arguments are not very useful to the practical critic. For the purposes of discussion here let us assume that there is a real difference between form and content in a literary work. One of the ongoing dialectical processes in literature comes about because of the necessity to use established forms in order to be able to communicate coherently while at the same time struggling to break and remake these forms because they are arbitrary restrictions and not an *a-priori* part of literary "knowledge". Each generation of writers, it seems, struggles to break free from the perceived fetters of the past generation. As criticism has taught us, it is helpful to know where a particular form came from, or what its ancestors were like, in order to understand the new form. Romantic poetry can be studied as a rebellion against the Neo-classical poems that came before. Wordsworth, striving to break free from Pope's couplets, created a new poetic line; and, of course, many of today's poets fight to be free from Wordsworthian influence.

In any case, the form of a literary piece can be important to understanding the piece. It is important to notice that the "Song of Songs" is a wedding idyl, and that "The Book of Job" is a play. "Ruth" is the first short story. "Type-scene" is the name of a literary device worked out for Homeric poems by Walter Arend and used by Alter in his analysis of the Old Testament.[13] The idea is that there are certain fixed situations which the writer is expected to include in his/her narrative and which he/she is expected to perform according to a set order of motifs - situations like the arrival of a messenger, the hero's voyage, the oracle, the arming of the hero and several others. The type-scene of the visit, for example, should be presented according to a conventional blueprint which includes: a guest approaches; someone spots him, gets up and hurries to greet him; the guest is taken by the hand, led into a room, invited to take the seat of honour; the guest is enjoined to feast; the ensuing meal is described. Almost any description of a visit in Homer will reproduce more or less this sequence not because of an overlap of sources but because that is how the convention requires such a scene to be rendered.

In the Bible we find several common type-scenes. As Alter says: "Some of the most commonly repeated biblical type-scenes I have been able to identify are the following: the annunciation...of the birth of a hero to his barren mother; the encounter with the future betrothed at a well; the epiphany in the field; the initiatory trial; the danger in the desert and the discovery of a well or other source of sustenance; the testament of a dying hero."[14]

When one looks carefully at the many betrothal scenes in the Old Testament a pattern emerges. A young man must find a mate in the outside world; hence, he travels to a foreign land. The well or oasis where he meets his future mate is an obvious symbol of fertility and life, a clear and powerful female symbol. Drawing water from the well establishes a bond between male and female, host and guest, benefactor and benefited, and leads to the excited announcement and the actual betrothal.

---

[13] *Op. Cit.* Alter, pages 50 and following.
[14]   See   Chapter   3   of   *The   Art   of   Biblical   Narrative.*

What is interesting is not the recurring form of the type-scene but the variations writers use for character development and emphasis. These variations of the application of this pattern yield rich interpretive differences which can be seen by comparing the betrothal of Jacob and Rachel, Moses and Zipporah, Boaz and Ruth, and Samson and the woman in Timnath. In each case a careful analysis will reveal (as Alter does so well in his book)how slight variations of the pattern can light the story with new meaning and subtle change. Far from being primitive, the biblical stories are rich in narrative complexity and subtlety of character.

An intelligent reading of any work of art requires some knowledge of the grid of conventions the work is laid out on and against. Though we have lost some of the conventions of the biblical writers we can come to see how they define the story after coming to appreciate these old and different conventions. And remember, the conventions change but the stories remain the same.

CHAPTER 4: HISTORY AND THE BIBLE

In Genesis 12 Yahweh[1] appears to Abram and orders him to leave his own country and people to go to a new country that he is to be shown. There Abram will be blessed by Yahweh and given a great name. With this order in mind Abram, without hesitation, organizes all of his affairs and leaves Harran with Sarai, his sister-wife, and with Lot, his nephew, and all of their dependants. Yahweh's appearance to Abram there in the desert is the initial indication of a promise or covenant between Yahweh and Abram.

> That very day the Lord made a covenant with Abram, and he said, 'To your descendants I give this land from the River of Egypt to the Great River, the river Euphrates...(Gen. 15.18)

When Abram is ninety-nine years old Yahweh appears to him again to say:

> 'I make this covenant, and I make it with you: you shall be the father of a host of nations. Your name will no longer be Abram, your name shall be Abraham, for I make you a father of a host of nations. I will make you exceedingly fruitful; I will make nations

---

[1] "Yahweh" is the English version of the ancient Hebrew name "YHWH" for God. It is sometimes translated as "Jehovah." In some ways the name used by the writers to refer to God is a history of the concept of God. The conceptual shift from tribal god to universal God is evident in the changing terminology. Names and naming are an important sub-plot of the stories.

out of you, and kings shall spring from you. I will fulfil my covenant between myself and you and your descendants after you, generation after generation, an everlasting covenant, to be your God, yours and your descendants after you. As an everlasting possession I will give you and your desccendants after you the land in which you are now aliens...(Gen. 17.4-8)

Abraham's special son, Isaac, given to Sarah so late in life, carries on the seed and the covenant is passed on from father to son, although the selection, or choice, of son to receive the blessing and the responsibility of the covenant is not always according to the conventions of the time (that is, sometimes the first born son does not receve the boon). Isaac and Rebecca have the twins Jacob and Esau and the question arises: which of the two will be chosen to carry on as covenant bearer? Jacob is a dreamer, a visionary of sorts, who also is marked for heroism by images of stones and dreams of angels. He will be chosen. Yahweh says to him:

'Jacob is your name,
but your name shall no longer be Jacob:
Israel shall be your name.' (Gen. 35.10)

and then Yahweh renews the covenant promise:

'The land which I gave to Abraham and Isaac I give to you; and to your descendants after you I give this land.' (Gen. 35.11-12)

By the end of the book of Genesis the scene has shifted to Egypt and the Hebrews are enslaved in an alien land. It seems that Yahweh has forgotten about them and about the covenant until Yahweh chooses Moses as the new Abraham and announces his intention:

'I am the Lord. I appeared to Abraham, Isaac and Jacob as God Almighty. But I did not let myself be known to them by my name Jehovah. Moreover, I made a covenant with them to give them Canaan, the land where they settled for a time as foreigners. (Ex. 6.2-5)

The history of the Old Testament is the history of the covenant promise for land. Always at the narrative centre of the stories we find an unbroken cord which is the covenant between Yahweh and his chosen people. Revelation of divine intention, frustration on the part of the chosen people as the intention seems thwarted by time and chance, violation of the covenant agreement by the chosen ones - these are the narrative beads strung on the strong cord of the covenant. The story holds our attention on one level to the extent that we wonder how the covenant promise for land will be fulfilled, for, after all, Canaan is already occupied by a thriving civilization. How will this collection of Hebrews, beaten down by hundreds of years of slavery, ever be able to escape from slavery in Egypt, come together as a people, wage battles of occupation, and take and hold a country of their own? The stories of the Pentateuch answer this question in dramatic fashion.

Covenant provides the plot line for these stories and covenant provides the clue to the structure of the basic elements of the story. Evidence of other covenants, treaties, and agreements between a powerful king, a suzerain, and his people, have been found which provide us with narratives of the type the biblical writer repeats. Hittite documents show various kinds of agreeements and reveal a pattern to the treaties. The primary purpose of the suzerainty treaty was to establish a firm relationship of mutual support between the two parties (especially military support), in which the interests of the Hittite sovereign were of primary and ultimate concern. It established a relationship between the two, but in its form it is unilateral. The stipulations of the treaty are binding only upon the vassal, and only the vassal took an oath of obedience. Though the treaties frequently contain promises of help and support to the vassal, there is no legal formality by which the Hittite king binds himself to any specific obligation. Rather, it would seem that the Hittite king by his very position as sovereign is concerned to protect his subjects from claims or attacks of other foreign states. Consequently for him to bind himself to specific obligations with regard to his vassal would be an infringement upon his sole right of self-determination and sovereignty. A most important corollary of this fact is the emphasis upon the vassal's obligation to *trust* in the benevolence of the sovereign.[2]

Six main elements can be distinguished in the texts of most of these Hittite treaties:

---

[2] See George E. Mendenhall, *Law and Covenant in Israel and the Ancient Near East,* Pittsburgh: The Biblical Colloquium, 1955, p.30. for a discussion of these early documents.

1. A preamble which identifies the author of the covenant, giving his titles, attributes, and genealogy. For instance: "Thus speaks X, the great king, king of Hittite land, son of Y, the valiant, the great king." Here emphasis is laid on the majesty and power of the king who is conferring a special relationship on the vassal.

2. A historical prologue which describes in detail the previous relations between the two parties. It outlines the benevolent deeds which the king has already performed for the vassal, not vaguely, but very specifically and factually. The implication is that the vassal is already obligated to the great king because of the favor and protection experienced in the past. Thus there is a real mutuality of contract; but the vassal is pledging future obedience and loyalty in return for past benefits which he received without having any claim to them. Strict obligation is on his side; on the great kings', there is no obligation other than the presumption and implied promise that he will continue his benevolence.

Notable is the personal form of this prologue. The great king addresses the vassal directly: "I have sought after you; although you were sick and ailing I put you in the place of your father and made your brothers and sisters and the whole Amurru country subject to you."

3. The stipulations which spell out in detail the obligations accepted by the vassal. These usually include:

a. Prohibition of service to any other great king.

b. Promise to be on friendly terms with the king's other vassals; if disputes arise they are to be submitted to the overlord's arbitration.

c. Promise to send contingents to support the great king when he goes to war.

d. Promise to trust the great king completely, and not to tolerate rebellious or critical language.

e. Promise to bring yearly tribute in person, and on that occasion to renew fealty.

4. A directive that the treaty be deposited in the temple of the vassal city, and periodically read in the hearing of the people.

5. The invocation of the gods both of the Hittites and of the vassal as witnesses to the treaty.

6. Finally, the pronunciation of curses upon the vassal if he breaks the covenant, and the promise of blessings for its observance. These are the only sanctions expressly mentioned; that is, the Hittite king does not threaten military proceedings and destruction. The treaty is a sacred document, and it is

the gods who will see to its enforcement and vindication.[3]

Perhaps the most historic of books in the modern sense of "historic" are the two Samuels and 1 and 2 Kings. The Septuagint[4] called the books "1 and 2 Kingdoms" and "3 and 4 Kingdoms" respectively; names which emphasize the continuity of story in the now four books called "1 and 2 Samuel" and "1 and 2 Kings". Changing the titles from the kings to the prophet in 1 and 2 Samuel is understandable, as the canon would have been shaped under the immediate influence of rabbis and not kings. Israel's shift from prophet-judges of Samuel's type to kings is indeed the subject of the books of Samuel, and that shift is an important political and historical development in Israel's early days. The story also includes the personal life of Saul and David and the divine intervention of Yahweh in the events of history. In some ways Samuel resembles Genesis in its preoccupation with founding families who are placed at the centre of historical change in the unfolding story of Israel.

Historical causation and divine justice are woven into this story of three central characters: Samuel, Saul, and David. The books focus on three major struggles or conflicts: Saul and Samuel, Saul and David, and David against the combined forces of the two. The history of David's rise to kingship is personal as well as historical and the kind of "evidence" we are given to consider is a mixture of prophecy, internal musings, messages from Yahweh, and claims about the world which can be verified in extra-biblical ways. Recent literary study of the books has corrected a misconception inherited from historians to see the story as straightforward reporting by an eyewitness to the events.[5] Instead we see the work now as a combination of chronicle, legend, projection, and above all *story* in the fullest sense of that word.

In Second Samuel we read:

---

[3] See, for example, the discussion in R. A. F. MacKenzie, *Faith and History in the Old Testament*, Minneapolis: University of Minnesota Press, 1963, pps. 39,40.
[4] The Septuagint is the main Greek translation (abbreviated as LXX) and was begun in the third century B.C.E.
[5] Julius Wellhausen, *Prolegomena to the History of Israel* (1878; reprint, Gloucester, Mass. 1973), page 262, speaks of events "faithfully reported"; Ernst Sellin and George Fohrer, *Introduction to the Old Testament*, translated David Green (Nashville, 1968) page 163 talk of a writer who was "undoubtedly an eyewitness to the event and a member of the royal court."

After this David inquired of the Lord, 'Shall I go up into one of the cities of Judah?' The Lord answered, 'Go.' David asked, 'To which city?', and the answer came, 'To Hebron.' So David went to Hebron with his two wives, Ahinoam of Jezreel and Abigail widow of Nabal of Carmel...The men of Judah came, and there they anointed David king over the house of Judah. (2 Samuel 2.1-4)

Meanwhile Saul's commander in chief, Abner son of Ner, had taken Saul's son Ishbosheth, brought him across the Jordan to Mahanaim, and made him king over Gilead, the Asherites, Jezreel, Ephraim, and Benjamin, and all Israel. (2 Samuel 2.8-11)

Abner...marched out from Mahanaim to Gibeon, and Joab...marched out with David's troops from Hebron. They met at the pool of Gibeon and took up their positions one on one side of the pool and the other on the other side. Abner said to Joab, 'Let the young men come forward and join in single combat before us.' ...There ensued a fierce battle that day, and Abner and the men of Israel were defeated by David's troops. (2 Samuel 2.17-20)

The war between the houses of Saul and David was long drawn out, David growing steadily stronger while the house of Saul became weaker and weaker. (2 Samuel 3.1)

At first reading, this passage, like most of the so-called "historical books" from Genesis to Kings, appears historical. We are given a lot of "facts". Some suggestion of the causal relationships between events is also given. Saul and David are struggling for the throne; David will win because he is the chosen one of Yahweh. The overriding impressions in the Old Testament are that (1) Yahweh is directly involved in history; (2) what has happened had to happen to allow Yahweh's plan to unfold properly; and (3) the literary structure of the books follows the form of a treaty or covenant document between Yahweh and Israel. Time after time we are given scenes depicting Yahweh's participation in the human drama, although these do tend to become more subtle in the later books. For example, the direct contact of the early parts of Genesis are replaced by the device of having "an angel of the Lord" speak to characters and then by having the message imparted by means of a dream. One of the basic reasons why the Old Testament can not be considered history, in any modern sense of the word, is clear in the above: for how could a writer be privy to the dreams of his characters? Or, in the passage from Samuel, how could the writer know what Abner said to Joab by the side of the pool? Too often we are presented with material from the omniscient point of view, are told of intent, dreams, thoughts, conversations with others in private, and find ourselves, through the narrative skill of the writer, inside the character's head. Good literature; bad history.

History attempts, at least, to be objective. That means, among other things, that modern historians feel much better if they can verify events in the past from multiple sources. They like to find extra-biblical sources to corroborate biblically suggested events, characters, and causal relationships. The historian is interested in human recorded past and deals principally with written records. When the inquiry is based primarily on oral and/or artifactual evidence, we refer to the researcher as an anthropologist, archaeologist, or something other than a historian. Modern historians, for the most part, tend to dismiss elements of the supernatural as explanatory devices for the interpretation of the events recorded in the documents of the past. Biblical sources receive essentially the same treatment, although some historians are more cautious than others in their sifting out of the supernatural and miraculous elements. Regarding the account of the Hebrew escape at the Red Sea, for example, even those historians who are inclined to accept the account as essentially accurate in its present form will, in their own recounting of the incident, tend to emphasize the natural rather than the supernatural aspects of the story. That is, they usually speak in terms of low tide and high winds and either suggest that Yahweh worked "indirectly" through these natural phenomena or leave the question of his involvement open altogether. The following quotation from John Bright's *A History of Israel*, is typical:[6]

> Concerning these events, to be sure, we can add nothing to what the Bible tells us. It appears that Hebrews, attempting to escape, were pinned between the sea and the Egyptian army and were saved when a wind drove the waters back, allowing them to pass (Ex. 14.21,27); the pursuing Egyptians, caught by the returning flood, were drowned. If Israel saw in this the hand of God, the historian certainly has no evidence to contradict it!

---

[6] John Bright, *A History of Israel,* 3rd edition, page 122.

But such a comment merely begs the question of causality, since nothing will count as evidence for or against such an interpretation. Did the wind blow at the Red Sea while the Hebrews were making good their escape? Who knows? Did God cause the wind to blow? Who knows? Within the mythical architecture of Exodus the answer is simple. Yahweh parts the waters and then collapses them on the Egyptians. 'Did this really happen?' is the question of the literalist, depending on a misunderstanding of the nature of the text: remember, these are not factual claims *about* the world, but performatives within a story true *to* the world. The defeat at the Red Sea is the defeat of the Pharaoh-god by the Hebrew god, Yahweh. At the level of story this defeat is "evidence" of the power of the Hebrew god. For centuries after, the Jew can point to this story as "evidence" for chosen tribe status and as a reminder of the covenant between Israel and Yahweh. The stories in the Old Testament are forming and shaping a people just as the writers of the stories are forming and shaping the people *through* the stories. Egyptian records do not indicate anything about Moses and the escape at the Red Sea, but if we found them and if such a person as Moses existed to take the Hebrews out of Egypt, then we could expect the Egyptian story to be a much different story with a different line about causality offered to explain the events. We have difficulty sorting out the *real* causes of events in our own time, and we still tell stories to reassure ourselves that there is indeed some understandable cause for events that affect us. And some of us today continue to offer god as the cause for things we do not understand or cannot see except in some purposeful way.[7]

Many recent discoveries in archaeology have sparked historical interest in the Old Testament. Since about 1890 archaeologists have been constantly active in "the holy land" and have provided us with a wealth of non-written sources for information on such things as weapons, dress, foodstuffs, ceramic wares, architectural styles and other silent artifacts that help us to put together the past. They have also discovered a number of written documents from the ancient Near East which have proved to be especially relevant for the study of Israel's history during Old Testament times. These include:

---

[7] Some Christian fundamentalists have claimed that A.I.D.S is god's punishment for evil behaviour. They are silent on the reasons for their god afflicting those who contracted the virus through blood transfusions or hospital accidents.

1. The Amarna tablets
2. Royal Egyptian Inscriptions
3. The Mesha Inscription
4. Royal Assyrian Inscriptions
5. The Babylonian Chronicles
6. Hebrew and Armaic Ostraca

The Armana Tablets were discovered in 1887 in the El-Amarna district of Egypt, about ninety miles south of Cairo. Written in Akkadian, most of them are letters belonging to the correspondence between the Egyptian court during the reigns of Amenophis IV, and the vassal rulers of city-states in Syria, Phoenicia, and Palestine. They reflect the political and sociological circumstances in Palestine during the first half of the fourteenth century BCE (before Common Era). References to the "apiru" in the Amarna Tablets have generated much discussion among Old Testament scholars, since this Akkadian term may be related etymologically to the designation "Hebrew" used in the Old Testament.

The royal Egyptian Inscriptions comprise the official Egyptian reports of Asiatic campaigns and lists of conquered cities. These documents are of some importance to early Israeli history though the age of Egyptian empire and conquests had already passed by the time of the settlement of the Hebrew tribes in Palestine. The hymn of victory of Merneptah (c. 1236-1223 B.C.E.), discovered in Thebes in 1896, is an especially interesting exception in that it provides the earliest known non-biblical reference to Israel:[8]

> The princes are prostrate, saying: "Mercy!"
>   Not one raises his head among the Nine bows.
> Desolation is for Tehenu; Hatti is pacified;
>   Plundered is the Canaan with every evil;
> Carried off is Ashkelon; seized is Geyer;
>   Yanoam is made as that which does not exist;
> Israel is laid to waste, his seed is not;
>   Hurru is become a widow for Egypt!
> All lands together, they are pacified...

---

[8] Quoted here from *The Old Testament and the Historian*, J. Maxwell Miller, Fortress Press, Philadelphia (1973), page 7.

The Mesha Inscription is a stele erected by Mesha, King of Moab, during the mid ninth century B.C.E., and discovered in Jordan in 1868. It memorializes the King's reign and celebrates his recovery of Moabite independence from Israel (cf. 2 Kings 3.4ff). Many other inscriptions from the period of the Divided Kingdom have been discovered and each makes a contribution to our understanding of the history of Syria-Palestine during Israel's monarchial period.

Records have been discovered from Assyrian Kings and from Babylonian and Persian Kings which also assist us in understanding the time of the ancient Near East and provide us with valuable information, useful to historians and biblical commentators alike, to assess certain "historical" sections of the biblical stories. Finally, the ostraca (potsherds which bear messages) provide lists, letters, etc. which give additional information about Hebrew life. Some claim a special relationship between the Bible and archaeology[9], pointing out that "the Bible describes public life and the 'word of the spirit;' archaeology fills in a knowledge of everyday life and culture, [and] both are necessary if we are to comprehend ancient Israel in its full variety and vitality." To the extent that the Bible is a text presenting radical theology it can not be judged as a book of history or a record of everyday life. One obvious limitation that flows from the theological intentions of the writers/editors is that they tell us next to nothing about the daily life of the average Hebrew. Archaeology has dramatically changed our understanding of the everyday life of those people who are in the background in the biblical stories.

Professor Dever says of the relationship between the Bible and archaeology, "the legitimate archaeologist (in contrast to the "raider of the lost ark") will...not attempt to date the creation, or set out to locate the Garden of Eden and excavate the bones of Adam and Eve, or establish flood levels and dig up the timbers of Noah's ark." Those who do from time to time announce that they are setting out to find the ark, or to search for Joseph's bones, are making the basic mistake of misunderstanding the nature of the text. Once again, these stories are not literal social or economic history, but are fundamentally theological stories which present a particular *official line.* In the first five

---

[9] See "Archaeology and The Bible", William G. Dever, *Biblical Archaeology Review,* May/June 1990, pages 52 ff.

books of the Old Testament this official line has to do with the "saving acts" of Yahweh on behalf of his chosen people Israel. These stories are not just descriptions, but are always description plus theological explanation. In a recent movie about a veteran of Vietnam ("In Country") a U.S. general "blesses" his men who are on their way to the war. He says: "You are chosen to fight godless communism...you men have been chosen to be the leaders in a fight that will never be forgotten...you are chosen...America is never going to forget you...you are the best...good luck and go with God." It makes no sense to ask if what the general says is true or false; these are not statements of fact. They are part of the official line *of the time*. And as we have seen in relation to the war in Vietnam the official line has changed. But the *story line* has not changed; the horrors of that war, the people who fought in it, and the human costs, these are as real as the stories in the Old Testament.

There are many non-biblical sources of written and "silent" artifacts which can aid the student of the Bible in recreating the time of the biblical patriarchs and of the monarchs of the Great Kingdom. To return to the passage at the beginning of this chapter, we can say that even though the narrative is embellished with legend and with omniscient point of view it does nevertheless provide some firm historical facts: there really was a David who fought a civil war against the house of Saul, achieved undisputed sovereignty over the twelve tribes, conquered Jerusalem, founded a dynasty, created a small empire, and was succeeded by his son Solomon. These facts are facts not because the Bible says so, but because they are facts. These stories are not, strictly speaking, historiography, but rather the imaginative reenactment of history by a gifted writer who organizes his material along certain thematic biases and according to his own remarkable intuition of the psychology of his characters. He feels entirely free, as did Shakespeare, to invent interior monologue for his characters; to ascribe feeling, intention, or motive to them when he chooses; to supply verbatim dialogue for occasions when no one but the actors themselves could have knowledge of exactly what was said. If history at all, this is a special genre of history.

One other characteristic of the text that makes it difficult to consider as history is that of selection. The main story is of Israel and of the House of David. This concern means that at times when the events do not fit those patterns they receive short shrift. For example, here is the story of Manasseh:

> Manasseh was twelve years old when he came to the throne, and he reigned in Jerusalem for fifty-five years...he did what was wrong in the eyes of the Lord, in following the abominable practices of the nations which the Lord had dispossessed in favour of the Israelites....the Lord spoke...:'Because Manasseh ...has done these abominable things, outdoing the Amorites before him in wickedness, and because he has led Judah into sin with his idols, this is the word of the Lord the God of Israel: I will bring disaster on Jerusalem and Judah..." (2 Kings 21.1 ff)

From twelve years old to sixty seven years old Manasseh reigned as King, and yet we get his entire life's history in just a few hundred words. His son, Amon, is dismissed by the writer in even fewer words so that we can get to the events of real importance for the writer in Josiah's reign: the discovery of the Deuteronomy ("I have found the book of the law in the house of the Lord.").

It is as Professor Alter says[10] "what the bible offers us is an uneven continuum and a constant interweaving of factual historical detail (especially, but by no means exclusively, for the later periods) with purely legendary "history"; occasional enigmatic stories; archetypal fictions of the founding fathers of the Nation; folktales of heroes and wonder-working men of God; verisimilar inventions of wholly fictional personages attached to the progress of natural history; and fictionalized versions of known historical personages." The history in the Bible should not be confused with history and the Bible.

THE EXODUS

Without the Bible we would know nothing of Moses. He is not mentioned anywhere else. From the time he first appears in Exodus until we are told of his death in the last chapter of Deuteronomy we are dealing with a fictional character stiched to some real historical events. The exodus from Egypt was probably a real event. The entry into the "Promised Land" was likely a real event although most scholars today would suggest that the Hebrew take-over of Canaan was a slow process and not the dramatic and nearly instant

---

[10] Robert Alter, *The Art of Biblical Narrative,* Basic Books, New York, 1981, page 33.

event recorded in the Bible. The religious experience that Moses underwent alone with his flock of sheep in the wilderness of Midian is certainly a genuine experience of turmoil, resolution, and commitment to a task. How can we know this? From inference and conjecture arising from putting together information from archaeologists, historians, linguists, anthropologists, we are able to have a fairly clear picture of the events telescoped into the Biblical Moses story. We know a great deal about conditions in Egypt at the time when the events recorded in Exodus took place; we know a great deal about the conditions in Mesopotamia and Palestine at that time and about the relations - cultural, social, political, economic - between Semitic peoples and Egyptians.

The account of Israel's slavery in Egypt, with which Exodus begins, is presented as a part of a continuing story which goes back to the Patriarchs in Genesis. The story really opens with God's call to Abram to leave Haran (northwest Mesopotamia) and migrate to the country later known as Palestine.

> The Lord said to Abram, 'Leave your own country, your kinsmen, and your father's house, and go to a country that I will show you. I will make you into a great nation, I will bless you and make your name so great that it shall be used in blessings:
>
> Those that bless you I will bless,
> those that curse you, I will execrate.
> All the families on earth
> will pray to be blessed as you are blessed.

Abram's (later Abraham) son Isaac was provided a wife (Rebecca) by his father. The Lord appeared to Isaac also and renewed the promise he had made to Abraham. Jacob, the chosen son of Isaac and Rebecca, carries on the tradition and the special agreement; he is sent back to his grandfather's original home of Haran to find a wife, and on the journey there he has his own special encounter with God. In fact he gets two wives, his cousin Leah and her younger sister Rachel, since his uncle would not let him have the younger without first taking the older. But he loved Rachel, who finally bore him Joseph and Benjamin. Joseph's brothers were jealous of his special status and arranged to have him sold as a slave into Egypt.[11] Once there Joseph rose quickly to power as a result of his remarkable powers of interpreting dreams and his abilities in administration. Joseph like his father Jacob is a dreamer, one in tune with the intellectual side of life, one who is aware of life as process through time. Soon he was the second in command to the Pharaoh. During a famine in Canaan Jacob sends his sons to Egypt to buy corn and they meet the now mighty and powerful Joseph, whom they do not recognize but who recognizes them. Eventually Joseph forgave his brothers for what they had done to him and persuades Pharaoh to invite them and his father to come live in that part of Egypt called Goshen. There they prospered. Jacob died and eventually Joseph died, saying to his brethren:

> 'I am dying; but God will not fail to come to your aid and take you from here to the land which he promised on oath to Abraham, Isaac, and Jacob. He made the sons of Israel take an oath, saying, 'When god thus comes to your aid, you must take my bones with you from here.' So Joseph died at the age of a hundred and ten. He was embalmed and laid out in a coffin in Egypt. (Genesis 50.24-26)

Exodus opens with an account of Jacob's descendants, the children of Israel, prospering and multiplying in Egypt. On this stage Moses, representing that which is universally human in our stories, is implanted in a historical setting. It is the tiny ark on the Nile that, through Pharaoh's daughter's pity, penetrates the headquarters of the oppressors.

Who were these Hebrew people? The word 'Hebrew' does not appear to be the name of a race or a nation, but of a class of people who worked the caravan routes of the middle east - the word probably means something like 'donkey-men' or 'caravan-men'. They travelled and traded with their families and flocks and herds, never in one place for long. The Biblical picture of the Patriarchs wandering in Palestine between the hill country and the desert, maintaining contact with their ancestral Mesopotamia and moving south to Egypt when food became scarce is supported by, among other extra-Biblical evidence, the 450 clay tablets unearthed at the ancient city of Alakh, some

---

[11] See Chapter 5 for a closer examination of these heroes. The link between Genesis and Exodus is Joseph, and we are told in Exodus 1.8 that "a new king ascended the throne, one who knew nothing of Joseph." It is this time indicator that has suggested that this king is Ramses II, although his name does not appear in the Bible.

dating from the 18th century B.C.E., illustrating the social, economic, and political life of the times. The so-called Execration Texts dating from about the end of the Middle Kingdom of Egypt (18th century B.C.E.) record the enemies of the country as well as listing the lands and territories adjacent to Egypt.

The patriarchal period, the age of Abraham, Isaac, and Jacob and their semi-nomadic wanderings, is thus roughly assigned to about 1950-1800 B.C.E. in the Middle Bronze Age.[12] The Middle Kingdom of Egypt collapsed about 1786 B.C.E. in chaos and civil war. When the smoke clears the Hyksos are in control of the country. They rule until about 1550 B.C.E. when in a war of liberation the Egyptians pushed them out and replaced their rule with the Eighteenth Dynasty. Now the Hyksos and the Hebrews were racially connected. Many scholars now agree that there is some connection between Hyksos rule of Egypt and the settling of the Hebrews there. It seems reasonable to assume that the Hyksos, who themselves had travelled the caravan routes to Egypt for centuries before they took power there, favoured other 'Apiru'[13] groups and encouraged them to settle in Egypt. When the Pharaoh Amosis (1552-1527 B.C.E.) expelled the Hyksos from Egypt, the Hebrews in Egypt were left without protectors. Contemporary documents show that the Hyksos who escaped slaughter were enslaved. It is reasonable to assume that the Hebrews, now unprotected by the Establishment, were also enslaved at this time. This would place Joseph's rise to power under Hyksos rule and make Amosis the Pharaoh who knew not Joseph.

The Bible account is not always consistent and the chronology difficult to pin down. We must remember that the Bible is not history in the modern sense, but presents the traditions of a people, their national and religious origins, and a fair amount of so-called sacral history (of or pertaining to sacral rites and observances). The account is more an imagined sense of the past

---

[12] There is a great deal of dispute about dating these events in current scholarly circles. See, for example, the debate between Piotr Bienkowski and Bryant G. Wood in the September/October 1990 issue of *Biblical Archaeology Review* (Volume XVI no. 5).

[13] 'Apiru' or 'Habiru' seems to identify a class of people of the Near East who have been a part of discussion about Hebrew origins. References to them appear in late third and second millennium sources from all over the Near East. See Moshe Greenberg, *The Hab / piru*, New Haven, American Oriental society, 1955.

which exhibits ideas to be valued, characteristics to be emulated, traits to be developed. The Exodus probably took place in the reign of Rameses II between 1280-1250 B.C.E. We are told the Israelites spent 430 years in Egypt which means they came into Egypt in around 1700 B.C.E. which is when the Hyksos established themselves. Recently discovered archaeological evidence shows that the Palestine city of Hazov - destroyed by fire by the invading Israelites under Joshua (Joshua 11.10-13) - was destroyed in the latter part of the 13th century B.C.E. We can be reasonably certain that by the end of the 13th century B.C.E. the Israelites - now really the people of Israel - were settled in parts at least of Palestine, and the Egyptian experience was behind them, though never to be forgotten.[14] In some ways it does not matter what the dates are: the story has taken on a timelessness that makes it the myth to inflame any suppressed peoples anywhere.

What of this Moses? What kind of man is he? First of all the story gives us Moses the Hebrew who also in some sense is an Egyptian - and in this paradox lay his special powers.[15] We are told of his genealogy in simple terms: "A descendant of Levi married a Levite woman who conceived and bore a son." Levi was one of the sons of Jacob. Martin Buber in his book *Moses* has this to say:

> "...in order that the one appointed to liberate his nation should grow up to be the liberator...he had to be introduced into the stronghold of the aliens, into that royal court by which Israel has been enslaved; and he must grow up there. This is a kind of liberation which cannot be brought by anyone who grew up as a slave, not yet by anyone who is not connected with the slaves; but only by one of the latter who has been brought up in the midst of

---

[14] Martin Noth in his *The History of Israel* (Harper and Row, New York, 1958) says: From all the more detailed references and especially from the relevant section in the Pentateuch it appears that 'bringing forth out of Egypt' connoted not merely the point of departure of the migration of the Israelite tribes but a mighty deed of the God of Israel. Israel had been enslaved in Egypt and was to be held there, but its God had wonderfully delivered it from bondage and saved it from the power of the Egyptians. there is no doubt that the concrete statement in this confession is based on a definite historical occurrence and it is not difficult to discern the circumstances in which it took place." (page 112)

[15] Sigmund Freud wrote of an Egyptian Moses in his book, *Moses and Monotheism*.

the aliens and has received an education equipping him with all
their wisdoms and powers, and thereafter 'goes forth to his
brethren and observes their burdens.'. (page 27)

The marvellous story of Moses' deliverance from the Nile has caught
the imagination of many a child. It is told quickly: "Pharaoh's daughter came
down to bathe in the river, while her ladies-in-waiting walked along the bank.
She noticed the basket among the reeds and sent her slave-girl for it. She took
it from her and when she opened it, she saw the child. It was crying, and she
was filled with pity for it. 'Why,' she said, 'it is a little Hebrew boy.'" The
human cry of the child strikes a responsive chord in the woman and she saves
the child from the river. How she explains this child from the river we are not
told. And when he is grown, educated and raised in the Pharaoh's household,
he still has Hebrew blood coursing through his veins. All of this is compressed
and then we are told of the pivotal episode in his life when he slew the
Egyptian. In this act, in the words of Christopher Fry, "he killed his Egyptian
self in the self of that Egyptian."[16]

Moses, excited by a presumably newly realized sense of identity with his
fellow Hebrews, takes the side of an abused Hebrew slave and kills the
slave-driver who is abusing him. The next day he learns that there is no
necessary gratitude on the part of the oppressed. The Pharaoh discovers the
murder; Moses must flee to save his life. This gets him to Midian, home of his
mother's people, where he helps the daughters of a priest of Midian who are
being harassed by other male shepherds at a well. Moses, the future saviour of
the Hebrews, takes sides with the women in the dispute, foreshadowing the
part he will play in the larger drama in Egypt. The land of Midian to which
Moses fled was probably in the south-eastern part of the Sinai Peninsula.
Midian represents for Moses a simple way of life and a stern desert code in
contrast to the cosmopolitan polytheism of Egypt. The life there was much
more like that of his Hebrew ancestors before they settled in Egypt. Moses
needs time to recover his past and discover his roots. The story has to get
Moses to Midian, for it is there, alone in the wilderness, that his encounter
with God takes place.

---

[16] Christopher Fry, *The Firstborn*, a play in three acts, Oxford University Press, London,
1952, page 34.

Moses was minding the flock of his father-in-law Jethro, priest of Midian. He led the flock along the side of the wilderness and came to Horeb, the mountain of God. There the angel of the Lord appeared to him in the flame of a burning bush. Moses noticed that, although the bush was on fire, it was not being burnt up; so he said to himself, 'I must go across to see this wonderful sight.'(Exodus .1-5)

After God has Moses' attention (here again in the image of the burning bush one can sense the human author at work: in the right sunlight this phenomenon happens often, it is the cause that is added here) he tells him of the covenant with Abraham, Isaac, and Jacob binding Moses to this past, this promise. He then tells him of the future and the part that Moses is to play in it. A reluctant hero, Moses responds with "But who am I that I should go to Pharaoh, and that I should bring the Israelites out of Egypt?" The answer does not speak of Moses' special worth or of his special skills, but is about being chosen: "I am with you," says God. If "I am with you" is present then you are a hero in the full sense of the word. What is 'god'? 'God' is the name for the heroic virtues, the commitment to the future, the change to be brought about as the hero brings a boon to his people, or in this story brings his people to a boon. In answer to Moses' question about his name, God says, "I AM; that is who I am. Tell them that I AM has sent you to them." "I am" is *being* itself; "I am" is the necessary frame within which any story can exist, it is the very ground of being for a narrative of any kind. "I am" is the simplest declarative statement possible, and every one of the infinite sentences that proceed depends upon the truth of "I am".

Moses is to lead the Hebrews out of slavery not because they are his brethren but because they are unjustly oppressed. He becomes a national leader because of a universal principle.

Fry represents the conflict between Moses and Pharaoh as a clash between two ideals: Pharaoh stands for civilization, Moses for humanity and the rights of the individual. What is more important, the pyramids or the men who build them? Fry's Moses says:

A man has more to be than a Pharaoh.
He must dare to outgrow the security
Of partial blindness...(Fry, page 14)

...What have we approached or conceived when we have conquered and built a world? Even though civilization became perfect? What then? We have only put a crown on the skeleton. It is the individual man in his individual freedom who can mature with his warm spirit the unripe world. (Fry, page 15.)

The conflict between Moses/Aaron and Pharaoh (Moses, the reluctant hero, has been given his brother Aaron to speak for him since Moses is a "halting speaker") is at times a childish competition in conjuring tricks, but its function in the story is clear: this Pharaoh has power and is thought to be a god. Many commentators make a point of showing that the conflict between God and Pharaoh is a one-sided conflict, unfair because God has all the power. But Pharaoh was thought to be a god also, and so we have here the conflict between two equal combatants. The story tells of the ascendancy of one tribal god over another, tells of victory and special care by the Israelite god for his people. After this the bull god of the Egyptian valley is no longer to be worshipped, for I AM has triumphed.

I AM has triumphed by direct intervention into human affairs. The account of the ten plagues is rich with conviction of "divine" power working for the Hebrews and against Pharaoh. The object of the plagues is expressed with forceful directness:

> Then the Lord said to Moses, 'Go into Pharaoh's presence. I have made him and his courtiers obdurate, so that I may show these my signs among them, and so that you can tell your children and grand-children the story: how I made sport of the Egyptians, and what signs I showed among them. Thus you will know that I am the Lord. (Exodus 10.1-3)

The plagues are not magic, nor are they presented as merely natural events. Based on natural events they represent a heightening and ordering and a deliberate turning on and off of events that *could* occur, but are given a meaning within the story by showing us god at work behind the scenes, manipulating the events to the end of freedom for the Israelites and honour for himself in the future story. They represent POWER - YAHWEH at work on nature herself. These events give the exodus a sense of something very special - divine intervention in the aid of a particular cause. Divine intervention is always easier to write about *after the fact*, when one knows how things come out. God's will or intention, like narrative intention, is revealed *in* the story. God's intention is clear: tell my story to future generations of Israelites. And, of course, it is in the story that this story is molded and formed.

The final plague is the most devastating- the killing of all Egyptian first born:

> 'At midnight I will go out among the Egyptians. Every first-born creature in the land of Egypt shall die: the first born of Pharaoh who sits on his throne, the first-born of the slave-girl at the hand-mill, and all the first-born of the cattle. All Egypt will send up a great cry of anguish, a cry the like of which has never been heard before, nor ever will be again. But among all Israel not a dog's tongue shall be so much as scratched, no man or beast be hurt.'

God has given Moses and Aaron detailed instructions for the passover sacrifice using for the first time the phrase "all the congregations of Israel" and associating the ritual of the passover sacrifice with means of preventing the slaughter of the Israelite firstborn. This is an echo of the original passover ritual, a festival of nomadic shepherds at which a sheep or goat was sacrificed and the blood sprinkled to ward off evil powers, which especially threatened the firstborn. The narrative recipe: take an ancient ritual, wrap it in a new story, and bring the new ritual into history as part of an ongoing story. Another part of the ritual, that of unleavened bread, is brought into the story at this point. A pastoral festival and an agricultural festival are historicized in narrative and establish (constitute) the Passover Feast as a ritual of remembrance of the deliverance from Egyptian slavery. Moses rediscovers himself, his god, his relationship with the Israelites, and he will recast and revitalize the law for the Israelites.

A defeated Pharaoh finally lets the people go (with, one imagines, a sigh of relief) and they become the charge and responsibility of Moses. He is to provide; they will consume. Moses is not a new master, he is their leader: in matters religious and spiritual it is Moses who imposes the way of life. An unbroken chain from Abraham to Isaac to Jacob to Moses: this bond between Yahweh and Israel is welded in images of contact between the worlds of history and of the "divine" story to be unfolded in history. And what we know of Moses we know through the story.

After breaking free from the bondage of Egypt the "children" of Israel now face the problems of sustaining life in the desert. They need food and water. They will cry for a return to the known from this new position of hunger and freedom and the unknown. They will exhibit all of the weaknesses and fears of a people on a new trek toward identity. The miraculous feeding stories fold together all the traditions of miraculous feeding in the wilderness available to the narrator: manna from above, quail from above, and a constant thirst. The symbolic meaning is clear: the God of Israel is providing for the sustenance of the people of Israel by direct intervention in natural events. Manna may be the secretion of insects and be an edible substance made up of glucose, fructose, and pectin; but its function in the story is to proclaim that Yahweh is manifest in its presence.

A group of tribes, a collection of individuals, is formed into a people at Mount Sinai where the covenant between Yahweh and the patriarchs is extended to include all of the people who have struggled through the desert of despair to a place which will become the sight for the giving of the constitution that binds the people together as a congregation. Imaged in lightning and thunder, shown to be special by purification rituals, offered to the people on chunks of stone, these commandments are intended as absolute: everything in the imagery surrounding the giving of the law is intended to emphasize the importance of the law. "And he wrote upon the tables the words of the covenant, the ten commandments." The Decalogue is presented in a narrative package that is distinguished by its images of power, mystery, and the absolute. The WORDS are put in writing in tablets of stone and the writing is attributed to God or at least to Moses acting on God's behalf and eventually these tablets are placed inside the Ark of the Covenant to be stored in the holiest part of the tabernacle. These words become the symbol of the meeting and contact between God and his chosen people.

So goes the official line. And the power of the story of the giving of the law can work to wipe out of our memory the larger story: on both sides of the narrative devoted to the giving of the law we find stories of destruction and death. This Yahweh who now gives the law is also capable of violating many of his own laws. "You shall not commit murder" is ordered by the wrathful god who previously has killed the firstborn of all the Egyptians. The official line states the laws are absolute; the story line reveals that in fact the laws can be broken. What is officially intended as a list of duties prescribed by God as absolute, definitive of morality, and constitutive of the proper relationship between human and god, turns out to be relative, dependent upon an understanding of morality, and vague in its expression of proper action. Yes, it is wrong to murder. But what does that tell us? When is killing to be classified as murder? When you kill Egyptians? Obviously not. When you kill Canaanites? Obviously not. Although the official line announces a "truth", the story line reveals a need for *interpretation*.

Is this god of Exodus *worthy* of worship?

CHAPTER 5: "THEY WERE THE HEROES OF OLD..."

Let us look more closely at some of the stories to see how the general introductory material presented in earlier chapters might be of use in reading the Bible. Every speech act;[1] can be thought of as requiring three conditions to be completely successful: intention, text, and interpretation. When a person uses language to inform another about a state of affairs the information may be generated in language and begins with an intention on the part of the speaker. A simple thought experiment serves to show that intention is a necessary condition for a speech act to occur. Imagine walking along the beach and seeing many lines in the sand made by the outgoing tide. You might consider those lines from an aesthetic viewpoint, and point to interesting patterns in the sand made by the lines; you might even speak metaphorically about how the water is "writing" in the sand, but it would not occur to you to consider them as a new language that needed translation. The reason such an approach strikes us as absurd is that it is impossible to consider the ocean water as having *intention*. The lines in the sand are just that: lines in the sand. But now imagine that on the same beach walk you find a bottle washed ashore by the water and in the bottle you find a piece of paper covered with lines. In this case you have reason to believe that effort spent attempting to translate the lines into a language that you understand will not be an irrational

---

[1] A speech act is an act performed by using either written or spoken language to bring about any one of a number of intentional consequences. People use language to do many kinds of things: to promise, to predict, to pray, to prophesy, to politicize, to proclaim, or to report. John Austin and John Searle have both written on the subject of speech acts; see *How to do things with Words* and *Speech Acts*.

act because it is likely that an intentional act of communication has occurred. In the second case we would consider the lines a text and proceed to read it in quite a different way than the first set of lines. It is not the medium that is crucial here, for it is quite possible to make temporary texts in the sand with a stick (who hasn't written her name in the sand and probably thought how apt such an act is in capturing the human condition?), but it is the intention that makes the one a speech act and the other a non-speech act.

Readers invest time and effort in texts because of a belief that meaning, in the form of information or inspiration, either resides in or is triggered by the text at hand. By applying everything we know to the text we begin to create an interpretation. 'Intention, text, interpretation' is a bit like an unknown in an algebraic expression: its meaning is determined by the context and conventions of the language of algebra. Think of meaning as the unknown x of an algebraic expression. X is not ambiguous; its value is determined in each "sentence" - thus the value of x is not constant, but it is not arbitrary either. Consider:

$$1. \ 3x = 12, \text{ so } x = 4$$
$$2. \ 2x = 12, \text{ so } x = 6$$
$$3. \ .5x = 12, \text{ so } x = 24$$

where the meaning of x changes from statement to statement but is fixed in the statement in which it is used. Speech acts do not yield their meaning in such a mechanical way, but when a reader reads a text, some value for x, some interpretation, will necessarily follow. Just as we can solve algebraic expressions for unknowns only if we know the conventions, so too with speech acts. Reading is a creative act as can be seen in the way we use the word "reading" to refer to a construct, another text, as in "my reading of the curse of Ham story is that it is a story about homosexual incest," or, "most everyone reads Abraham's test story as an expression of blind faith but I think that it is a story of rational self-interest." Writers and readers are driven by intention, and they meet on a grid of conventions.

We have seen how repetition of a key phrase is used to effect the reading of the creation myth which opens Genesis. The form of that story is clearly an important part of its complete impact: repeated phrases emphasizing the phases of creation and the valuing of those things created; formal imperatives which move from word to world; and the utterances of the creator-god, which are the commands of a separate, transcendent power, and which mediate between nothingness and being. We have seen also how the author presents various other myths: the flood story presents a covenant myth, the tower of Babel story presents an origin myth to "explain" why there is "a babble of the language of all the world" and fantastic stories of giants and hints of many gods populating the .... the place where gods live. These many gods behave like Greek gods moving in with Bacchanalian thoughts on the beautiful human women. These stories come to us from a distant past, and bring with them roots from a vast storehouse of images. They are told as part of our universal need to explain and understand the experiences of our life by telling stories. Were there really giants on earth? No. Did Noah's ark float around filled with pairs of animals (or sevens of animals)? No. These stories do not claim a truth; rather they proclaim it.

The balance of Genesis establishes the beginnings of the line of heroes which people the next several books, heroes who, through the covenant promise, are chosen to bring a boon to the community. Everyone of importance to the story of Israel springs from Terah, and we are given the requisite genealogy to proclaim this line. These are the bare bones of the stories, but let us see how the flesh is put on the bones.

Consider Yahweh's "test" of Abraham. In a brief narrative one of the central stories of the Judeo-Christian belief system bursts out of the page and into human consciousness:

> The time came when God put Abraham to the test. 'Abraham', he called, and Abraham replied, 'Here I am.' God said, 'Take your son Isaac, your only son, whom you love, and go to the land of Moriah. There you shall offer him as a sacrifice on one of the hills which I will show you.' So Abraham rose early in the morning and saddled his ass, and he took with him two of his men and his son Isaac; and he split the firewood for the sacrifice, and set out for the place of which God had spoken. On the third day Abraham looked up and saw the place in the distance. He said to his men, Stay here with the ass while I and the boy go over there; and when we have worshipped we will come back to you.' So Abraham took the wood for the sacrifice and laid it on his son Isaac's shoulder; he himself carried the fire and the knife, and the two of them went on together. Isaac said to Abraham, 'Father', and he answered, 'What is it, my son?' Isaac said, 'Here are the fire and the wood, but where is the young beast for the sacrifice?' Abraham answered, 'God will provide himself with a young beast for a sacrifice, my

son.' And the two of them went on together and came to the place of which God had spoken, there Abraham built an altar and arranged the wood. He bound his son Isaac and laid him on the altar on top of the wood. Then he stretched out his hand and took the knife to kill his son; but the angel of the Lord called to him from heaven, 'Abraham, Abraham.' He answered, 'Here I am.' The angel of the Lord said, 'Do not raise your hand against the boy; do not touch him. Now I know that you are a God fearing man. You have not withheld from me your son, your only son. (Genesis 22.1-12)

One way of reading this story is as a myth signifying the end of human sacrifice: there will be no human sacrificed in this story. But such a reading is flat and does not do justice to the levels of narrative tissue to be found. Concentrate on the story: once again this god speaks: "Abraham," he calls. Abraham replies: "Here I am." What else could one say to the power represented here? There is no place to hide from this god; Adam and Eve learned that. And he issues commands: "Take your son Isaac, *your only son, whom you love*...." In the command there are two phrases (emphasis mine) which are completely redundant. Abraham certainly does not need to be reminded either that Isaac is his only son or that Isaac is beloved. Isaac is, remember, a "special package", a miracle that arrived from this god who now demands the miracle's sacrifice. Isaac arrived very late in Abraham's life from a wife beyond child bearing days, and he is the repository of the seed that is to carry on the chosen people. 'Isaac' means 'he laughed' and the charming story in which he is announced has Sarah laughing at the idea that she can give birth to a child at her stage of life. No, these non-restrictive phrases are for the reader's benefit: "Remember, reader, this command to this old man is to take his *only* son, his *beloved* son, to the land of Moriah, there to *kill* him." Abraham's response? "So Abraham rose early in the morning...and set out for the place which God had spoken."

In the scene just after the announcement of Isaac's birth and before the test story we were shown Abraham's reaction to God when told of the impending destruction of Sodom and Gomorrah. Abraham argues with his god: "Wilt thou really sweep away good and bad together? Suppose there are fifty good men in the city..." And further: "May I presume to speak to the Lord, dust and ashes that I am: suppose there are five short of the fifty good men? Wilt thou destroy the whole city for a mere five men?" Finally Abraham negotiates so aggressively that God that "For the sake of ten I will not destroy it." But the angels of the lord are unable to find the people who would in their goodness save Sodom and Gomorrah and God destroys the place. And Lot's wife does not obey the order "do not look back" and is turned into a pillar of salt. Do not obey and die.

This man Abraham, who had argued effectively with God in order to try to save unknown men in Sodom and Gomorrah, says nothing to try to save his only son. He says nothing; he does obey. We are told nothing of his conversation with Sarah or of her reaction to the order to kill *her* only son.[2] Can you hear?

> "Sarah, I have to go on a journey."
> "Where are you off to now, dear Abraham?" "
> "Oh, I have to go out into the desert and sacrifice
> Isaac, but I should be back in about six days."
> "Sacrifice Isaac! No, let us take him and hide from
> this god."

But there is no place to hide. "Here I am." And Sarah's reaction in the story? Well, we can only guess at any of this because we are not told. Here the writer has compressed the narrative to the breaking point. We are told, "On the third day Abraham looked up...." He has been travelling, head down, for three days, ever since receiving the crushing command to sacrifice his son. The narrative provides no details, presents no psychological profile. What happened on that three day journey?

Do you see young Isaac running along, playing, whistling, throwing stones, puzzled that his loving devoted father is so depressed? We are not told that Abraham is depressed; we are just told that he "looked up" on the third day. What a wealth of narrative detail has been omitted in order that our attention be riveted on this old man Abraham, obedient and unquestioning, walking toward this place of sacrifice. Do you identify with Abraham? Is this story filled with verisimilitude? Can you imagine being ordered by your god to sacrifice your child? Would such an order tell you something about your god?

---

[2] Abraham has another son, Ishmael, but Isaac is Sarah's only son.

Isaac's direct question to his father, who has not spoken for the entire journey, is an ironic one: "...where is the young beast for sacrifice?" And Abraham's answer is ironic, "God will provide himself with a young beast for a sacrifice, my son." Replace that final comma with a colon and the answer is as honest and complete as Abraham can give. More irony. Or is it? Why doesn't Abraham argue with God on this occasion when he did so before to save people he did not even know? Perhaps Abraham knows exactly what part he is to play here. Unquestioning obedience, required by this god in the Garden of Eden story, is required here also. Failure to obey has led to severe punishment in the past. Abraham knows that Lot's wife looked back and was turned into a pillar of salt. Knowing what he knows about this god, Abraham proceeds with the best action based on a rational analysis of his situation. Earlier, when faced with an order from Abimelech, king of Gerar, Abraham also acted out of rational self-interest; he told the king that Sarah was his sister and did nothing to stop the king from taking her.

A current textbook on the philosophy of religion[3] is typical in its assessment of the story of Abraham: "This story is the archetypal example of faith as trusting obedience to God." Penelhum, like others, takes the story out of context to assess it. But this story of Abraham and Isaac is a part of a larger narrative, a narrative which has shown important events that have already occurred in the earlier relationship with God. For example, in an earlier scene God has said to Abraham: "I will maintain My covenant with him [Isaac] as an everlasting covenant for his offspring to come." (Gen. 17.19) Thus, Abraham has reasons to believe that God will not kill Isaac - in fact, he has the word of God. Instead of a set piece on blind obedience the story is a report of rational action.[4]

Reading Abraham as a rational self-interested hero instead of as a "knight of faith" may be objectionable because to do so shrinks him to mere

---

[3] *Faith,* edited by Terence Penelhum, Macmillan Publishing Company, New York, page 5.

[4] A fascinating book on the subject of rational assessment is *Biblical Games: A Strategic Analysis of Stories in the Old Testament,* by Steven J. Brams, MIT Press, Cambridge, Mass., 1980. Brams writes: "One conclusion I draw from these stories is that "rational" interpretations of biblical actions are no more farfetched than "faith" interpretations." (page 36)

human size. Where is that fearful "teleological suspension of the ethical"[5] that Kierkegaard writes of so movingly ? Where is the knight of faith in a reading like this? Where? It resides in the Kierkegaard interpretation, in *his* official line, but not in the story line given in the Bible. Kierkegaard writes of Abraham:

> Yet Abraham believed and did not doubt, he believed the preposterous. If Abraham had doubted - then he would have done something else, something glorious; for how could Abraham do anything but what is great and glorious! He would have marched up to Mount Moriah, he would have cried out to God, "Despise not this sacrifice, it is not the best thing I possess, that I know well, for what is an old man in comparison with the child of promise; but it is the best I am able to give Thee. Let Isaac never come to know this, that he may console himself with his youth." He would have plunged the knife into his own breast. He would have been admired in the world, and his name would not have been forgotten; but it is one thing to be admired, and another to be the guiding star which saves the anguished.[6]

What would it mean to believe and not to doubt? Would doing so have any survival value? To believe the preposterous is just what the salespersons of channeling, E.S.P., out of body experiences, and other nonsense depend upon. How passionately one believes that x has no efficacy whatsoever in making x true, where x is a proposition about the world. Either God exists or God does not exist; and what I believe about the proposition 'God exists' has no effect on its being true. We can tell another story, as Kierkegaard does in his retelling of the Abraham story; we can put forward another *official line* as Kierkegaard does in *Fear and Trembling*, we can escape into the irrational or into subjectivity, and "believe the preposterous," or we can listen to the ancient voice of the poet who is telling the Abraham story, and who reveals its human meaning in the details of the narrative and in the overall

---

[5] Kierkegaard, Soren, *Fear and Trembling and The Sickness Unto Death,* translated, with an introduction and notes, by Walter Lowrie, Princeton University Press, Princeton, page 15.

[6] Kierkegaard, op. cit., page 35.

structure. Hear Sarah laughing outside the tent as the angel announces to Abraham that they will have a child. That laugh is the laugh of this tale: human and skeptical.

The human sized Abraham is in the biblical text; the knight sized Abraham is in Kierkegaard's text. Fear and trembling flow from Kierkegaard's reading while the story tells of fear and surviving. Two different stories are at play here. One proclaims that this god (the establishment, authority, the official line) values unthinking obedience above all else, and, indeed, will reward blind faith with the ultimate prize. A second reports on how to live, and how to survive, in an arbitrary world filled with powerful and tyrannical forces. Abraham, who earlier was Abram, carries not only two names, but also two radically different intentional "lines": one with the authority of the religious doctrine which it proclaims, the other with the authority of the human voice it can not drown. What one must do to survive or advance oneself is not always identical with what one believes in one's heart or says in public. There is always an official line, proclaimed as true by priests and kings, and it is often in conflict with the story line that makes up a human life. Official lines change: now blind obedience is of utmost importance, later it will not be enough. Official lines change because they are based on a complex of beliefs and doctrines, which as we all know are relative to time and place. But each of us realizes that some things never change; these things are not to be found in official lines because they reside in story lines. In part the story line reveals ways of surviving in spite of the official line.

Patriarchy is the official line of Genesis. Men's names and men's stories make up much of the Old Testament. Yahweh appears to Abraham, to Isaac, to Jacob, to Moses. We have come to think of God the *father*. This privileging of the masculine over the feminine is also part of the official line, and although it is, it is countered by the story line. Who are the characters with sparkle, intelligence, and ability? The women. Rebecca over Isaac in every way - except in the official line.

And what does it mean to choose Rebecca over Isaac? Look at the story: Sarah dies. Isaac is devastated by the loss of his mother. Abraham sends a servant back to his homeland to get a wife for Isaac. The servant meets a virgin by a well and by good fortune she is of the right tribe. When we first see Rebecca it is clear that she is a lively, intelligent, alive young woman. "The girl was very beautiful, a virgin...She went down to the spring, filled her jar and came up again." She moves quickly and decisively, draws water for the servant, for his camels, answers all questions, and runs to her mother's tent to report. Here is a type-scene for a betrothal. But what is different; what is the writer telling us about character and story through the variations in the pattern for a betrothal scene?

First, it is a servant and not the husband-to-be who is present at the well. Isaac is back at home moping about at the loss of his mother. Actually he is even further removed from the center of the story than that, for it was Abraham, not Isaac, who sent the servant in search of a wife. And when the servant returns home with Rebecca, (who announces her decision to leave her mother and family and travel with him with a "Yes, I will go,") then we finally see Isaac, the bridegroom. "One evening when he had gone out into the open country hoping to meet them he looked up and saw camels approaching." He looked up? There is some confusion in the text here, and one reading of the Hebrew is, "One evening when he had gone out into the open country to relieve himself...". Isaac is out there either to meditate or to urinate. Either action is a good measure of this bridegroom. Of Rebecca we learn, "So she became his wife, and he loved her *and was consoled for the death of his mother*" (emphasis mine). Isaac the special; Isaac the spoiled. He will have a wife to replace the mother he has lost.

JACOB AND ESAU

Abraham remarried after Sarah's death and his wife, Keturah, bore him six more sons. These six plus Ishmael and Isaac and several sons by his concubines provide dozens from whom he can choose when he dies. He chooses Isaac to carry on the special relation with Yahweh, or, better yet, Yahweh chooses Isaac to carry on the special seed, or, even better, the writer presents a story in which *choosing* is given to us in the form of a narrative. Just as Yahweh had chosen Abraham for his covenant so too Abraham chooses Isaac. These choices are made; we are given the heroes. And do these particular people have any particular virtues? The stories tell us: no. Neither is exceptional. Neither is endowed with extra-human courage or special insight (the image that remains in both cases is bowed head), neither is particularly bright. But here are the choices. This is the god of choice; whatever else he does in these stories he is always choosing. He chooses to create the world. He chooses to accept Abel's sacrifice but reject Cain's sacrifice. He chooses Abraham and in so doing chooses Israel over all other tribes. He chooses Isaac over Ishmael, Jacob over Esau, Joseph over all of his brothers. Why? It is important that we look carefully for the answer to this question. Is there something special that leads to each of these choices? No. This god of choice is also the god of chance. Never are we given reasons for these choices.

> Here a choice is announced to Rebecca:
> Two nations in your womb,
> two peoples, going their own ways
>   from birth!
> One shall be stronger than the other;
> the older shall be servant to the
>   younger. (Gen. 25.23)

And "when her time had come, there were indeed twins in her womb. The first comes out red,[7] hairy all over like a haircloak, and they name him Esau ("Red"). Immediately afterwards his brother is born with his hand grasping Esau's heel, and they call him Jacob ("he caught by the heel"). The boys grow up, Esau a hunter of skill and Jacob a stay-at-home. We are told that Isaac favoured Esau and that Rebecca favoured Jacob. Given what we know of these two characters it is obvious that Jacob has the stronger backer. Jacob, remember, is at home with his mother while Esau is out hunting. Jacob trades some soup for Esau's birthright and we are given an explanatory comment from the writer: "Thus Esau showed how little he valued his birthright." Here we see clearly an attempt to show a causal relationship between character and outcome: Esau deserves what he gets (or does not get) we are told. At yet another level we are told how it is that Israel flourished and their close kinsmen, the Edomites, did not. David will subdue the Edomites (2 Sam. 8.13-14). Writing *after the fact* has the same effect as writing before the fact with foreknowledge.

Because of a famine in the land God orders Isaac to move to Gerar. Notice how we are given two explanations for the action: 1. famine, 2. god's command. This dual explanation for the actions of the heroes is typical in the

---

[7] Medical science has attempted to diagnose conditions depicted in the Bible. For example, J.R. Gwilt writes, "It seems likely that Esau suffered from congenital adrenal hyperplasia; this is based on his appearance at birth...his exhaustion due to vigorous exercise with a feeling of immanent death, and his rapid recovery after a high protein meal of lentil soup and bread." "Biblical ills and remedies" in *Journal of the Royal Society of Medicine,* Volume 79, Dec. 1986.

Old Testament. We are often given a natural as well as a supernatural reading of the forces at play. Thus, God is always present in the story, controlling events and characters directly. God appears to Isaac as he had done with Abraham and reaffirms the covenant, "Thus shall I fulfil the oath which I swore to your father Abraham. I will make your descendants as many as the stars in the sky; I will give them all these lands..." And we are told of the continuing story of Israel: from Abraham to Isaac to Jacob. This connection between Abraham and Isaac is emphasized with one brush stroke in chapter 26: "When men of the place asked him about his wife, he told them that she was his sister; he was afraid to say that Rebecca was his wife; in case they killed him because of her; for she was very beautiful." Like father like son: both are capable of lying to save their own skins. These are characters of human dimension.

The famous deception story of Genesis 27 begins with a reminder to the reader that Isaac is old "and his eyes became so dim that he could not see". With Rebecca assisting Jacob, and with a nearly blind Isaac, it is easy to accept that Jacob in his costume, with wool over his smooth arm, can deceive his father. Once again we are given a natural explanation for the events of the story, a story which is intended to show how it is that the chosen seed of God will be carried on from generation to generation in violation of the conventions of primogeniture. One measure of a god is to have the god break human conventions. Although Isaac and his choice, Esau, can not see, this Jacob can see even at night while asleep. He dreams the famous ladder dream in which he makes contact with the spirit world. In the dream he is told that the land will be given to him and his descendants, who will be as countless as the "dust upon the earth". Jacob will become Israel, and will father the twelve tribes. The image of fruition used in the Isaac story came in "as many as the stars" but now the promise to Jacob is expanded to as "countless as the dust upon the earth." Not only is the image expansive, it is also a part of an imagery pattern that goes back to the creation story and forward to the united kingdom, when all of the land is brought under one kingship and is the pinnacle of power for the Hebrews. The promise God makes to the heroes of the Old Testament stories is always a promise of land - a place here on this earth, a place of dust: real, solid and actual.

Jacob, who receives this promise, is imaged as one who is real, solid, and actual. He is aggressive, but a dreamer. He is tenacious (he will work twenty years to get Rachel), brave, strong, physical, wily, self-reliant and shrewd. He is the Hercules of the Old Testament, lifting stones, wrestling with angels, tested and successful, climbing in his dreams to touch the other world but always of this world (he uses a ladder with its feet firmly on the ground). If fire identifies Samson, then stones identify Jacob. He lifts them, builds with them, finds water in them, and above all, *has* stones. From these stones will come a nation. A comparison between the meeting of Isaac and Rebecca and Jacob and Rachel brings out the character differences. Rebecca was a burst of energy and vitality in the scene where she is first discovered by the well. Isaac is not present. In Genesis 29 we find a parallel scene when Jacob meets Rachel. Travelling through open country Jacob spots a well which has a huge rock over it. He discovers that all the herdsmen gather at the well daily and when they are all there then together they can roll this rock off the well shaft to water their flocks. He makes contact with these herdsmen, discovers that they know Laban, the grandson of Nahor, and asks about him. "Yes, he is well," they say, "and here is his daughter Rachel coming with the flock." A well, a woman, and a group of herdsmen - a scene to watch carefully and to compare with others like it. While the herdsmen wait for the rest of their number in order to jointly roll the "huge rock" off the well Rachel arrives. "When Jacob saw Rachel, the daughter of Laban his mother's brother, with Laban's flock, he stepped forward, rolled the stone off the mouth of the well and watered Laban's sheep. He kissed Rachel, and was moved to tears....she ran and told her father." The scene is filled with action, exhibited through the series of active verbs. The sight of Rachel brings a surge of energy to Jacob allowing him to do that which several men can not do: roll the huge stone off the well. Once that well is opened, water, the life force, can flow. The images of male and female sexuality and the promise of new life are obvious in the well, the stone, the uncovering and the release, and the two characters are brought together by the kiss. There is power here. Sexual power, imaged in the well, the rock, the flocks, the young people, the actions, is palpable in the story.

Jacob the deceiver, who with his mother had tricked Isaac into giving him the birthright over his older brother, is now deceived himself by Laban who exchanges Leah for Rachel on Jacob's wedding night. Jacob works for twenty years for Laban in order to pay for Leah and Rachel. With his two wives and the two slave girls given to him by his wives he fathers thirteen children, twelve of them the sons who will become the twelve tribes of Israel. Thus Israel is founded and the act is signalled by a change of name for Jacob, who becomes Israel. The story must get the Israelites into Egypt, and it does so by having Joseph sold into slavery in Egypt by his brothers. Chapter 37 begins with "And this is the story of the descendants of Jacob." First we are told of Joseph, who is Jacob's chosen son, and we see how disharmony arises in the family because of this special treatment. Here again the story is struggling with the stated principle which it carries, namely, that God has chosen a particular tribe for special covenant treatment. The concept of choseness, as we see in the Joseph story, is fraught with problems. Joseph's brothers are jealous of him and hate his overbearing presence. He acts as a spy for his father, and he is given a special long sleeved robe by his father. This robe becomes an identifying feature for Joseph and when he is sent to spy on his brothers in Dothan it serves the writer well as a way of focussing the brothers' hatred when they first spot the cloak coming across the fields.

Joseph's story is an excellent example of sophisticated narrative structural devices used in support of story. In the opening passages we are told of a dream of Joseph's in which his brothers bow low before him. This dream serves to give motivation for the jealousy and hatred the brothers feel for him, and to mark the particular skill of Joseph's which will bring him into power in Egypt. At the end of the story "his brothers also wept and prostrated themselves before him," saying, "You see, we are your slaves," and the motif introduced at the beginning is closed at the end. Dreams, interpretations, insights, seeing, are all a part of the story, as are their opposites, to be found in deception and trickery. Jacob, like his father Isaac before him, cannot see very well and does not notice that his special treatment of Joseph is a cause of disharmony in his family. Choosing one over another for good reasons is one thing and could be understood by rational people. But choosing for no reason is arbitrary and the seeds of destruction are contained in the act of arbitrary choice. Chapter 38 is a good example of structural integrity and of sophisticated choices made by the writer/redactor. Writers, like the characters in stories, must make choices. Each sentence is a choice. A footnote in the New English Bible (page 40) says of Chapter 38, "The account here interrupts the flow of the Joseph narrative." It interrupts the story, but for good aesthetic reasons. In the brief story we are told about Judah's treatment of Tamar. He had promised her his younger son to replace an older brother who had died. Judah forgets about his promise to her and she is forced to take action to get what is due to her. Part of her scheme has to do with deceiving Judah by veiling her face and passing herself off to Judah as a prostitute. Judah, driven by sexual desire, does not see as he should, just as Jacob, overcome by excessive grief, had leapt to the conclusion that the bloody cloak shown him by his sons meant that Joseph was dead. By getting a pledge from Judah, Tamar is later able to get him to recognize that he is the father of her twins. In the next section Joseph will exhibit sexual restraint in dealing with Potiphar's wife because he does see clearly. The stories are thematically related and play one on the other while reminding us of the idea of *seeing* which is central to the entire series of stories. Seeing the pledge reminds Judah that he has made a promise to Tamar. Seeing what dreams mean brings Joseph to a position of power that enables him to send for his family and thus bring the Israelite tribes into Egypt for the Exodus. When God speaks from a position of knowledge of the future, as the author of all stories, then seeing and interpreting become of great importance. "What is in store for me, what is my future?" are questions to be asked by every character in the narrative, and he who can see the plan through dreams or any medium is a hero. Jacob's family, torn apart by jealousy and hatred, must find itself before harmony can be restored; must see and recognize each other by dealing with the sins of the past. This family, now Israel, is united by the end of Genesis: "He [Joseph] comforted them and set their minds at rest." To see is to read. The Old Testament hero is, above all, one who can read intention and offer correct interpretation. Abraham reads Yahweh's intentions in the sacrifice story and interprets the story correctly. Israel prospers when its heroes see clearly.

CHAPTER 6: "WHO SHOULD I SAY THAT YOU ARE?"

To read is to interpret. To interpret is to seek intention. Good readers offer consistent readings of texts. Biblical heroes are good readers who read Yahweh's intentions. Who is this Yahweh that we read of from the very beginning of the text?

"In the beginning of creation, when God made heaven and earth..." is the first thing we read. Not only is there a time indicator functioning like "once upon a time" but also it seems right to call it *the* time indicator - not once *in* time but at the beginning *of* time. "In the beginning of creation" signals an ongoing creation, a continuous creation in time, and not just a creative act of instantaneous power inserted and withdrawn.

In the Genesis 1 creation story we find authority, brevity, and solemn majesty presented in the character of God, the transcendent and creative commander of the universe. But already in Genesis 2 we meet a sudden switch in form and style. Now the relationship of the characters rather than the tabulation of events or commands is primary. Here is a personal God, immanent and knowable, instead of transcendent and imperial. The language is picturesque and flowing: this God breathes life into dust sculpted man and plants a garden, this God responds to the loneliness of Adam and creates Eve, this God walks in the garden and talks to his creations. The God who issued commands in Genesis 1 speaks only once here and then to himself, "It is not good for man to be alone." While in Genesis 1 God appears as a being who stands outside of his creation and controls it with his mighty word, in Genesis 2 the portrait of God is very different. Here his immanence, personal nearness, and local involvement on the human scene are basic features. Yahweh is not a detached sovereign overlord but a god at hand as a loving master. He is a god with whom man has a ready contact. He *molds* with his hands like a potter; he *breathes* into the mouth of a clay model, he *searches* through the garden for Adam and Eve, he *converses*.

These two differing notions of God have been described as the Priestly and the Yahwist conceptions. The priestly account is claimed to run from Genesis 1.1 through 2.4a and the Yahwist account from Genesis 2.4b through 4.26. They differ in these ways: while the Priestly account is solemn, repetitive, and majestic in style, the Yahwist account is told in story form with an evocative and economical use of words which appeals to the imagination instead of the intellect. While in the Priestly (P) account God creates things, in the Yahwist (J) account he forms them. P has male and female created in the likeness of God; J has man and woman formed as living beings from the dust. P offers a cosmic perspective of an ordered world with God outside it, and J presents an intimate and involved God creating not by order but by hand. In P documents the name for God is 'Elohim' and in J documents the name for God is 'Yahweh'.

Quite different conceptions of god are to be seen in these different renditions. Detached or involved, or both? In the final combination of stories the answer is both. One set of stories likely arose from the priestly concerns of ritual and intellectual justification for a certain conception. The so-called Yahwist story teller has differing intentions, is as we say, of the people, and tells the story in a more personal way. The difference here could be described as the difference between a sermon and a drama. By the time the redactor has woven the stories together the result is a more complex god than either P or J envisioned. From the very beginning it seems that talking of God was in part a matter of projecting self-interest on to the screen. Talking of god is not a matter of getting the description accurate but always is a matter of proclaiming what is to be described. If two people (or two nations) disagree on the proper description of god, they have no place in the physical world to go to check for descriptive accuracy - they go instead to texts, they return to their story and not to the laboratory.

The Hebrew God appears on several occasions in the stories of the Old Testament. In one sense these books are the record of the covenant between God and his chosen people. He reveals himself to the patriarchs and to Moses - appears as himself to the tribal heroes. For example:

When Abram was ninety-nine years old, the Lord appeared to him and said, 'I am God Almighty. Live always in my presence and be perfect, so that I may set my covenant between myself and you and multiply your descendants.' Abram threw himself down on his face, and God spoke with him and said, 'I make this covenant, and I make it with you: you shall be the father of a host of nations. Your name shall no longer be Abram [that is, High Father], your name shall be Abraham [that is, Father of a Multitude], for I make you father of a host of nations. (Gen. 17.1-5)

Later God appears to Abraham at Mamre in the form of visitors to his tent to announce that Sarah will give birth to a son. The Lord also reveals to Abraham his plans for Sodom and Gomorrah, explaining that he should not conceal from Abraham what he intends to do since Abraham is his choice to father a great and powerful nation, and knowing of God's intentions will be further proof that Abraham is the chosen one. Later God will also appear to Jacob and also rename him. God identifies himself this time as "the God who appeared to you when you were running away from your brother Esau." In the famous scene in Exodus God once again appears to man, this time to Moses. Here, in answer to Moses' question, 'If I go to the Israelites and tell them that the God of their forefathers has sent me to them, and they ask me his name, what shall I say?' we hear, 'I AM; that is who I am. Tell them that I AM has sent you to them.' I AM is who I am; and YHWH is my name. And these puzzling words have been written about more than any others in literature . Here in the story we have God himself uttering his name, providing us with a clue to his nature. What might these words mean?

Names are of great importance in the Old Testament. Several of the heroes of the tribes have name changes when the covenant is renewed. Often the name given, as, for example, in Abraham's case, is not only used to refer but is also a word with meaning. 'Abraham' means 'father of a multitude' and 'Isaac' means 'he laughed.' We do not usually think of names as having connotations, but as tags to be used to denote or refer to a particular person. But here, in addition to referring, these names often carry a meaning that tells us something about the character in the story. 'Yahweh' (the probable pronunciation of the Hebrew consonants YHWH) is the unpronounceable name, the name that cannot be said. The name of God is unique in that it is one word that cannot be pronounced. The difficulty of talking *about* God is literally in the story - to refer to God is to have to employ a word that cannot be pronounced. From the very beginning of the story we see the acknowledged difficulty of god-talk, for we are cut off from either referring to him or from giving some meaning to his name. The name he gives Moses has neither sense nor reference. The story tells us that God is beyond language in the most basic of ways: he is going to be impossible to talk about because the word used to name him cannot be pronounced, and if it could be pronounced it would have no meaning.

But this has not stopped people from talking about God, for the message of the story is always subject to and object of interpretation from a particular point of view. One Catholic writer[1] offers a reading of the Old Testament passage quite different from mine. He says that there are three possibilities of readings from the 'I AM that I AM' passage. First, "I am who I am" is god's affirmation of himself "to be the Absolutely existent One to whose being there is no limit or restriction."[2] In the Greek version this comes out "I am he who is." Father Murray says these meanings are too academic for the story and the times. What Moses is really asking, he says, "was to know not his [God's] nature but his role in their community and his mode of action in their history." Therefore he puts aside this interpretation. A second possibility is "I make to be whatever comes to be." He writes:[3]

> The belief that God is the Maker of All was present among the Israelites from the beginning. In fact, in all primitive religions the belief prevailed that the god stood at the origin of the world. It may, however, be doubted that the original hearing of the divine name caught this cosmological sense in it. To them, Yahweh was in the first instance the God of their fathers, who created the people, who was the Lord of the people, the power behind their history.

It is yet a third interpretation which Father Murray finds the correct one. This reading he asserts "yields a more adequate exegetical understanding." What does it mean to find a reading that "yields a more adequate exegetical understanding?" It means to consider many readings from the point of view of an already established official line and then to select as

---

[1] John Courtney Murray, S.J., *The Problem of God,* Yale University Press, New Haven and London, 1964.
[2] Ibid. page 8.
[3] Ibid. page 9.

correct that one which promotes the official line. This approach is not to read out of the work but to read into the work from a set of preconceptions, and one of its problems is obviously that what you read is what you are. Murray's reading proceeds like this: "...in the enigmatic play on words and in the Name Yahweh that embodies its sense, Moses and his people heard not the affirmation that God is or that he is creator but the promise that he would be present with his people." I have argued that 'Yahweh' is without sense. And in this senselessness lies the "meaning" of the story. How would we decide who is right? Look at the story - or to paraphrase D. H. Lawrence, "Never trust the teller; trust the tale." Murray's three readings and my fourth are not disagreements about what is there in the story but are disagreements about the *meaning* of the story. By "meaning" here I mean the most sensible and natural reading of the story as it appears in the complex narrative without importing a preconceived scheme of dogmatic interpretation.

Our first responsibility is to read sensitively and with care what the writer has written. It is difficult because we do indeed look through a glass darkly - the glass being darkened by the layers of interpretations offered up over the centuries, interpretations which have evolved into the official line. For example, we talk about god as if she were male. All those Sunday School pictures show a male, a sort of larger than life Abraham, with flowing beard and human features. But there is powerful imagery in the Bible that offers us a female god. A recurring image in the Old Testament is of a god who is like a hen, gathering its chicks under its protective wing ("as an eagle watches over its nest," Deut. 32.11). Images of birth are used to compare the birth of a new nation or of a new idea to childbirth:

> Long have I lain still,
> I kept silence and held myself in check;
> now I will cry like a woman in labour,
> Whimpering, panting and gasping. (Isaiah 42.14)

The divine feminine[4] is also present in the New Testament. Jesus says (John 16.21) "A woman in labour is in pain because her time has come..." and later says of himself that his "time has come." In that story Jesus is bringing

---

[4] Virginia Ramey Mollenkott has a book of interest on the topic called *The Divine Feminine*, published by Crossroad Press, New York, 1981.

forth a new way of relating to God, a new idea. The male dominated language of the church is found in the official line - the concepts of god in the texts are beyond sexist projections. And just where does the meaning of a story reside?

Three possibilities present themselves for consideration and discussion: 1. intention, 2. text, 3. interpretation. The meaning, argue some, is to be found in the *intention* of the author. If we could only know what the author intended then we could know what the story means, or, we could then measure the intention against the accomplishment. This approach is seen in the "let's call the author" approach to literary criticism. "If anybody knows what's going on it's bound to be the author." This approach would have us study history, psychology, biography and anthropology in order to understand texts. The New Critics reminded us that the text itself is important, although they emphasized it to the exclusion of all else. Authorial intention, they argued, is difficult if not impossible to ascertain, while the artifact itself, the text, is present to be studied. Reader response critics point out that meaning resides in the mind/brain of the reader. Everyone has sat in a literature class and wondered if there was indeed any answer to the problem of multiple interpretation other than the cynical one of giving the teacher what you think she wants.

Here is a record of such a debate centering around a modern and brief poem. "Aren't you just reading that into the poem?" Very often the English teacher cannot prove the validity of his/her interpretation, try as s/he might to build a logical case: the design s/he has just traced out in the webwork of a poem's connotations and reverberations (perfectly logical in her eyes) begins to waver as students fire at him with alternative connections, last year's high school teacher's equally logical structure, and antagonistic literary critics ("Well, if you're so hot why haven't you published?"). As the design melts back into a flow of possible meanings, the teacher stammers his/her appeals to justice, then to mercy, but the class has passed sentence: ring-binders snap shut like so many hungry alligators, and the students march off to physics where issues are clear. The teacher exiles herself to an hour of solitary confinement in her office.

Below is a record of a similar trial, with some concluding judgements.

The bone of contention is a poem by Robert Frost:

Dust of Snow

The way the crow
Shook down on me
The dust of snow
From a hemlock tree
Has given my heart
A change of mood
And saved some part
Of a day I had rued.

The first testimony took place in the classroom of Norbert Artzt, who had written the poem on the blackboard, and proceeded to reveal its perfectly logical pattern. Here is part of his report (printed in *College English*, April 1971):

> "What is on the board?" I ask again.
> Someone says "words."
> We have taken the first step. "What do these words do?"
> "They make a statement." ...
> I digress. "Is the statement a complete one?"...
>
> The answers come. They are seeing the words.
> "In what time of year does the thing take place? Is winter a time of life and growth? What about snow? What about dust?"...
>
> The young man with the long hair is in a frenzy. "The bird is scattering dust on the poet's head. He is burying him. Good grief! He is burying him."
>
> Everyone feels the chill. They are cold now. They are afraid. Winter, dust, crow, snow, hemlock tree- the images are coalescing. The deep structure of the poem is emerging in their heads.
>
> Suddenly the momentum stops.
>
> "But why?" someone asks. "Why if the man gets a premonition of death does his mood change for the better?"

We move back to "the way". I ask how the bird shakes the snow down on the man, why he does it....

The bird is drying his wings or landing or taking off. The bird is indifferent to the man walking beneath him. I ask what this bird's indifferent act might mean in the context of the experience. Some-one suggests that the meaning may lie in the man's feeling about what has happened. The man recognizes that nature is indifferent to the life of any particular man.

I ask again what the thing on the board has said. The long-haired boy speaks. He is a genius. He will burn down the White House some day. "The poet has realized through this experience that death is inevitable and incalculable. It can come at any time, any place, to anyone. The poet knows he's wasting his time in regret, wasting life." The boy becomes prophetic; his name is Jeremy. "The poet has had an epiphany. That is why his mood changes."

Counter-testimony came from Laurence Perrine - after reading Artzt's report he wrote, in *The Explicator*, March, 1972:

"The way" in which a crow shakes down dust of snow on Frost's speaker is left unspecified, thus permitting several possibilities. I can see them chiefly as four: Beautifully, animatedly, cheerily, and humorously. First the poem presents a scene of visual beauty, black etched   against white, the movement of the scattered   snow counterpoint against the immobility of the evergreen tree. Second, the action of the crow   presents a bit of life and animation in a scene otherwise frozen and without life. Third, the scattering of the snow on the speaker is almost an acknowledgment of his presence, a greeting, a communication between the two living actors in the scene. Fourth, the snow's falling on the speaker suggests a touch of humor, as if the sly crow were playing a practical joke on him. The beauty of the action, its evidence of life, its suggestion of a greeting , and the touch of humor in it combines to lighten the mood of the speaker....

Recounting a very simple incident, Frost strove to give it an utter simplicity of form and language. His one sentence poem has only one word with as many as two syllables.

Two additional points. First, the fact that the crow's action saved only part of a day the speaker "had rued" does not imply that his sorrow was too pervasive. He may have made a social blunder, for instance, and his wife may have spoken sharply to him; but he is hardly mourning his wife's death or the loss of a child. Nevertheless, the point of the poem lies in the discrepancy between the smallness of the crow's action and the extent of its effect: it is this that tells us most about the sensitivity of the speaker, his responsiveness to beauty and life, and his love of nature.

To judge this case, what voice could be more authoritative than Robert Frost's? In the film *Lover's Quarrel With the World* (1963) he states:

> There's a little poem of mine, an old one. It goes like this. (He recites "Dust of Snow".) See now. Let's look at that fair and square. (He recites it again, more slowly.) And someone says to me,"Very sinister poem!" And I said, "Sinister?" "Yes, the crow, the crow is a black bird." And I said, "The crow figures all sorts of ways, but all right , I don't argue. And what more?" "The hemlock tree." And I said, "Yes?" And he said, "but Socrates, Socrates - death of Socrates." Well you get surprises in this world. I never thought of that. I live with hemlock trees, and it's not the weed that Socrates drank at all. And it's all wrong with the tree. I'm partly just as much from the city as the country. But I'm a little more country than city. And I know what a hemlock tree is.

Yet there is a higher appeal. Here is Auden:[5]

> One sign that a book has literary value is that it can be read in a number of different ways. Vice versa, the proof that pornography has no literary value is that, if one attempts to read it in any other way than as a sexual stimulus, to read it, say, as a psychological case-history of the author's sexual fantasies, one is bored to tears.

---

[5] W. H. Auden, *The Dyer's Hand,* Random House, New York, 1962, page 4.

> Though a work of literature can be read in a number of ways, this number is finite and can be arranged in a hierarchical order; some readings are obviously "truer" than others, some obviously false, and some like reading a novel backwards,   absurd. That is why, for a desert island, one would choose a good dictionary rather than the greatest literary masterpiece imaginable for, in relation to its readers, a dictionary is absolutely passive and may legitimately be read in an infinite number of ways.

Need Frost be aware of this hierarchy? In fact, need he be aware of fairly basic implications of his poem? We often need others to help us grasp the meaning(s) of our own dreams. Often the creative work functions as an "other" to the one creating it.

But in case the issue seems to be resolving or dissolving into valid subjective realities, here's a new confrontation, revealed by a broader context. After the appearance of Perrine's attack on him, Artzt (author of the first article) wrote to Jeremy for moral support. Jeremy was then at a Federal Correction Institute for burning draft cards and a draft office. His reply:

> What really craps me out is that guys like you and Mr. P. take these things so seriously. Both of you ought to take a long walk in the snow.

> What matters in this world is action. When words turn into action you have poetry. When they sit on the page or in the classroom you have nothing.

> I'll tell you what you can do for me - you can stop the war. When the murders are done with, write me again and tell me what you did to stop the killing.

When an eight line poem can stimulate such discussion is it any wonder that the stories from the Bible are interpreted in so many different ways? Would it help to be able to talk with the author? Where is the authority for a reading that is true? Do we look to a priest or a rabbi? Would not that be to substitute one reading for another? In a sense the claim of authority for the biblical stories, namely that they are written by God, should be taken as metaphoric truth. The truth is in the stories - not in the interpretations offered by others who add their voices to the stories. Reading the Bible is to read a complex narrative, with all the subtlety and complexity that requires, but it is not merely to choose to accept someone else's reading on authority. Reading any complex text requires that we bring to it everything that we can, effectively, all we are: a critical mind, a sensitivity to literary structures, an awareness of the time and place from which the text arises, our little knowledge of life itself. In reading the Bible, too often, instead of a critical reading based upon intention, text, and reaction, we are seduced by the *official line*, which does all of the work for us. Adding the official line to the formula of intention, text, and reaction means we are faced with the difficulty of attempting to read the intention, text, and reaction of the official line!

What a beautiful thing it is to read the bible stories without the layers of interpretive stuff that many of us bring to them from the chapel or the synagogue. It is difficult to read these texts with fresh eyes from within our culturally imposed official line, but it is the only way to read them.

As I write this two armies are facing each other in the Persian Gulf. Saddam Hussein has recently invaded and taken Kuwait. George Bush has responded with the assistance of the United Nations by moving a multi-national force into Saudia Arabia. The self-interest of the nations involved is beginning to be hidden under rhetoric about "holy wars" and "sacred places" and "evil forces" - rhetoric that tries to make this grab for oil by both sides into some kind of religious encounter between two gods: the God of Islam and the God of Christianity. Are we to believe that God, any god, is concerned about the price of a barrel of oil? The number of religious wars fought on this earth is staggering. Millions of people have died in defense of some conceptual projection or other. We have fought over subtle matters of doctrine, over what shape the temple should have, over what sacrifices are appropriate. And in every war each side claims that God is on their side. As Lincoln said in the American Civil War: "They say that God is on their side; we say that God is on our side. We could both be wrong, but at most one of us is right." Belief in god can be a powerful force in the affairs of men and women. Such belief can bring us to our knees, can arm us with a sword of fire as we march off to war, can bring us fear of the future, can fill our minds with expectation, can provide peace and acceptance. One can also believe in ghosts, devils, secret powers of the mind, the power of crystals to cure cancer, the existence of witches, or the green cheese theory of the moon's construction. What is the difference, if any, between a belief in these fantastic notions and a belief in a god?

Nothing and everything. On the one hand there is no difference, in the sense that there is no evidence for the existence of devils or gods. On the other hand there is a difference in the tenacity with which people hold on to the belief in god. With many beliefs we are willing to let them go when we are provided with sufficient evidence. Strictly speaking, of course, it is impossible to hold a false belief. Once I know that a given belief of mine is false I can no longer hold it as a belief. If I do, then doing so counts as evidence that I am irrational. But just as I cannot know that God exists, I also cannot know that God does not exist. 'Know' is the key word here. How does it function? We say that we know P (a statement) just when we believe that P, we have evidence that P, and P is true. In formal dress:

X knows that P is true if and only if:
1. X believes that P,
2. X has good evidence that P, and
3. P is true.

Knowledge then is justified, true belief. Belief is a necessary but not a sufficient condition for knowledge, which means that no matter how hard I believe that P, P's truth is independent of my belief. It also means that the number of believers is also logically independent of the truth of the proposition. The strength and the number of believers cannot guarantee the truth of a proposition. It may well be that millions of committed persons once believed strongly that the earth is flat. But that didn't make it flat. So it is with God. Millions of people seem to believe in Allah, and millions of people seem to believe in the Christian God. Millions believe in Buddha. Millions believe in no god. But we do not believe that this issue will be settled by a world wide vote.

Besides going to "sacred" texts to prove our god's existence, which is question begging ("I know that God exists because it says so in the Bible and God wrote the Bible!"[6]), how do we proceed?

---

[6] In one sense the claim that God exists because the Bible says so is true. God exists as a character in the stories in just the way Hamlet exists in Shakespeare's *Hamlet*.

One way is to posit another way of knowing, a way of knowing that is not subject to the same rigor as is factual knowledge and its repeated claim for verification. Faith is often suggested as way of knowing religious truths which is different from the way of knowing other kinds of truths. "The invisible is always visible to faith," writes Father Murray,[7] and there does seem to be a widespread belief that faith is a way of knowing that should be included as a third logical category in answer to the question 'how do you know that x?' One way we know that x is through experience and another is through reason. Perhaps a third way is faith. All three answers have been offered as ways of knowing about God. Experience, it is argued, offers evidence that God exists. Because of the complexity of the created world, in the beauty and design of the created product is some evidence that a creator must exist who created the whole of it. Nothing as complicated as a human eye or human brain could possibly exist unless there were some creator behind the creation, but incremental evolution over vast expanses of time would be a counter hypothesis that explained the coming into being of things in the world without the need for special creation. Design itself is a slippery concept - it is hard to say where it resides, in the thing that has it or in the thing that views it. The believer seems to "see" something else in experience that the non-believer cannot "see."

John Wisdom, in a famous paper published in 1944,[8] argues that "the existence of God is not an experimental issue in the way it was," primarily because of "our better knowledge of why things happen as they do." While in the past we may have thought of God as a power that pulled the levers of the natural order, today, with the advances of science, we are not so apt to believe that prayer is the best solution to end a drought or heal a cancer. Wisdom's paper, which generated a new interest in the philosophy of religion, offers an explanation of how it is that "an explanatory hypothesis, such as the existence of God, may start by being experimental and gradually become something quite different." He offers a story about two men who return to their long neglected garden to find that among the weeds are some of the old plants growing strongly. One suggests that a gardener must come and tend them. The other says there is no gardener. They experiment by examining the garden very carefully, studying other unattended gardens, and asking neighbours if anyone

---

[7] Op. cit., page 113.
[8] John Wisdom, "Gods," *Proceedings of the Aristotelian Society,* 1944-45.

is secretly tending the garden. The two discover exactly the same facts, but one continues to say "There is a gardener" and the other to say "There is no gardener." Wisdom says, "with this difference in what they say about the gardener goes a difference in how they feel towards the garden, in spite of the fact that neither expects anything of it which the other does not expect." One man feels one way about the garden and the other feels another way. Is this all it means to assert a belief in God?

People who argue about the existence of God and attempt to convince others of their position are arguing about something they take to be fundamental and important - they do not seem to be talking just about how they feel. Each wants to offer some kind of reasons for his/her belief, or as Wisdom puts it, "The disputants speak as if they are concerned with a matter of scientific fact, or of trans-sensual, trans-scientific and metaphysical fact, but still of fact and still a matter about which reasons for and against may be offered, although no scientific reasons in the sense of field surveys for fossils or experiments on delinquents are to the point." However, not every dispute that we have is one that can be settled by experiment. In mathematics, logic and literary interpretation we may offer reasons in support of our beliefs, but be unable to offer experimental results that support the interpretation or solution. In law cases the same facts may be accepted by both parties and there still be a dispute as to what they mean. In these kinds of cases, argues Wisdom, "the solution of the question at issue is a decision, a ruling by the judge."

Is belief in God equal with belief in mathematics or logic? Over the centuries many have thought so and many attempts have been made to provide the deductive argument that would win the day. In the eleventh century Saint Anselm offered a brilliant argument based upon a definition of God as "that than which nothing greater can be conceived." He argued:

> 1. By God we understand that than which nothing greater can be conceived.
> 2. That than which a greater cannot be thought cannot exist in the understanding alone.
> 3. Therefore, there exists both in the understanding and in reality something than which a greater cannot be thought.

Anselm's argument is not dependent upon experimentation or observation of scientific facts; it is an argument based upon definition. He believed he had provided the knock down argument for God's existence. His joy of discovery is evident in his comment, "Thanks be to thee, good Lord, thanks be to thee, because I now understand by thy light what I formerly believed by thy gift, so that even if I were to refuse to believe in thy existence, I could not fail to understand its truth."[9] Anselm was subject to almost immediate criticism on the ground of a parallel argument that seemed to lead to absurdity: Lost Island is an island of perfection that I can conceive of in my understanding, and it is greater than any other island, therefore it must exist, for if it did not then I could conceive of an existing island that would be greater than Lost Island because it would exist! But either there is such an island or there is not, my conceiving it cannot bring it in to existence.

Anselm's argument and all other a priori arguments fall victim to the Kantian observation that existence is not a predicate. When one says 'Bob is tall' one uses 'tall' to predicate something of Bob. But if Bob is tall then 'Bob' must already refer to someone who exists. To say 'Bob exists' is not only odd it is also redundant. Existence is not a matter of logic but a matter of fact. Arguments for God's existence which are based upon reason in this way turn out to be unsatisfactory - they always seem to be about language but not about God.

What then of faith? Is faith a different kind of faculty that some of us may enjoy which somehow provides direct access to knowledge? 'Faith' is both quite an ordinary word and quite an extra-ordinary word. On the one hand it functions to describe the epistemic relationship we have with all sorts of things we do not understand: 'I have faith that my automatic transmission will work,' or 'I have faith that the Canadian dollar will continue to have some value.' On the other hand it is used in this way: 'I have faith that God spoke to the patriarchs in the desert,' or 'Faith tells me that Christ died for my sins.' Are these usages the same? Not exactly, for in the first examples we could in principle come to know whether the faith was well placed by pursuing study of a certain kind. But in the latter examples there is nothing further to study, even in principle; faith in those examples is hope. Not all faith is rational.

---

[9] Quoted here from *Philosophy: Paradox and Discovery*, edited by Minton, Arthur J. and Shipka, Thomas A., 2nd edition, McGraw Hill, Inc., page 9-10.

patriarchs in the desert,' or 'Faith tells me that Christ died for my sins.' Are these usages the same? Not exactly, for in the first examples we could in principle come to know whether the faith was well placed by pursuing study of a certain kind. But in the latter examples there is nothing further to study, even in principle; faith in those examples is hope. Not all faith is rational.

Belief in God appears more an aesthetic experience than anything else. One either sees the beauty in a painting or one does not. Is the beauty really there? Yes and no. As Wisdom says, "We have eaten of the fruit of a garden we can't forget though we were never there, a garden we still look for though we can never find it."

God, like beauty, is to be found in the stories, the works of art, of the Bible. When our first son was about four he went to play school one day and immediately went over to an easel and stood there holding a brush ready to start painting. The teacher came up behind him and said, "What are you going to paint?" "God," he said. "And do you know what God looks like?"

"I will when I finish the painting," he said as he began to paint.

CHAPTER 7: THE CLOUD OF THE LORD

> For the cloud of the Lord hovered over the Tabernacle
> by day, and there was fire in the cloud by night, and the
> Israelites could see it at every stage of their journey.
> (Ex.40.38)

The Old Testament narrative paints a picture of God. He is never far away; is, you might say, the subtext of the stories. He is the creator-god, the avenging-god, the choosing god, the covenant god. The promise he makes to Abraham which launches the narrative is renewed and thus brought back to our attention at the introduction of each new hero in the line from Abraham to Jesus. Even when he is not participating as a character in the action of the story his presence is felt. From the beginning we have been told how the events of the story are under the control of this god, and at the conclusion of *Exodus* we find that his presence will be constantly, visually on the canvas - day and night - omnipresent. "And the Israelites could see it at every stage of their journey." This cloud and the Tent of the Presence are constant reminders to the newly freed Israelites of the power and presence of their tribal god. Not only did he free them from slavery but he is also guiding them to their promised land. He reveals the way to his people and they are never lost in the desert.

Just as Yahweh reveals the way through the desert to the rich valleys of Canaan, so also does he reveal the way to religious and political riches. A priestly account of the origins of the sanctuary, its personnel and rituals follows in *Leviticus*. Time after time the formula "the Lord spoke to Moses and said," announces a new set of rules concerning offerings, installation of priests, sacrifices, sexual conduct, purification and atonement, preparation of food offerings, and the approved slaughtering techniques. The Tent of the Presence is the center of the religious life of the tribes and from it come the laws that will bind the tribes together into a people. Negotiating meaning between the Presence and the People - that is, the approved readers of the subtext - are the priests, the members of the tribe of Levi.

The patriarchal religion was patterned after the patron deity of the clan - the "god of the fathers" - and its rules and patterns are developed in the stories in the post exodus books. Religion in the early Near East consisted not so much in certain beliefs as in common patterns of ritual enactment.[1] The recurring prophetic metaphor shows a relationship of parent to child:

> When Israel was a child, I loved him
> and out of Egypt, I called my son. (Hosea 11.1)

where the desert sojourn is viewed as Israel's childhood and where Yahweh taught his children the necessity for discipline and trust. In the stories of conquest we see the most basic form of the contract theory of political obligation: obey the laws of the divine ruler and the consequences will be good, disobey and chaos will follow. Contract theory as developed later by Hobbes and Rousseau is implicit in the Old Testament stories although never specifically offered as a political theory. Why does one have an obligation to Moses, Joshua and the Judges? Because they are divinely appointed and speak the words of Yahweh. The battles that go against the tribes are ones where the will of Yahweh has not been followed. Good consequences flow to those who obey and are righteous; when events turn out bad the reasons are to be found in the disobedience of the people who have broken the contract.

Throughout the forty year "childhood" the lack of food and water and the risk of attack by hostile tribes were constant threats. Time after time Yahweh provides for his people through miraculous delivery of manna and quail in the midst of a barren desert and through the equally miraculous ability to produce

---

[1] S.H. Hooke, *In the Beginning*, Oxford, Clarendon Press, 1947, p.132 ff.

water from the dry and barren landscape. In one story (Num. 20) we are given the reason why Moses will not be able to enter the promised land and it revolves around water.

> The Lord spoke to Moses and said, 'Take a staff, and then with Aaron your brother assemble all the community, and, in front of them all, speak to the rock and it will yield its water. Thus you will produce water for the community out of the rock, for them and their beasts to drink.'

Moses makes a fatal, human error. Responding to the community with impatience (and who wouldn't given the constant complaining of the community?) he does not speak to the rock as commanded, but strikes the rock twice with his staff, saying, 'Listen to me, you rebels. Must we get water out of this rock for you?' This one loss of patience, this human response to a toilsome situation, costs him dearly:

> 'You did not trust me so far as to uphold my holiness in the sight of the Israelites; therefore you shall not lead this assembly into the land which I promised to give them.'

No one, not even the faithful, long serving, reluctant hero, Moses, is immune from the commands of Yahweh. Moses disobeys and is denied access to the promised land.

Moses' ability to inspire is dramatically shown in the story of the battle against the Amelekites. While Joshua led the attack, Moses stood on a hill in full view of his army holding his arms over his head and as long as his arms were outstretched the Hebrews were successful, " and Joshua mowed down Amalek and his people with the edge of the sword." A constant theme throughout the story of the conquest of Canaan: it is the divine power of Yahweh that is responsible for success.

According to the Priestly account (Ex. 19.1; Num. 10.11) the Hebrews spent nearly a year at Mount Sinai before finally breaking camp and striking out toward the Wilderness of Paran. With them on the journey goes the portable ark and the tabernacle as evidence of Yahweh's presence as they push on to the vicinity of Kadesh where the official forty years in the wilderness is spent. Throughout Yahweh faithfully produces water, manna, and quail.

The Balaam story (chs. 22-24) provides a delightful interlude in the Numbers narrative and is the one case in the Bible of a talking animal and a touch of humor - for here the dumb beast is more enlightened than the learned master. Talking animals are not unusual in the literature of the time (e.g., Achilles' horse Xanathus in the Iliad) but the only other Old Testament example is the serpent in the Garden of Eden. The emphasis in these oracle stories is on the fact that an oracle is only as good as Yahweh allows him to be and foreshadows the later prophetic conception of the divine Word.

The words of Deuteronomy are the words of the ritualistic covenant agreement with an emphasis on the timeless and contemporary nature of the agreement. Each new generation stands before the God of Sinai to hear the words of the lawgiver and renew the covenant:

> Hear, O Israel, the statutes and the ordinances which I speak in your hearing this day, and you shall learn them and be careful to do them. The Lord our God made a covenant with us in Horeb. Not with our fathers did the Lord make this covenant, but with us, who are all of us here alive this day. (Deut. 5.1-3)

The story of the time in the wilderness emphasizes the ongoing power of Yahweh and his covenant promise to the chosen people. It also tells of victories and defeats as the tribes seek a way of entering Canaan to settle in the promised land. The laws that will bind the tribes together and the rituals that will be constant reminders of the power and glory of Yahweh are a part of the official line of these books, establishing as they do the many priestly observations that will be apart of the history and celebration of the covenant. The beginning story for one of the important Jewish holidays is described as follows:

> Along with the annual feasts stipulated in the Covenant Code, Levitical law added the Day of Atonement (Yom Kippur), the most solemn of all Hebrew fasts. Observed on the tenth day of penitence at the beginning of the New Year, when forgiveness was sought for the sins of the past year. Although it was not until the post-Exilic period that it received a fixed place in the liturgical calendar, its rituals appear to be quite old. Sin offerings were made by the high priest for himself, his family, and "for all the assembly of Israel," after which the nation's sins were symbolically laid upon the scapegoat (goat for "Azazel"), which was driven into the

wilderness to die. The day of Atonement was the one day in the year when the high priest entered into the Holy of Holies, the inner shrine of the temple.[2]

The book of Joshua tells us the official story of the conquest of Canaan. Although all the extra-biblical evidence indicates a long and gradual encroachment by the Hebrew tribes here we are given three swift and decisive campaigns to bring the whole land into Israelite control. The battle of Jericho is a prime example of the point of these stories. On the way to the city the tribes must cross the Jordan River. As they approach the river the waters miraculously stop and allow their passage in a story reminiscent of the Red Sea episode on the way out of Egypt. After observing the Passover the assault on the city begins. With the priests in the front, carrying the Ark and blowing trumpets, they march around the city seven times and then miraculously a mighty shout is sufficient to bring down the walls of Jericho. The city is then totally destroyed as a sacrifice to Yahweh.

Narrative conquest of the promised land is portrayed as a sudden and complete victory but all of the evidence, even other biblical evidence, indicates a much less thoroughgoing victory as we see at the beginning of the book of Judges where the question raised after Joshua's death is "Who shall go up against the Canaanites, to fight against them?" indicating that the victory is not complete, the lands not yet secured.

After the death of Moses the mantle of authority passes on to Joshua, the warrior hero, who will reign over the conquest. The climactic entry into the promised land, a land that Moses will see but never enter, is promised again in Yahweh's charge to Joshua at the beginning of the book of Joshua:

> 'My servant Moses is dead; now it is for you to cross the Jordan, you and this whole people of Israel, to this land which I am giving them. Every place where you set foot is yours: I have given it to you, as I promised Moses....Be strong, be resolute; it is you who

---

[2] James King West, Introduction to the Old Testament, The MacMillan Company, New York, 1971, page 155.

are to put this people in possession of the land which I swore to give to their fathers....for the Lord your God is with you wherever you go.'

And indeed the story offers evidence that Yahweh is with Joshua, for he is not only able to capture and destroy Jericho and Ai, but he is also able to defeat the combined forces of all of the Amorite kings in the battle outside of Gilgal in Gibeon (Joshua 10). It is in that battle that the power of Yahweh is exhibited in a most dramatic way - the sun itself stands still "until a nation had taken vengeance on its enemies."

Signs, miracles, victories, all signal the proclamation that the chosen people are the instrument of a powerful god, a god who is fulfilling a promise made to the patriarchs so many hundreds of years before. In the ongoing covenant story of the Pentateuch we see a simple ethic: follow the rules and good consequences will come; break the rules and bad consequences will come. But the Hebrew writers also knew that this simple explanation of good and evil was unable to explain all the real events in a community's life. Sometimes the bad prosper. Sometimes the good suffer. This conflict between the official line and the story of a real life is wrestled with in the Wisdom literature. Proverbs, for example, tells us of a practical wisdom to employ in everyday life, while the books of Job and Ecclesiastes offer a counterpoint to the official position that God always rewards good and punishes evil.

CHAPTER 8: THE LAND OF UZ

We find many literary genres in the biblical texts: legend, poem, letters, legal documents, short story, song, prayer - but nowhere do we find real philosophical argument. The texts with the most philosophical themes are the so-called Wisdom Literature texts which include *Job* and *Ecclesiastes*. A number of presuppositions, beliefs, claims and judgments rest just below the surface of the stories however, and these are never explicitly stated but are assumed as common ground. Through the stories we see a structure of implicit claims about the world and our experience of it: Yahweh exists; birth and death are a part of a mysterious external plan; time and chance exist but appear to be subject to Yahweh's control; life's meaning comes from outside, from an external source or authority; human fulfillment comes from being a part of a collective of people who comply with the commands of a supreme suzerain, who, in return for fealty promises land and protection. The single theme that ties together all of the Old Testament stories is the theme of the covenant between Yahweh and his chosen people. Once we see this theme as the focal point of the stories we can begin to see order and meaning to the structural sprawl. The Mount Sinai experience is the dramatic climax to the covenant announcements in *Genesis*. At that moment in the story the external force announces and records the suzerainty treaty, an act which constitutes the people of Israel. The Ten Commandments become the first constitution. "Have no other gods before me and I, the god who took you out of slavery in Egypt, promise you land and life."

Yahweh's promise to Abraham, Isaac, Jacob is fulfilled through the prophet-mediator, Moses, in the desert after the daring escape from Egypt.

'How do you know that Yahweh appeared to Moses?' 'Because it says so in *Exodus*. 'How do you know that Yahweh spoke to the patriarchs?' 'Because it says so in *Genesis*.' Saying so does not necessarily make it so, unless of course one has already accepted that the stories are true because they were "written" by an infallible being. 'How do you know that God exists?' 'Because the Bible tells me so,' is an exchange that is fatally flawed in its logic. As we have seen, the writers of the stories in the Bible are not arguing a position, but are proclaiming the truth of their narrative, claiming it has a special place in the area of human knowledge, a place which secures it from attack from skeptics and those who claim a different *revealed* truth. But how can one believe without evidence? How can one exercise a rational approach to all other areas of knowledge and then suddenly throw reason away in the arena of religion? Easily, it seems. By requiring less of religious claims than we do of any other knowledge claims we are able to insulate our deeply felt beliefs from any rational analysis - some people really *want* these claims to be true and then confuse the passion of the belief with the truth value of the claim. But, passionately believing that you have turned off the coffee pot before you left for work, is not a sufficient condition for it being turned off, no more than a passionate belief that you have won the big lottery is either necessary or sufficient for your having done so.

Contemporary philosophical discussions of truth insist that truth is a property of statements. We say, for example, that the statement: 'It is raining' is true just when it is raining. That is, a sentence is true when the statement made by the sentence corresponds to a state of affairs in the non-linguistic world. 'I have a headache' is true if and only if I do in fact have a headache. If I utter the sentence but do not have a headache then the statement expressed by the sentence is false. There are of course other possibilities based upon the usage of the sentence. I could have an arrangement with you that the sentence 'I have a headache' will be used by us to mean something else, say, a code for a message like 'the enemy has landed on our shores.' Or, the sentence could be a line in a play, uttered by an actor in a particular scene. In that kind of example we do not talk about the sentence being true or false. In general in literary texts we suspend these epistemic concerns as soon as we hear or read a signal like 'once upon a time', or 'long time ago', or 'in the beginning' which indicate we are in a fictional world where truth value functions in a quite different way than in much of everyday discourse. Literature provides us with possible worlds to reflect upon and to respond to, gives us a point of view to consider, and breathes "life" into characters just as surely as the creator-god of Genesis does.

Biblical writers are best read as poets not as philosophers. And as poets they do not have this correspondence theory of truth in mind. Those who claim that the Bible is "True", if by that claim they mean that every statement in the Bible is literally true, fail to respond to the fictional signals provided by the writers. What are these signals? More than just the introductory mode indicators are at work in these texts; for example, the narrator(s) often steps out of the story to say something directly to the audience: "There came a famine in the land - *not the earlier famine in Abraham's time* – and Isaac went to Abimelech the Philistine king at Gerar." (Gen. 26.1); "He named that place Beth-El, *but the earlier name of the city was Luz.*" (Gen. 28.19); "*(An omer is one tenth of an ephah.)*" (Exodus 16.36); "*In days gone by in Israel, when a man wished to consult God, he would say,'Let us go to the seer.' For what is nowadays called a prophet used to be called a seer.*" (1 Sam. 9.9) Breaking the frame in this way shows us the frame, and from time to time we are reminded of the fact that we are reading a story, reminded of intention and voice and other literary components at work in the narrative.

The stories in the Bible assume a certain official line and present the character of God through actions, images, and dramatic situations. From the beginning of story telling we have been seeking a way of expressing the inexpressible, of linguistically presenting the extra-linguistic. How do you talk about God? Through the Word. The New testament belief in "the Word" or "Logos which becomes flesh" comes directly from the Greek notion of Logos and provides the basic concept in terms of which the doctrine of the Incarnation was to be understood. The concept of Logos came directly from the Stoics, for whom it originally meant an immanent World-Soul. It was later fused with the Platonic idea of *nous* and so was conceived as acting in accordance with archetypal patterns. The basic problem was: how is it possible to have knowledge of a strictly transcendent being. A suggested solution came in terms of an intermediary, in this case a logos, which was posited to solve the question of knowledge. Throughout the early Christian centuries what we find is not philosophy of religion but theological writings employing various philosophical concepts. Revealing the character and plan of God to limited and finite human beings is a difficult problem solved by establishing a canon based on an authority of the highest order. Hence, for a very long time it was believed that Moses was the author of the first five books. Books like

Ecclesiastes and *The Song of Songs* were included in the canon on the authority of Solomon. No serious biblical scholar any longer believes that these books were written by Moses and Solomon.

Philo, the gifted Jewish philosopher of the first century, was largely responsible for the idea of logos or "the Word" entering into Christian thought. Many theologians, then as now, resented the intrusion of philosophy into the domain of faith (the most outstanding was Tertullian who said, "I believe because it is absurd.") Early Christianity also flirted with mysticism which was another Greek contribution. The so-called Neoplatonists reverted to a profound sense of the Oneness or Unity of Universe in a way which put particulars and plurality in jeopardy, as they had been to some extent in the philosophy of Plato. In order to account for particulars the difficult notion of emanation was developed . God is the ultimate unity and He/She transcends all forms of thought, but finite beings exist as a falling away from the original perfection.[1] The problem here is that it is very hard to make sense of the notion of emanation without calling in question the all-embracing nature of the one ultimate reality. The insistence on the latter did influence mystic thought and the influence produces Oriental mysticism with its attempt to draw away altogether from our present existence, with its limitations and evil, and to pass beyond into a union with the ineffable Being. One way of turning the ineffable into the "effable" is through story.

In strong contrast to the Eastern belief that evil is illusory and particulars are mere shadows stands the Hebrew-Christian doctrine of creation. The Old Testament, as we have seen, is full of stories which express the elusive and transcendent nature of their god. The Hebrews believed that a true discernment of God's transcendence required the recognition of our own distinctness as beings independent of God. This in turn sharpened the question of how such limited and finite beings could in anyway come to know God. The Hebrew answer was in terms of God's disclosure of Himself in history and experience, and this was deepened and extended in specifically Christian claims about the works and words of the man-god, Jesus Christ.

---

[1] John Milton's *Paradise Lost* has this notion embedded in the fall of Satan from grace. Dante's *Divine Comedy* is the literary high point of mystical Christianity.

One of the central problems within the Judeo-Christian theological story centers on epistemology: how can we finite and limited creatures have a knowledge of this infinite and all-powerful transcendent being? The question is not merely philosophical or to be dismissed as an academic puzzle. The search for authority is a real human search and includes passion and desire, fear and need. When we humans seek the divine we are looking for an experience not an argument. And yet it is our experience which makes the search so difficult. How do we - how can we - understand a god-sponsored world in which little children suffer and die? Evil may be a worm in man's heart but it also eats away at comfortable belief. Evil has always been a problem for theologians because its existence brings into doubt either the nature of God or the existence of God. Bluntly put, the problem is: If God is all-powerful, all-knowing, and all-good, then why does evil exist in the world? If God cannot eliminate evil then God is not all-powerful. If God can but does not then God is not all-good.

One answer is to claim that evil is appearance only and not reality, but this hardly matches up with our experience. Another is to posit a dualism of good and evil locked in perpetual battle and equally matched in power. But this makes god a half-owner of the universe with limited powers. Some argue that evil is the responsibility and result of human free will - that because we are free to choose, and we are limited in knowledge, we sometimes choose wrong. Others, of course, argue that there is no god, and that cause and effect are all we need to explain natural catastrophes and human actions. The biblical stories which treat these questions are in the collection called Wisdom Literature. Can we know the nature of Yahweh? How would an existing divine force reveal itself? The continuing popularity of the book of Job shows that these problems are important. Job questions God's nature, his connection to morality and justice, and the relationship between the creator and his creation. A reading of the book of Job shows the way the Hebrew writers presented these philosophical problems in literary form. It will also suggest answers to the fundamental epistemological and moral questions. The Book of Job also serves as a transition between the Old and New Testaments. Many Christian writers have seen in Job the foreshadowing of Christ, and have argued that the answer to Job's questions is to be found in the man-god, Jesus.

To begin let us look briefly at a paper by Paul Weiss.[2] In this paper Weiss distinguishes ten different kinds of evil: sin, bad intention, wickedness, guilt, vice, physical suffering, psychological suffering, natural evil, and metaphysical evil. The first two are most characteristically human for they are privately inflicted. The ten are defined as follows:

1. Sin - he sins who is disloyal to a primary value accepted on faith. Blasphemy is one form of sin and treason another. He sins who denies his people just as surely as does he who violates the fiats of his/her god. Job shows us that it is not necessary that a man sin. Job is righteous. Job is not a sinner. Since he suffers, suffering and the multiple evils of the world ought not to be attributed to man's failure to avoid sin.

2. Bad intent - ethical evil, like setting oneself to break an ethical command. Like sin this is privately achieved. It is concerned with the good as open to reason. The man of bad intent fails internally to live up to what reason commands. (Steals, kills , lies). Evil intent and suffering do not necessarily go together.

3. Wickedness - the evil of carrying out evil intentions. Job is right in insisting that he was not wicked. He who is wicked does not necessarily incur the wrath of God. Nor does he necessarily suffer.

4. Guilt - We ought to love, help, cherish everyone, but since we are finite and have finite interest, funds and energy we can not. Each thus fails to fulfill an obligation to realize the good completely. We are hence necessarily guilty. We fail to do all that ought to be done. Eliphaz charges Job with the neglect of hosts of the needy, but we are all guilty in that respect.

5. Vice - The habit of doing what injures others; vice is produced by men and not by God, and need not entail suffering.

6. Social.

---

[2] Paul Weiss, "God, Job, and Evil", *Commentary,* Vol. VI (1948).

7. Physical.

8. Psychological.
Job suffers in all (6,7,8) these ways: torn in his body, by his mind, and from his fellows, Job has no rest.

9. Natural evil - an evil embodied in the wild, destructive forces of nature, as manifest in earthquakes, tidal waves, hurricanes, etc. These do not arise because there is something bad in man/woman. To suppose that nature is geared to the goodness and badness of men and women is to suppose either a mysterious harmony between ethics and physics, or that spirits really move mountains. God is responsible for "natural evil" says the Book of Job.

10. Metaphysical evil - As Weiss puts it: "What could not be avoided by the things in any universe whatsoever is the tenth kind of evil, metaphysical evil, the evil of being one among many, of possessing only a fragment of reality, of lacking the reality and thus the power and good possessed by all the others. Any universe whatsoever, created or uncreated, is one in which each part is less than perfect precisely because it is other than the rest, and is deprived therefore of the reality the rest contain."

Consider this list as a map for reading Job. But notice also that it is not an objective map. It too contains a certain story about ethics; and is not completely clear and separate from its official line. 'Sin' is a religious not a moral term. It is a sin to wear a head covering in some contexts, a sin not to wear a head covering in other contexts. To be disloyal may be a moral failing, but surely it depends upon what one is disloyal to. Disloyalty to an authority urging immoral acts is certainly not a moral failing. You have to make a moral judgment about which god is worthy of respect and worship. 'Bad intent' and 'wickedness' are moral terms and it is just here that Job is innocent - he has neither bad intent nor wickedness - the story makes that clear. 'Guilt' may be a moral term; that is, one may feel guilty if one has done something wrong, but to feel guilt in a general sense is a pathological, not a logical phenomenon. "But you should not feel guilt for that" is a perfectly reasonable and healthy corrective to the guilt ridden innocent. Weiss's fourth category seems to include the notion that ought implies can - one can not be held morally responsible for things beyond one's control. 'Metaphysical guilt' as described by Weiss is hard to understand. What sense does it make to hold a person responsible for not being all of reality?[3] Can one rationally blame one's dog for not being a camel? A human being? This concept would have evil built into the very fabric of the universe, a notion as puzzling as its counterpart of having good built into the fabric of the universe. Religious doctrine may assert such a position, but it is not clear precisely what would count as evidence for such a position. As Job discovers in the story, good and evil are the province of men and women, and have nothing to do with God. The universe is not good or evil - it is. For Weiss Job is guilty because he is a man and all men are guilty. But the Book of Job tells us that Job is innocent, and yet he suffers. What does this story tell us about the nature of the god it depicts as a major character?

Notice first that it is a piece of literature, a story of a particular kind. It is a play. It has a framing device. It has long boring speeches and little action. It is repetitive. The key images have to do with knowledge, wisdom and understanding. These are to be gained in a court room setting with God as judge and accuser, Job as wrongly accused defendant who aches for his day in court to prove his innocence. Job is a radical protestor, struggling against a system that strikes him as unfair and unjust. He is not patient, and he is not Jewish, though many think of him as the paradigm of Jewish patience. The existence of God is assumed; it is his nature that is in question. Suffering does not imply wrongdoing; the bad do sometimes prosper. There is no necessary connection between morality and the size of one's portfolio. The Book of Job is like some massive chunk of marble that has within it a beautiful sculpture which has not yet been completed: rich, extensive, suggestive, but incomplete. It has been praised as a great work:

> Not only its value as a work of art, displayed by the power of its language, by the depth of its feeling, by the grandeur of its structure, but also the subject with which it deals, the daring titanic struggle with the immemorial, yet ever new, questioning of mankind concerning the meaning of suffering, places this composition as regards its general significance beside Dante's *Divina Commedia* and Goethe's *Faust*.[4]

---

[3] This understanding of metaphysical evil and its logical problems comes from Dale Beyerstein.
[4] Arthur Weiser, *The Old Testament: Its Formation and Development,* D. M. Barton, tr., New York: Association Press, 1961, page 288.

The book consists of two distinct parts. The bulk of the work, and by far the more important, is the long poetic section which is framed by the brief prose narrative which relates the legend of the righteous man's travails, beginning in heavenly council, and the happy ending when the suffering man has everything restored to better than ever status. Biblical scholars[5] tell us that the framing device, written in an archaic style, bears all of the marks of an ancient and popular folk tale, while the dramatic interchange in poetic form is from a much later, probably post-exilic time. In any case, it is easy to see the difference between the two, even in translation, for the simplicity of the frame is even more obvious when set off against the complex and philosophical poetic debate between Job and his "comforters". An editor has molded the two parts together to form one literary whole, and as readers we must judge how successful the whole has been completed and how the two parts function together.

Look at the frame: we are told immediately that Job is "a man of blameless and upright life" who fears God and has his face set against wrongdoing. He is given as perhaps a bit too much of a good man; that is, he seems to approach the good life like an accountant, offering sacrifices for possible wrongs on the part of his children because he thinks "that they might somehow have sinned against God." William Blake in his illustrated edition of Job has the family at the beginning of the story reading the book to be sure that they are following all of the commands of God, but appearing to have a fairly bleak and stiff time of it. The musical instruments are not being used, there is no joy in this family life before the experience of the whirlwind. Blake's story is visually projected, and he gives us three characters: God, Satan, and Job, all of whom look alike. In Blake's vision God and Satan are forces in us, psychological parts of us. Suddenly in the prologue we hear of the members of the court of heaven who gather in the presence of the Lord, and this sudden shift from earth to heaven is presented with no transition and with no hesitation. In this heavenly court Satan challenges God to a contest to test Job. God will allow Satan to torment Job in order to see if he is steadfast. Satan takes his task seriously and destroys Job's flocks, his servants, and his children. Job's children are killed by a whirlwind sweeping across the desert which

---

[5] See, for example, James King West, *Introduction to the Old Testament,* pages 391 ff., The MacMillan Company, New York, 1971.

knocks their house down and crushes them. We will see a whirlwind again before this tale is over. "Throughout all this Job did not sin; he did not charge God with unreason." Satan tries further tortures, with God's approval, and attacks Job's body and mind. His three friends arrive and "for seven days and seven nights they sat beside him on the ground, and none of them said a word to him." So far a cracking good fairy tale: powerful forces are at work above who will interfere with events in the human world either to pass the time or to test a man to see what kind of torture he can take before breaking. These are the forces of some child-like, cruel and sadistic place, imaged in monsters and presented as powerful but without moral sense. A god who will break his own commandments against killing is not worthy of worship. What do we learn from the frame outside the frame? After seven days of silence Job breaks silence and curses the day of his birth, for "there is no peace of mind nor quiet for me; I chafe in torment and have no rest."

Job at this point seems to believe that there is a correlation between being good and being rewarded with the goods of the world. Follow the rules, be careful, take a few extra steps of precaution by sacrificing even if you do not need to and all will be well. His attitude seems to be one of an overly strict, rule-bound worrier, completely uptight about righteousness but forgetting about the joy of life itself. Yes, Job is righteous, and no, he has not sinned against the laws in the book of righteousness, but he has forgotten to enjoy life in all its bountiful glory. He is not really straight with life. He snaps at his wife, worries about his children's obedience to the book of rules.

It is one of the ironies of literature that the phrase "patience of Job" is now part of our linguistic heritage. Job is, in fact, not at all patient, but wants his problem dealt with now, right now - wants to face God and argue his case, not sit patiently awaiting resolution. This rebellious demand for a chance to plead his case can be seen in the complex of images that revolve around the key motifs of justice, balance, and scales of justice. Until he is able to do so the world and everything in it is flat and without taste. Notice the images in the following passages from the King James translation:

> But Job answered and said,
> 2. Oh that my grief were throughly
> weighed, and my calamity laid in the balance
> together!
> 3. For now it would be heavier than the sand of
> the sea: therefore my words are swallowed up.

4. For the arrows of the Almighty are within
me, the poison whereof drinketh up my spirit:
the terrors of God do set themselves in array
against me.
5. Doth the wild ass bray when he hath grass?
or loweth the ox over his fodder?
6. Can that which is unsavoury be eaten without salt? or is there any taste in the white of
an egg? (Job 6.2-6)

Even though Job is filled with grief and racked with pain he continues
to cry out for justice. His is a just cause and he wants to be heard in the court
of the Almighty, where he believes Justice resides.

11. Therefore I will not refrain my mouth;I
will speak in the anguish of my spirit; I will
complain in the bitterness of my soul. (7.11)

Lo, mine eye hath seen all this, mine ear hath
heard and understood it.
2. What ye know, the same do I know also: I
am not inferior to you.
3. Surely I would speak to the Almighty, and I
desire to reason with God.
4. But ye are forgers of lies, ye are all physi-
cians of no value. (13.1-4)

Job is not a coward; he faces his torment with a desperate strength fed
with moral outrage. One can almost see his inner conflict at work in the play;
the drama in this work is indeed in the mind of the protaganist.

15. Though he slay me, yet will I trust in him:
but I will maintain mine own ways before him.
16. He also shall be my salvation: for an hypo-
crite shall not come before him.
17. Hear diligently my speech, and my declara-
tion with your ears.
18. Behold now, I have ordered my cause; I
know that I shall be justified. (13.15-18)

Awash in tears, afraid of the threat of death, but constant in his assertion of innocence, Job cries out to earth and to heaven to allow him his day in court.

> 16. My face is foul with weeping, and on my
> eyelids is the shadow of death;
> 17. Not for any injustice in mine hands: also
> my prayer is pure.
> 18. O earth, cover not thou my blood, and let
> my cry have no place.
> 19. Also now, behold, my witness is in heaven,
> and my record is on high.
> 20. My friends scorn me: but mine eye poureth
> out tears unto God.
> 21. O that one might plead for a man with God,
> as a man pleadeth for his neighbour! (16.16-21)

Lack of understanding, of comprehension, is the real cause of Job's torment - he wants desperately to *know* what is going on in his presumed moral universe. Where is the moral centre of the universe to be found? How is it that the innocent suffer?

> Then Job answered and said,
> 2. Even to day is my complaint bitter: my
> stroke is heavier than my groaning.
> 3. Oh that I knew where I might find him! that
> I might come even to his seat!
> 4. I would order my cause before him, and fill
> my mouth with arguments.
> 5. I would know the words which he would
> answer me, and understand what he would say
> unto me. (23.1-5)

> 6. Let me be weighed in an even balance, that God
> may know mine integrity. (31.6)

We can not miss this recurring imagery pattern, and it supports the idea that Job feels he is a righteous sufferer who wants justice, who wants to argue his case before he who is (apparently) judging him. He continues to believe that there must be a moral connection between behaviour and benefits. Thus, his cry to be heard, to present his argument: if God is the final arbiter and is reasonable and comes to know the facts then he can not possibly continue to torment Job. In his balance ledger understanding, good should bring good and bad should bring bad. I can hear my German Lutheran step-father every time I read Job. I hear him crying out to his Lutheran God from the wheat fields in Colorado after a hail storm had just wiped out the entire crop: "Why are you punishing me? What have I done wrong? Why not the Renzelmens across the road? Why me?" There was, of course, never an answer. Otto, like Job, demanded to know the relationship between suffering and action, between deed and resulting reward or punishment. Job's friends, like my Lutheran pastor on those childhood Sundays, offer him old arguments about how there must be a correspondence between the way we live and the rewards we get. They offer the old notion of rewards for the good and suffering for the bad. See a man's condition and you can read off his spiritual status. But Job (and Otto) knew he was not guilty and feels outraged to be a citizen in a system of justice that seems to have gone crazy. We know what Job does not: that God has agreed to let the devil use Job in a test of loyalty. This ironic situation reveals a God who seems not interested in justice in particular or in morality in general. In the prologue God/Satan flagrantly violates at least three of the commandments he gave out on Mount Sinai.

And what do we discover when God, as the voice out of the whirlwind, speaks to Job in the dramatic conclusion of the "justice-scales" theme? Job, who has suffered in mind and in body, who has lost his children, his flocks, his health, has cried out to be heard by his tormentor. And when the answer comes what does God have to say about the nature of justice? What does he offer in explanation of the relationship between crime and punishment? What insights does God offer about the nature of good and evil? What does God say to Job about the reasons for his suffering? Absolutely nothing. Job, who wanted to reason with God, who wanted to argue his case in court, who wanted to understand the relationship between acts and rewards, has no chance for argument. Expecting a wise judge to debate his case with, he gets a God of power, sheer power. All of the long speeches of Job and his friends in which arguments were presented and analyzed, in which causes and effects are posited, are set against the voice from the whirlwind. And this voice does not present argument, does not offer explanation, provides no thesis on cause and effect; no, this voice does not speak as a rational first cause, but instead says:

> Then the Lord answered Job out of the
> whirlwind, and said,

2. Who is this that darkeneth counsel by
words without knowledge?
3. Gird up now thy loins like a man; for I will
demand of thee, and answer thou me.
4. Where wast thou when I laid the foundation of the earth? declare, if thou hast understanding.
5. Who hath laid the measures thereof, if
thou knowest? or who hath stretched the line
upon it?
(38.1-5)

The voice out of the whirlwind releases a whirlwind of rhetoric, a series of creation images of sheer brutal power, but has absolutely nothing to say about the situation that Job is in. What we have waited for throughout the play finally comes and it is totally unexpected. The human questions about morality and suffering, about justice and fairness, are not resolved, are not even directly addressed. What answer does the story provide? What of all these questions of the human spirit? A transcendent God is not concerned with justice - justice is a human concept and is to be worked out by humans in this world and in this life. This powerful urge, creative and destructive, is life itself, confusing, inexplicable, powerful, unknowable in detail, and not captured in words, but only imaged in whirlwind. The images in the voice out of the whirlwind's speech at the conclusion of the play resonate off the opening speech in Part I where Job says in the third chapter of the King James transla- tion:

After this opened Job his mouth, and cursed
his day.
2. And Job spake, and said,
3. Let the day perish wherein I was born, and
the night in which it was said, There is a man
child conceived.
4. Let that day be darkness; let not God regard
it from above, neither let the light shine upon it.
5. Let darkness and the shadow of death stain
it; let a cloud dwell upon it; let the blackness of
the day terrify it.
6. As for that night, let darkness seize upon it;
let it not be joined unto the days of the year, let

it not come into the number of the months. (3.1-6)

This lament, filled with images of darkness and death, is not so much suicidal as it is a cry for non-being. Job wants to blot out of history the night he was conceived and the day he was born. There is excess here - much like the excess piety hinted at in the prologue. To speak of changing history to blot out the day of one's birth is still to insist upon one's importance in the scheme of things. 'I must have been important; just look at all of the worldly goods that I had before my fall.' These are not the lines of a patient, long suffering man. Try reading them aloud with patience and quiet resolve. Notice the form of those poetic lines. They echo the opening passages of Genesis, the creation story: "Let there be light..." and "Let there be..." - a refrain for the creation of everything in that story. Job uses a similar imperative in his opening speech, but his statement is negative, black and destructive. The whirlwind will later refer to the creation also, and put Job in his place as a finite limited being because he was not present at the beginning. From the light of the creation story to the darkness of Job's spiritual condition is the distance from rational creativity to irrational destruction. Job's only sin is that before the whirlwind he believes that the universe is rational and moral, attributes which he believes its first cause shares. The Book of Job shows us a deep truth: mortals are cut off from any god-authority as the foundation for moral life. Justice, as King Lear also must discover, is not in the heavens but in men and women. And this lesson comes as part of a lesson in interpretation. Trying to *read* the world as a one-dimensional playground where the good boys and girls are rewarded with slices of cake and the bad boys and girls are punished is not a legitimate reading. Certainly Job learns something in the course of the play, and that lesson is about the nature of morality - morality is not founded upon God. This new knowledge is imaged in the motifs of "knowledge" - "wisdom" - "teaching" presented in a series of images which cluster around those words: "tell the creatures that crawl to teach you", "to give you instruction", "there is wisdom", and "long life brings understanding", "uncovers mysteries" and so forth. But as far as the key experience of the play - the voice from the whirlwind - none of these cliches bears any fruit (to use another cliche). Job's lesson comes in the form of a tempest, a powerful image of the irrational forces that the writer sees at work in life. You cannot make sense out of life any more than you can make cents out of life. "Who is this that darkens counsel by words without knowledge?" questions the voice. And the answer to the question is Eliphaz, Bildad, and Zophar, for in the epilogue God says to Eliphaz, "My wrath is kindled against thee, and against thy two friends: for you have not spoken of me the thing that is right, as my servant Job has."

The Lord admits here that Job has been right, but right about what? His "comforters" are given a light punishment for saying that which is not right, but what were they wrong about? Clearly, on one level, Job is right because he did not follow his wife's advice and "renounce God and die'. He continued to have faith beyond all reason, continued to believe in a just universe based upon some rational principles of fair play. His friends claim to know these principles, and in that must lie their sin. Time after time they tell Job that the righteous never suffer, only the evil suffer, and that therefore since he is suffering he must be evil, and that to stop the suffering he must correct his ways.[6] Job can not and will not accept this simple-minded "stimulus-response" theory of justice because he has seen too often that, in fact, innocents suffer and the corrupt prosper. He wants to know why the innocent suffer, but he does not claim to have the answer. He wants to plead his case in front of God in order to gain that knowledge and to understand how it is that God has arranged the moral world. As we have seen Job is to be disappointed for he never gets to have the kind of discussion that he hopes will untangle forever the problems of moral philosophy. Instead when God finally does appear to him as a voice out of the whirlwind[7] Job learns of God's power but not of justice as fairness or as the relationship between punishment and crime. Job is rewarded, finally, for his blind loyalty and for having faith beyond reason - and the point is: that is exactly what the official line of the book of Job proclaims, blind faith is re-warded by revelation. Eliphaz errs by claiming to understand the ways of God, as if mere and puny humans could possibly understand the mysteries of this creator god. Dogmatic explanation is punished; skepticism is rewarded. One can not read the condition of man in the outward manifestations of wealth and property. What does this experience mean? How can I read it? The meaning is

---

[6] Often one runs into this argument:

   1. If we are evil then we will suffer.

   2. We are suffering.

   3. Therefore we are evil.

but this is not a valid argument. It would make the following parallel argument valid, which it clearly is not:

   4. If I am Superman then I am a man.

   5. I am a man.

   6. Therefore I am Superman.

The fallacy here is called Affirming the consequent.

[7] Consider the image of the whirlwind. A whirl wind is capricious, powerful, inarticulate, a natural force.

in the revelation of the master story teller.

Read the clever little masque called "A Masque of Reason" by Robert Frost[8] for an interesting take on the story of the relationship between Job and God, and "Mrs. Job". For a more serious modern rendition read the play *JB* by Archibald McLeish. Artists throughout the world and at various times have found the Book of Job a rich source of inspiration with its deep and problematic questions and its powerful figures of God, Satan and their plaything Job, or everyman. It is hard not to respond to the searing passages in the play, for the human conditon is oten found to be just like it is portrayed here: irrational, unjust, and lying above or beyond the reach of the human mind.

Why do the innocent suffer? Why do time and chance function as they do? Why me? Where is order? Who is running this show anyway? Why does evil exist? Where has the promised innocence of the garden of Eden gone?

We can not fault the Hebrew writer for not being able to sort out the problems of evil in the world. Several centuries later we are still discussing these same problems. As philosophers and theologians have known for thousands of years, it is extremely difficult to explain the existence of evil in a world created by a God who is both infinitely good and infinitely powerful. Various attempts have been made: evil has been traced to the fall of Adam, or God permits unmerited suffering as a means of purifying the soul for eternal life. Some have tried to relieve God of the apparent responsibility for evil by supposing he is finite in knowledge or power or both. The god as revealed in the Book of Job simply asserts all of these propositions as being true together:

1. I am.
2. Suffering is.
3. So what.

A god who reveals himself in time is a part of many of the stories of the Old Testament. In the beginning we learn of him through his revelation to the patriarchs and to Moses. There is no way to tell when and if he will reveal himself to any particular character, for his ways are mysterious and the signs he provides are ambiguous. What is his intent? What does it all mean? These

---

[8] The piece can be found in *The Poetry of Robert Frost, op.cit.*, page 484,485.

questions are asked of all texts; it is no different here. For the Christian the answer to Job comes in the story of the man-god Jesus, another comes from Koheleth, in the book called Ecclesiastes.

THE WAYS OF GOD ARE INSCRUTABLE

In the Hebrew Bible Ecclesiastes stands alone in theology and in style. It probably never would have been included in the canon except that it was believed to have been written by King Solomon, and that authority was sufficient to assure it a place in the collection of "revealed" books. It is the most footnoted of books in the collection. On occasions the "footnotes" have become a part of the text as the redactor added a line here and there to try to force the story into the official line. For example, as the headnote to the book in the *New English Bible* puts it: "Glosses which relieve the gloom (and, indeed, the impiety) of the book seem to have been added in later times...." It has often been read as a gloomy and impious book because it departs from the official line in such a basic way. Right after the Speaker says "I saw under the sun that, where justice ought to be, there was wickedness, and where righteousness ought to be, there was wickedness," a gloss (at 3.17) is added which states that God's purpose is to test men "to see what they truly are." Or again at 7.18 after the Speaker suggests a balanced approach as the best psychology to pursue ("Do not be over-righteous and do not be over-wise") the "Explainer" adds, "for a man who fears God will succeed both ways." And at 8.12-13, after the Speaker has stated that wickedness is not punished, and goodness not rewarded the Explainer adds, "A sinner may do wrong and live to an old age, yet I know that it will be well with those who fear God..." and the "yet I know" rings false in the overall story of skepticism that it presented in the text. The dramatic question in both Job and Ecclesiastes arises precisely because the human characters do not and cannot *know* what, if any, plan surrounds and defines their lives. In the Speaker's response to this question we see it makes no difference whether there is a plan or not; it is not knowable in any case. "True, the living know that they will die; but the dead know nothing."

Once in an evening class I had the students listen to a recording of Ecclesiastes as read by James Mason and asked them to jot down responses as they were listening.. I too kept notes of what came into my mind while listening to the Mason interpretation of the text. My "reader's response" notes follow:

The opening passage with its circular images of cyclical activity without purpose: eyes not satisfied with seeing, appetite not filled, rivers that flow to the sea but the sea is never filled - all accurately describe a mental state of despair and weariness.

Obviously the speaker is a middle aged man who has attempted to live his life with some ideas and beliefs that have proved to be false. The path he has followed has been a long one with many attempts to make life meaningful by aiming at particular external goals. He has tried wisdom, madness, folly, pleasure, great works, money, sex, mirth, and found them all to be empty, because always was the reality of his own mortality.

The text is like a huge symphony with separate and identifiable movements. It opens with an emptiness of spirit that is palpable to the senses, but then it starts to move to a different level of acceptance and resignation and finally to an amazing finale of optimism, acceptance and joy. (Herb is asleep now; his head leaning further and further toward Cathy. He may be faking it just to lay his sleeping head on her shoulder. He wakes and looks at me, ah, did the instructor see me sleeping? Emptiness, all is emptiness.) Is it boring? Well, yes I suppose the beginning parts are boring to a twenty year old who still believes he is immortal. (How many people will drop off to sleep? The room is hot, the reading accurate but monotonous - oh, how right Mason is to read it just that way - David's book falls off his lap as he too drops off. What difference does it make? "One event happeneth to all." No one will remember or care tomorrow what happened today.)

The poem which The Birds stole to make "Turn, turn, turn" is the first move towards life and acceptance. There is a time for everything has a comforting sound to it. There is a time to sleep and a time to study. I think again of the large number of literary texts that are rooted in Ecclesiastes: *The Sun Also Rises, King Lear, Waiting for Godot* ("two are better than one"- see Beckett's clowns acting out that cosmic connection that holds people together; we need someone to help us up when we fall down. "He couldn't remember where his home is. But he wanted to go there anyway.") "So I hated life." Why? Because it didn't yield to my hopes and plans; it went on not paying attention to me, not caring about me. What is missing? Why this despair and hatred of life? An entire inventory of goals is given and none have produced the feeling of life, of value. Are there more goals that haven't been considered? Will it become clearer when I am older? Will Herb wake up? What is missing? Why is everything stale and flat?

And finally - and finally an answer:

"The light of day is sweet, and pleasant to the eye is the sight of the sun; if a man lives for many years, he should rejoice in all of them." (11.7)

Everyone should write her own response to this book. Read it; listen to it; write about it. It suggests to me these themes: Get rid of goals and life begins to flow, have goals and you get tied up in knots. This does not mean that you should not save for a rainy day. These are life-goals that the Speaker talks about. If you set out to find wisdom, labor, pleasure as ends in themselves, expects these ends to deliver results as an investment might, then you are doomed to emptiness, for happiness is always a by-product of doing something and not a thing to be sought out like a coin lost on the floor. Life, says the Speaker, is an attitude not a program, a scene and not a plot. With divine justice in human affairs an illusion, and truth unattainable, the Speaker is left with little upon which to build. All that is certain for man\woman is that there is a desire for happiness. Thus, the basic theme of the book is an insistence upon the enjoyment of life, of all the things in *this* world since it is the only world we can know. Live capriciously, do not calculate like Job did; joy is our categorical imperative and we must taste of life's joys without self-deception. The Speaker reminds us that the realities of life do not correspond to the yearnings of the heart. Often our deepest desires are thwarted by the hard facts of experience, and our timeless yearnings are frustrated by our time-restricted days.

The Speaker answers Job. The Speaker says: "Do not be over-righteous and do not be over-wise. And above all do not try to be God."

CHAPTER 9: PROPHET VERSUS KING

> *Prophet: One who speaks for God or for any deity, as the inspired revealer or interpreter of his will; one who is held or (more loosely) who claims to have this function; an inspired or quasi-inspired teacher....One who predicts or foretells what is going to happen; a prognosticator, a predictor....The 'inspired' or accredited spokesman, proclaimer, or preacher of some principle, cause, or movement. (Oxford English Dictionary)*

Prophets mediate between the divine and the ordinary. They are important figures in the Old Testament who interpret God's story to the people and to the leaders of the people. In the Book of Judges the judge of the tribal confederation is often gifted with prophetic powers and able to read God's story when making decisions that are important to the tribes. Deborah, for example, is able to predict the day for her commander's victory by being able to read the signs that tell her when the rains are coming. She tells Barak (Judges 4.14), "Up! This day the Lord gives Sisera into your hands. Already the Lord has gone out to battle before you." And the rains come. Sisera's chariots are mired down in the "Torrent of Kishon" and the victory goes to Deborah. In what is "the oldest surviving extended fragment of Hebrew literature"[1] Deborah and Barak sing a song of praise to their Lord:

---

[1] Footnote page 255, *The New English Bible*, Oxford Study Edition.

> For the leaders, the leaders in Israel,
> for the people who answered the call, bless ye the Lord.
> Hear me, you kings; princes, give ear;
> I will sing, I will sing to the Lord.
> I will raise a psalm to the Lord
> the God of Israel.
> O, Lord, at thy setting forth from Seir,
> when thou camest marching out of
> the plains of Edom,
> earth trembled; heaven quaked;
> the clouds streamed down in torrents. (Judges 4.2-4)

and later we hear "Be proud at heart, you marshals of Israel; you among the people that answered the call, bless ye the Lord." Deborah's song is for a particular audience: those "who answered the call." Not all of the tribes did answer the call, for we learn later in the song that "Gilead stayed beyond Jordan," that Dan tarried by the ships, and that "Asher lingered by the sea-shore." Those who did answer the call were rewarded with victory on that day because Deborah knew when to attack to bring the enemy with its heavy chariots into the river bottom to be caught by the sudden rain:

> The stars fought from heaven,
> the stars in their courses fought
>   against Sisera.
> the Torrent of Kishon swept him
>   away,
> the Torrent barred his flight, the
>   Torrent of Kishon;
> march on in might, my soul! (Judges 5.20-21)

A few stanzas later we are told of the other prophecy by Deborah which comes to pass. She had told Barak that the day would belong to a woman, and indeed it does, as we read in the King James translation:

> 24. Blessed above women shall Jael the wife of
> Heber the Kenite be, blessed shall she be above
> women in the tent.
> 25. He asked water, and she gave him milk;
> she brought forth butter in a lordly dish.
> 26. She put her hand to the nail, and her right

hand to the workmen's hammer; and with the
hammer she smote Sisera, she smote off
his head when she had pierced and stricken
through his temples.
27. At her feet he bowed, he fell, he lay down;
at her feet he bowed, he fell: where he bowed,
there he fell down dead.
(Judges 5.24-27)

Sisera dies at the hands of a woman and the prophesy comes true: the day indeed belongs to a woman as Deborah had said. Sisera, the great champion, the warrior in command of far superior forces is vanquished in a tent by a workman's hammer weilded by a woman.

Deborah, as Judge, is unable to get all of the tribes to answer the call to arms, but with the forces at hand and a brilliant battle plan (there is even the suggestion that she employs a spy) which depends on using the tactics of guerilla warfare to challenge a larger and heavily armed enemy, she is victorious. After drawing the chariots of Sisera into the valley for what they would expect to be a "duck-shoot" she awaits the sudden rain which will eliminate the advantage of Canaanite light armor.

Deborah's inability to raise an army from all the tribes signals one of the weaknesses of the political organization of a loose confederation and sets the stage for the cry for a king which we hear in the first book of Samuel. Samuel is the last of the judges and the first important prophet. The two books of Samuel and the two books of Kings form a single text in the ancient Greek Bible entitled "Concerning the Kingdoms." Modern texts break this section into the four books we presently have which tell of the establishment of David's dynasty and the consecration of the Solomonic Temple.

'Samuel' means "name of God," and Samuel's birth narrative is one which emphasizes his special status. His father Elkanah has two wives, Hannah and Peninnah. "Peninnah had children, but Hannah was childless." Hannah is childless and is tormented by her "rival." She weeps and refuses to eat. One year while the family is at Shiloh for sacrifices, Hannah goes to the temple to pray for help. She prays:

O, Lord of Hosts, if thou wilt deign to take notice of my trouble
and remember me, if thou wilt not forget but grant me offspring,
then I will give the child to the Lord for his whole life, and no razor
shall touch his head. (1 Sam. 1.11)

As Hannah prays her lips move and Eli the priest sees her and is
deceived: he thinks she is a drunken woman and orders her away from the
temple. Hannah is not to be ordered away by anyone;   she refuses and
announces her innocence, forcing Eli to apologize to her for not seeing her
true condition. She gives birth to a son. She takes him to Shiloh to serve the
Lord. Shiloh is an important center before the age of the monarchy, but not
much is heard of it after the monarchy is established. Now the narrative places
the young Samuel under Eli's control as his master. From the time of the
bondage in Egypt God had charged Eli's family with the priesthood for all the
tribes of Israel, had   given them the special task "to mount the steps of my
altar, to burn sacrifices, and to carry the ephod before me"; and "assigned all
the food-offerings to [Eli's] family." Although God had promised that Eli's
family would fulfill this function for all time there is a narrative requirement
here to elevate Samuel to this high position. We are told that Eli's sons have
been stealing the best parts of the offerings (these sons will literally eat Eli out
of house and home) for themselves and that Eli has not disciplined them
properly - thus showing that he honors his sons more than he honors his Lord.
Eli is visited by "a man of God" and told that his fortunes will change. God is
looking for a new and faithful priest - he is choosing again. The story is
resumed, with a "time passes" indicator, in Chapter 3: "So the child Samuel
was in the Lord's service under his master Eli." Next we can hear the narrator's
voice as it breaks through the frame: "Now in those days the word of the Lord
was seldom heard, and no vision was granted," which is followed by a vision
given to Samuel.

The story so far gives us a special kind of man. Special signs surround
Samuel's birth: a childless woman suddenly and unexpectedly has her prayer
for a child answered, at the birth of the child special gifts are given, and the
child is marked in a special way. All of these are images of uniqueness, are
intended to show that Samuel is the chosen one. Next we see that Samuel is
able to have visions, to make direct contact with the Lord. In a charming story
we are told how Samuel hears the Lord call him but mistakes that call for the
more natural call of his master Eli. On three occasions Samuel runs to Eli

saying "You called me, here I am." Eli finally realizes that it is the Lord calling the child and tells Samuel how to respond. Samuel's first message from the "other side" is not a pleasant one to report to his earthly master:

> The Lord said, 'Soon I shall do something in Israel which will ring in the ears of all who hear it. When that day comes I will make good every word I have spoken against Eli and his family from beginning to end. You are to tell him that my judgement on his house shall stand for ever because he knew of his sons' blasphemies against God and did not rebuke them. Therefore I have sworn to the family of Eli that their abuse of sacrifices and offerings shall never be expiated.

but report it he must, even though he is a frightened messenger. Eli's response at hearing that he and his family are permanently unemployed and in serious danger is calm and resolute: "The Lord must do what is good in his eyes." One prophet is gone, a new prophet is chosen: "As Samuel grew up, the Lord was with him, and none of his words went unfulfilled. From Dan to Beer-sheba, all Israel recognized that Samuel was confirmed as prophet of the Lord." The piece starts with Eli being unable to recognize that Hannah is the vehicle for a special birth and ends with all Israel recognizing that Samuel is the prophet of the Lord. There is a secret plan to be revealed to a chosen few - a plan for the chosen tribes of Israel - this bigger narrative also must have plot and story-line where events are related causally and the intent of the Author is revealed in the story.

Chapters 4 through 6 do not mention Samuel but instead relate the primitive story of the Ark of the Lord.[2] Samuel has authority and legitimacy as established by: his birth in answer to a prayer, his birth to a childless woman, his special identifying feature (no razor shall touch his head), and by the affirming instance of having a vision of the Lord at a time when "the word of the Lord was seldom heard." Now the narrative shifts to finish the story of Eli and his sons. The Israelites face the Philistines near Aphek and are routed by the Philistines who kill about four thousand of the Israelites. After returning to camp from the killing fields, the Israelites confer with their elders who come to

---

[2] The Ark of the Lord is a box-throne like object upon which the Lord of Israel manifested his presence. See Exodus 25.22, Numbers 7.89, and Joshua chs. 3-4.

believe that the defeat is because their army did not have the Ark of the Lord in its midst. They send to Shiloh to get the ark (referred to here also as "The Ark of the Covenant of the Lord") and when it comes into camp there is a great shout from the Israelite army, now sure of its victory. The Philistines are afraid and cry out, "A god has come into the camp. We are lost!...Be men and fight!" And fight they do. We are told simply, "The Philistines then gave battle, and the Israelites were defeated and fled to their homes." The Ark of the Lord is taken by the victorious Philistines and Eli's sons, Hophni and Phinehas, are killed. As prophesied in the vision that Samuel reported to Eli, Eli's line is ended - his sons are dead. In a parallel to the Marathon story of Greek literature, here a Benjamite runs from the battlefield to Shiloh with news of the defeat and the stunning loss of the Ark. Eli is seated by the gate to the city in a throne, and is so shocked by the combination of news of the death of his sons and the loss of the Ark that he falls over backwards and breaks his neck.

These are dark days. Not only is the Ark gone to the hated Philistines but the long time keeper of the Ark at Shiloh is dead, and his family almost erased from the earth. The Philistines, meanwhile, take their prize to Ashdod and place it in the temple of their god, Dagon. Here we are shown the power of the Ark when it is placed next to a competing god. "When the people of Ashdod rose next morning, there was Dagon fallen face downwards before the Ark of the Lord; so they took him and put him back in his place." But the next morning Dagon has been unseated again - and his fall from the throne has broken his head and his two hands and now he lies broken at the feet of the Ark of the Lord[3]. Yahweh's power destroys Dagon. Though Israel has been defeated by the Philistines, their god has defeated the god of the Philistines. As Simone de Beauvoir writes in one of her novels, "When a god falls, he does not become merely a man; he becomes a fraud." And the Philistines will pay. Rats swarm over the Philistine territory; people and animals are stricken with tumours. Death and destruction hits the city like the Egyptian plagues used by the Hebrew god in his struggle with the Pharaoh. Finally, in desperation, the Philistine princes realize it is the Ark that is responsible for the death and destruction in their midst, and cry out, "Send the Ark of God of Israel away; let it go back to its own place, or it will be the death of us all."

---

[3] Dagon has been broken by the Ark of the Lord, and it is his head and hands that are broken. Dagon's ability to formulate intention and his ability to carry out intention are destroyed.

Although the armies of Israel have been unable to defeat the Philistine armies, their god, in the form of the Ark of the Lord has defeated Dagon and the people of Philistine. This God of Israel is powerful, destructive, and the story shows us that the defeat of enemies is always the doing of the Lord and has nothing to do with the armies of the Israelites. Victory is the Lord's, and so is defeat. Some plan is present for the Israelites - a plan which is not easily seen or understood, but a plan to be manifest by their god in time and in his own way. The Ark of the Lord is the perfect image for this portable god who is still looking for a permanent home for his chosen people. Power without limit, destruction arbitrarily delivered, a plan that can be penetrated by no one - "no one is safe in the presence of the Lord."

The Philistine story is finished once the Ark is returned to the Israelites, but the Ark's power is still dangerous, as witnessed in the report, "the sons of Jeconiah did not rejoice ... when they welcomed the Ark of the Lord" and the Lord struck down seventy of them. The men of Beth-shemesh respond: "No one is safe in the presence of the Lord" and send a message to Kiriath-jearim,[4] "The Philistines have returned the Ark of the Lord; come down and take charge of it." The Ark finally finds a home and a custodian and remains in Kiriath-jearim for several years. It will be moved again to Jerusalem several years later (2 Sam. ch. 6). During this time the Ark and what it stands for are far removed from the lives of the Hebrews, who have taken up the worship of Baal and Astarte, Canaanite fertility gods. A transition, "So for a long while..." reminds us that time has passed and we are told once again of Samuel. When the Israelites decide to return to the worship of their god, it is Samuel who addresses the whole nation: "If your return to the Lord is wholehearted, banish the foreign gods and the Ashtaroth[5] from your shrines; turn to the Lord with heart and mind, and worship him alone, and he will deliver you from the Philistines." This is a refrain we have heard before. If your faith is strong enough then your reward will be .... And what is implied in the text is that if the reward is not forthcoming then it is the people's fault for not having enough faith. As we have seen this argument is fatally flawed. Samuel rises to power at

---

[4] Kiriath-jearim was located between Jerusalem and Gezer just a few miles east of Jerusalem. The Philistines were also a migrant people who had at this time control of the coastal area between the Shephelah and the sea, part of which is now the Gaza Strip. The Philistine cities were Gaza, Ashkelon, Ashdod, Gath and Ekron. The Philistines gave their name to this part of the Canaannite territory as 'Palestine'.

[5] Ashtaroth was a cult object (idol) representing Astarte, a god of fertility.

this point in the narrative, and in an assembly of all the tribes at Mizpah he exhibits his special powers of prophesy by fasting and interceding with the Lord for the Israelites who confess their sins in a day long prayer meeting. Now when the Philistines advance the Lord thunders out at them, and his chosen people are able to pursue and slaughter them. This narrative is the Hebrew writer's way of giving us the events of hundreds of years of struggle between the peoples who were established in the area and the encroaching tribes of Israel, who were eventually to occupy the land and to form it into a country. We are reminded of the opening story in Genesis where formlessness is given form in the act of creation - in Exodus, the Book of Judges, and here too we see images of a crowd of individuals being formed into a congregation and then into a nation - a nation which, like the others around it, wants a king to rule it.

"Samuel acted as judge in Israel as long as he lived," and appointed his sons to be judges in his older years. His sons did not follow in his footsteps, however, and took bribes and profited from their judgeships. The Israelite response is to ask for a king. In what follows we see a hint of the conflict between the monarchist and anti-monarchist positions expressed in the story. Samuel warns the people that a king will take taxes from them and will enforce a universal draft when he needs soldiers. Their sons will serve in the army whether they want to or not. The people refuse to heed this warning and cry again for a king - "a king to govern us, to lead us out to war and fight our battles." After hearing the will of the people Samuel confers with his Lord and is instructed to give them a king. The Lord reads the peoples' will as a rejection of his kingship and there is a sense of jealousy in his acceptance of the new relationship between the tribes. The loose confederation of the judges is about to be replaced by a new political arrangement, a centralized monarchy. Samuel has served as a transition between the judges and the kings. Like him Saul will serve as a transition between the time of the power of the priests and the time of the power of the kings. Compare the relationship between Saul and Samuel with the relationship between David and Nathan to see in narrative terms the shift in power from the priest/prophet/judge to the king, or from church to state.

After some appropriate prophetly mumbo-jumbo in the form of signs and raptures, Samuel anoints Saul as king of Israel. Saul is anointed, appointed and installed. We are shown how this is to be played out. First Samuel anoints Saul in the name of the Lord as the one chosen by the Lord to be the king. Then we are shown the appointment which is by lot. The tribe of

Benjamin is selected by lot and then the family of Matri is chosen by lot, and finally from that family Saul is chosen by lot. When he is chosen he stands forth in the crowd as special. He is a head taller than anyone else. Once again the recurring theme of chosenness is built right into the narrative. Saul is from the Benjamite tribe which is the smallest tribe of the twelve tribes and thus his choice is also politically astute. It is doubtful that a king from the larger tribes would be acceptable, but a Benjamite, like today's selection of Secretary-General of the United Nations, must come from a small tribe. Finally we read another version of the choice of Saul, for after Saul's stunning victory over the Ammonites (ch. 11) the people cry out to have this victorious warrior as their king: "So they all went to Gilgal and invested Saul there as king in the presence of the Lord, sacrificing shared-offerings before the Lord; and Saul and all the Israelites celebrated the occasion with great joy." Unfortunately for Saul, this great joy will soon turn to bitter despair, for though he reigns over Israel for twenty-two years (we are told in 1 Sam. 13.1), he spends the last several years out of favour with the Lord, devoured by fear, jealousy and evil spirits, torn between hatred and love for David, and unsure of his power.

Many traditions are at play in the narrative. We read of Samuel's special birth and of his commitment to the Lord which emphasizes the unpredictability of the choice of the Lord. We are told of Samuel's visions and shown how he will replace Eli as the prophet of the Lord, but we are told almost nothing of his years as a judge for the tribes of Israel. 1 Samuel concerns itself with Saul and David. Samuel plays a small part in the narrative although his name is attached to the final text. Although Samuel has a small part in the story-line he serves a major part in the official line: he is the reader of the higher text, the reader of the Lord's plan; he will provide the current reader with the *correct interpretation*. The correct interpretation, Samuel's story tells us, is that the Lord is behind all of the events of importance in the history of the chosen tribes. Yahweh will choose to allow the desire of the people for a king even though he is their king. Yahweh will choose Saul; will turn away from him. Yahweh will choose David. The overlay of the Samuel story gives us motives and reasons for the events described in the Saul and David stories. Imagine for a moment cutting out the story of Samuel from the book of Samuel. How much havoc would such an incision cause?

The first important act of Samuel is to select a king when the people cry out for one. We read of Samuel going alone to anoint the one that the Lord has chosen. The choice of the Lord is revealed in a strictly arbitrary way to Samuel. The real king is not so easy to pick out for mere mortals, but Yahweh can see deeper than humans and his choice will be the best. None of the Israelites would have selected their first king from the smallest tribe - the tribe of Benjamin, only Yahweh could see how the virtues of Saul shone out from his humble beginnings "from the smallest of the tribes of Israel" and from a family which "is the least important of all the families of the tribe of Benjamin." Samuel's second important act is to kill Agag when Saul has failed to carry out the orders of the Lord completely and with dispatch. Saul's failure to obey (the original sin) loses him the favour of the Lord, and it is Samuel who provides us with this reading of the events.[6] Samuel stands between the Lord and his people reading the "text," which contains the Lord's intentions, to the people. He also stands between the text and us - providing a reading which makes sense of the narrative from a particular point of view. Samuel's function in the story is clear. But is it necessary?

No. Everything that he provides us is also given in another way in the narrative. His choice of Saul as first king can be explained without divine intervention in a straight forward manner. There are good reasons to choose Saul - reasons given in the story: Saul is a head taller than anyone else, a useful characteristic for a warrior king; he is selected by lot, a way of indicating that everyone had an equal chance; he is from the smallest tribe,[7] a way of placating the larger tribes, each of whom would have had its favourite candidate who would have been unacceptable to the other; he wins a decisive battle against the Philistines, an act that is at the center of the desire for a king. In other words it is possible to read the story in a realistic manner without the introduction of a puppet master who is controlling the strings which cause the actors to move. Samuel's function in the story is to offer a reading of the events of the story, a reading which proclaims the intentions and plans of Yahweh. Take that away and all that is lost is the official line.

---

[6] Note also that Samuel's sons are not worthy of following him as judge. There is no other contender for the leadership.

[7] During all of the years of the "cold war" we had no Secretary-General of the United Nations who came from the United States or the Soviet Union. The position was always filled by someone from a "smaller tribe."

Saul's story is a tragic one. He is chosen by Yahweh as the first king, given the task of uniting a loose confederation of tribes while fighting against the established and well armed Philistines, and is to do this while still under the direct control of the prophet Samuel, who is opposed to the monarchy. Saul is a brave warrior and leader who is capable of making decisions and acting quickly. These very characteristics which make him a strong king are also his downfall. After one battle with the Philistines he and his army are pursuing the enemy from Michmash to Aijalon. "But the people were so faint with hunger that they turned to plunder and seized sheep, cattle, and bullocks; they slaughtered them on the ground, and ate the meat with the blood in it." (1 Sam. 14.32) When Saul is told that the people are breaking the dietary rules of Yahweh he immediately acts. He has a large stone rolled into camp and set up as a temporary slaughtering place to drain the blood and purify the meat. In doing so he takes on a priestly function. This is the beginning of his downfall. His major sin, however, is *the* sin of the stories of the Old Testament: he disobeys. Told to 'Spare no one' in the battle against the Amalekites, Saul and his army spare the king and the best of the sheep and cattle. For this he loses Yahweh's favour. Remember that commandment: "Thou shalt not kill"?

Yahweh, the god of choices, now chooses again. He chooses David: "Then the spirit of the Lord came upon David and was with him from that day onwards." Several traditions converge in the David story. One has it that David is brought to Saul as a musician to provide Saul relief from his bouts with depression. In this story David kills Goliath in the most famous "underdog wins against incredible odds" story in literature. Confusion arises when a second strand of the story has Saul asking Abner, his commander-in-chief, who the boy David is, after we have been told that David is loved by Saul. In any case David and Saul's son, Jonathan, become friends bound together by love. This friendship proves important in the David story as on several occasions Jonathan assists David in his struggle against Saul. And what is the nature of the struggle? David has been blessed by the Lord and will be king. But Saul is king. The marvellous story of David's ascendancy to the throne is the stuff of movies. He is in constant danger; he has the opportunity on two occasions to kill Saul but he does not;[8] he is the leader of a guerrilla band living in the hills; he hires out to the enemy kings, but never fights against the Israelites; he is a

---

[8] It is obviously in David's interest to maintain the principle of the divine right of the king.

powerful sexual force who can turn Abigail's head and steal her from her husband; he is cunning, brave, powerful, and has stones. David has all the qualities (we are told) of the early patriarchs: he has the tenacity and strength of Jacob, the vision and wisdom of Joseph, the loyalty of Abraham, and the sexual appetite of all of them put together. It is only fitting that in his death bed the cure offered by his attendants is to place a young virgin in bed with him. They expect to see David get up once more.

David triumphs by the end of 1 Samuel. Samuel is dead. Saul is dead. Long live King David.

At the end of 1 Samuel we are told that Saul commits suicide by falling on his sword. At the beginning of 2 Samuel we are told of an Amalekite who comes to David and tells of the defeat of the Israelites and the death of Saul and Jonathan. This man claims to have killed Saul after seeing him "leaning on his spear with the chariots and horsemen closing in upon him." Is this an example of a contradictory report? One page has Saul falling on his sword and dying and the next has him falling on his spear and not dying. How are we to read this seeming discrepancy? The Amalekite is obviously a mercenary in the Israelite army. He comes to David hoping to be rewarded for killing the old king. Expecting a reward he gets killed. This mercenary does not see that though the death of Saul may be in David's interest, the murder of the king is not in David's interest. "How is it," said David, "that you were not afraid to raise your hand to slay the Lord's anointed?" The Amalekite's boastful lie, offered as a calculated attempt at currying favour, is his death warrant. "Your blood be on your own head," says David, "for out of your own mouth you condemned yourself when you said, 'I killed the Lord's anointed.'" What follows is the famous lament of David: (King James, 2 Sam.1.19-27)

> 19. The beauty of Israel is slain upon thy
> high places: how are the mighty fallen!
> 20. Tell it not in Gath, publish it not in the
> streets of Askelon; lest the daughters of the
> Philistines rejoice, lest the daughters of the
> uncircumcised triumph.
> 21. Ye mountains of Gilboa, let there be no
> dew, neither let there be rain, upon you, not
> fields of offerings: for there the shield of the
> mighty is vilely cast away, the shield of Saul, as
> though he had not been anointed with oil.

22. From the blood of the slain, from the fat
of the mighty, the bow of Jonathan turned not
back, and the sword of Saul returned not empty.

23. Saul and Jonathan were lovely and pleasant
in their lives, and in their death they were not
divided; they were swifter than eagles, they were
stronger than lions.

24. Ye daughters of Israel, weep over Saul,
who clothed you in scarlet, with other delights,
who put on ornaments of gold upon your apparel.

25. How are the mighty fallen in the midst of
the battle! O Jonathan, thou wast slain in thine
high places.

26. I am distressed for thee, my brother Jonathan:
very pleasant hast thou been unto me:
thy love to me was wonderful,passing the love
of women.

27. How are the mighty fallen, and the weapons
of war perished!

This dirge over Saul and Jonathan is to be taught to the people of
Judah. It is a fine lyric poem, a lament on the deaths of these two who have
been so intimately involved in David's life. It opens with a greeting to Saul and
immediately expands that to include all who have fallen. "Laid low", "fallen",
"death" are keys words in the opening which are picked up again in the closing
pair of lines, where the men of war are no more than the armour they have left
behind on the killing field. Let no enemy know of this downfall, for their
rejoicing and exulting at the deaths of these heroes would be an insult to their
memories. Let not the rains fall on the hills that bear their shields so that rust
cannot wear away all that is left of them: their armour, weapons and shields.

These men, powerful in life, are now reduced to mere tools, but their deeds and their spirits live on for they "were swifter than eagles, stronger than lions." In those images Saul and Jonathan rise above the Hills of Gilboa and become not only objects of lament but also subjects of love. David the new king is magnanimous in spirit and sensitive to the requirements of a good story. We stand with King David at the high point of Israelite Old Testament history. King David will soon unite the tribes and lift them on eagles' wings to the apex of their historic relationship with Yahweh: the promised land has been achieved.

David's story completes the transition from judges to kings. The Israelite cry for a king has been answered. Samuel, who, as we have seen, reads the Lord's story, is the last of the prophet/judges and the administration of the nation is now centralized in the hands of a divine-king. While Saul was constantly under the control of Samuel, not so with David. David's power is complete. He will turn to the priest/prophet for advice and will be brought up short for his more outrageous behaviour, but he is in command. "David came to the throne at the age of thirty and reigned for forty years. In Hebron he had ruled over Judah for seven years and a half, and for thirty-three years he reigned in Jerusalem over Israel and Judah together." (2 Sam. 5.4)

Samuel's story mediates between the "divine" and "history," offering us a reading of Yahweh's intentions in the unfolding of history in time. When Saul, in despair, goes to the Witch of Endor (1 Sam. 28) in an attempt to contact Samuel we see that Samuel, even in death, continues to "read" the future and to give a causal explanation of events. His spirit says to Saul:

> Why have you disturbed me and brought me up?...You have not obeyed the Lord, or executed the judgment of his fury against the Amalekites; that is why he has done this to you today. For the same reason the Lord will let your people Israel fall into the hands of the Philistines and, what is more, tomorrow you and your sons shall be with me.

Samuel the prophet can read the intentions of the Lord, and the proof of his reading will be in the accuracy of his predictions. Indeed, the story tells us that the next day Saul and his sons are killed and the Philistines are victorious. The very structure of the story proclaims the status of Samuel, and yet it is obvious here as before that the privileged position offered by writing about the past is presented as a knowledge of the future. One of the functions of prophets is to "read" the intentions of the gods and to provide us with reasons for our misfortunes - reasons which in the Old Testament most often turn out to be some form of disobedience. But Samuel is small potatoes compared to the prophets to follow.

THE TEST AT MOUNT CARMEL

> *The establishment of David's dynasty and the building of Solomon's Temple bring to a completion the Lord's work of establishing Israel in Canaan...Israel's prosperity has a condition, however: that the Lord's commandments be carefully obeyed. Hence, the rest of Kings tells how disaster finally came upon the Israelite kingdoms through their failure to meet that condition. While individual kings were guilty of various offenses, two particular violations of the Lord's cultic requirements condemned the two kingdoms. In the Northern Kingdom of Israel, the violation was the "sin" of Jeroboam I, namely, his establishment of the cult of the golden calves at Bethel...In Judah, the violation was permitting the local sanctuaries, called the hill-shrines, to continue after the Temple was built...*(Headnote p. 349, *New English Bible*).

The story in 1 Kings 1 that has Nathan talking to the dying King David about the succession rights emphasizes the power shift from prophet to king. When Saul went to the witch of En-dor (1 Sam. 28) and had her call up Samuel from the dead we saw how Saul responded: "Then Saul knew it was Samuel, and he bowed low with his face to the ground, and prostrated himself." At David's death bed it is Nathan who prostrates himself before "the presence" of King David: "The king was told that Nathan was there; he came into the presence and prostrated himself with his face to the ground." This yielding image indicates in the action of prostration the shift in power relationships between the prophets and the kings. King David enjoys the support of Yahweh, of course, and is a king by "divine right."

David and Solomon rule over the United Kingdom for some eighty years; the period is now known as the golden age of Israel (c1010 B.C.E. to c931 B.C.E.). David's capture of Jerusalem, his choice of Jerusalem as the

capital, and Solomon's construction of the Temple in Jerusalem signal the end
of the story of the nomadic chosen people and the fulfillment of the covenant
promise for land. Now the Hebrews have a permanent location for the Ark of
the Covenant, a king to offer central administration, and a settled way of life in
the promised land. Solomon not only builds a Temple for the Ark but he also
fortifies many of the cities in the kingdom by building thick walls such as are
seen at Megiddo, Hazor, and Gezer. These are the golden years: we read of
the wealth of Solomon imaged in gold and thousands of concubines, in massive
building projects employing thousands of slaves, in visits to the king made by
emissaries from other countries and by the Queen of Sheba herself. But at his
death in 931 B.C.E. the unification of the Hebrew tribal groups (traditionally
12 in number) falls apart - Kings David and Solomon will be the only kings to
reign over a union of all the tribes. Much of the Old Testament is written
during the years of civil strife, invasion, and exile which follows the death of
Solomon. How could a nation ruled by Yahweh's chosen ones decline so
rapidly? What had gone wrong? These "chosen people" are led out of slavery,
purified in the desert, given a "constitution," provided with a chosen king, enjoy
the results for some eighty years, and then tear themselves apart in internal
quarrels about shrines. Israel and Judah seem unable to agree on one reading
of the covenant text - competing readings break them apart into different
bunches, each claiming to have the Truth. This conclusion to the "promised
land" narrative is inevitable; it is to be found in the concept of "chosenness" -
choosing without reasons is destructive. Today we would call it privileging.[9] All
of those arbitrary choices made by Yahweh throughout the stories of the Old
Testament produce an attitude of intolerant arrogance as each tribe asserts its
own special claim to be *the* chosen vessel of the proclaimed divine. The
united kingdom crumbles because the tribes cannot agree on where and how
to worship their god.[10] The prophets, as opposed to the royal priests,
sympathized with the northern desire to reduce the power of the kings and the
Temple priests. As the monarchy falters the prophets return to prominence.

---

[9] The deconstructionists have pointed to the cultural and hence relative values that are bound
up in some of our pairings of terms: truth/fiction, philosophy/literature, male/female,
thinking/feeling. If one cannot provide a good argument for valuing one over the other then the
privileging is arbitrary.

[10] In addition to religious squabbling there were economic reasons for the split. Solomon's
ambitious building programs tended to "choose" the southern part of the kingdom to the
exclusion of the more nomadic northern tribes.

Consider Elijah the Tishbite: a series of stories about Elijah enter the narrative at 1 Kings 16 and relate the first stages of the overthrow of the dynasty of Omri. Elijah appears as a mature and complete figure who announces his authenticity to King Ahab by way of a nature miracle: he will cause a drought to occur in Israel, a drought which will eliminate both rain and dew until Elijah gives the word. On command from Yahweh he goes to Zarephath where he is told that a widow has been instructed to feed him. He goes; he meets the widow. She tells him, in response to his request for food, "I have no food to sustain me except a handful of flour in a jar and a little oil in a flask." Elijah tells her to make a small cake for him from the scarce supplies, and she does. But the food is not used up, for "the jar of flour did not give out nor did the flask of oil fail," and "there was food for him and for her and for her family for a long time." After some time the son of this woman fell ill and his breathing ceased. The woman is devastated by the loss of her son and blames Elijah for interfering with her life and bringing this sad consequence to her. He takes the boy in his arms, carries him to the roof-chamber, brings him back to life, and announces to the boy's mother, "Look, your son is alive."

"Now I know for certain that you are a man of God and that the word of the Lord on your lips is truth," she says, having seen his power in the act of bringing her son back to life. Immediately after this the narrative shifts to a larger arena where Elijah will demonstrate to all of the people that he is a prophet of Yahweh, a "true" prophet of the "true" god. In an amazing display of verification as a means of determining truth, Elijah sets up a contest between himself/Yahweh on one side, and King Ahab's prophets/Baal on the other. Four hundred and fifty prophets of Baal answer the challenge. The test is simplicity itself: "Bring two bulls; let them choose one for themselves, cut it up and lay it on the wood without setting fire to it, and I will prepare the other and lay it on the wood without setting fire to it. You shall invoke your god by name and I will invoke the Lord by name; and the god who answers by fire, he is God." Here is a real test, a test that looks like a scientific test. The hypothesis is something like this: The real god will have the power to start a fire and will do so on a request from a real prophet. Common sense tells us that fires do not just start spontaneously, but must be ignited by flame. No human hand will provide the ignition, and if the fire bursts out it must be the work of a god. Prediction: the real god will respond to the request of the real prophet by starting a fire to consume the offering.

Just before this test is conducted we read of Elijah's power (through Yahweh) in a series of stories which include nature miracles and a resurrection miracle. Based on the narrative we have no doubt that we are reading about a real and powerful prophet. He is alone against four hundred and fifty prophets of Baal - one voice against a multitude of voices. Just to be sure that the test is accepted as proof of the claim that Yahweh is God, Elijah stacks the deck against himself. After the wood has been laid, the bull prepared for sacrifice, and the trench dug around the altar, he orders the people to soak the wood with water. Not once, but three times, they carry water to the altar and soak the wood and the sacrifice. After the prophets of Baal have cried out to Baal all morning and most of the afternoon to no avail, Elijah tries. He addresses his god, "Lord God of Abraham, of Isaac, and of Israel, let it be known today that thou art God in Israel." And the result? "Then the fire of the Lord fell. It consumed the whole-offering, the wood, the stones, and the earth, and licked at the water in the trench." The prediction comes true at the appropriate time; therefore there is good reason to believe that the hypothesis is true.

Does this mean that we have been given evidence for the existence of god? It certainly would count as evidence if it happened. But, of course, this "test," no matter how objective and fair, is contained in a story, a story which has as its intention the desire to prove that Yahweh is God. The test is so dramatic, the result so compelling, that we would expect it to be recorded in all sorts of documents. But, alas, none of the four hundred and fifty "prophets" of Baal are left to testify to the miracle, for Elijah has the people of Israel take them down to the river valley below Mount Carmel. "They seized them, and Elijah took them down to the Kishon and slaughtered them there in the valley." Shortly after this successful display of power Elijah outruns King Ahab's chariot in a race to return to Jezreel.[11] After a short time in Beersheba hiding from Jezebel, Elijah is given new orders by Yahweh and sets off to anoint a new king and to find a new prophet. He finds Elisha ploughing the fields with twelve pair of oxen, throws his cloak over him and in that way includes him as his new disciple and Yahweh's new prophet. Elisha leaves his oxen, kisses his mother and father good-bye, slaughters a pair of oxen for the

---

[11] The interesting and popular movie, *Chariots of Fire*, gets its title from these stories in the Old Testament. The Christian runner, who will not run on Sunday for religious reasons, tells his sister that he feels the "power of the Lord" when he runs, just as Elijah did when he outran Ahab's chariot. Elijah is also taken to heaven by a chariot of fire.

people to eat, and follows Elijah.

At the beginning of The Second Book of Kings Elijah is still a "trouble" to Ahaziah, the king of Israel. The king sends a captain and fifty soldiers to get Elijah down from a hill-top where he is sitting. In response to the captain's orders Elijah says, "If I am a man of God, may fire fall from heaven and consume you and your company!" And we are told, "Fire fell from heaven and consumed the officer and his fifty men." Look closely at this passage. It is presented as a formal argument. 'If P then Q' and 'Q' therefore 'P'. Or,

> If I am a man of God then fire will consume you and your company. (premise)
>
> Fire consumes you and your company. (premise)
>
> Therefore, I am a man of God. (implied conclusion)
>
> which can be written:
>
> If P then Q
>   Q
> Therefore, P.
>
> which is not a valid argument form. (The fallacy it commits is called 'Affirming the Consequent'.)

Elijah, the one true prophet, alone against incredible odds, perseveres against the king's men (in spite of his bad logic!) and fire falls to consume a total of one hundred and two men before Elijah feels safe enough to come down the hill. It is really not so much a matter of logical error here in the story as it is an indication of the writer's attitudes. These "tests" are not to be taken as verification that god exists, but instead god's existence is taken for granted, is a given. We see that here, in the logical error, for at no time is it even a question whether or not "I am a man of God" is true. The truth of that "proposition" is given in the story. Read it like this: "Given that God exists, and given that I am a man of God then everything is possible for me. The physically impossible is possible; the ability to destroy is possible; the ability to outrun horses is mine." In the confusion of the divided kingdom Elijah's voice must be strong and clear, and one. The centre must hold. Elisha will carry on. "[A]nd suddenly there appeared chariots of fire, which separated one from the other, and Elijah was carried up in the whirlwind to heaven." The Elijah story looks back to Moses - with Elijah leading the Israelites from the slavery of Baal as Moses led them from the slavery of Pharaoh and with Elisha taking the place of Joshua - and it looks forward to the Jesus story.

"The spirit of Elijah has settled on Elisha," we read, and with it the power to control natural events, to intercede miraculously in the natural order of things, and to deliver life from death. Elijah is taken up by Yahweh in the same geographical area in which Moses was buried (Deut. 34.5-6) tying the two stories together in yet another way. Over and over again we read the fundamental story of the Hebrews: Israeli disobedience leads to Yahweh's anger, which leads to Israeli repentance and then to Yahweh's salvation. The heroes - Moses, Joshua, Samuel, Elijah, Elisha - have access to Yahweh through visions, dreams, and messengers and relate the text of history to the people who do not always pay close attention to the reading they are offered. The hero is always identified in some special way - a special birth, a special sign, a unique physical mark, a special power - so that we readers can identify the true prophet from the false prophet. The story is based on fact; that is, a united kingdom did exist as the high point of the Israelite experience, but it existed for less than eighty years before falling into pieces. The chosen people were to have the promised land for all time, but instead had it for two generations. Why did the kingdom fall? The *official line* tells us: Yahweh offered the promised land; he delivered; the contract demanded obedience on the part of Israel; Israel fell apart; therefore the reason must be that Israel has failed to keep its contractual obligations. In a word, plot. Story is made up of events; plot offers causal connections for those events. Prophets are readers of plot.

CHAPTER 10: "THERE IS A VOICE THAT CRIES"

THE PROPHETS OF OLD

Prophet	Approximate dates B.C.E.	Kings	Kingdom
Samuel	1050 - 1000	Saul, David	United Kingdom
Elijah	870 - 850	Ahab, Ahaziah	Israel
Elisha	850 - 795	Jehoram-Jehoash	Israel
Micaiah	853	Ahab	Israel

Prophets of the monarchs:

Prophet	Date	Kings	Kingdom
Amos	760	Jeroboam II	Israel
Jonah	760	Jeroboam II	Israel
Hosea	760 - 722	Jeroboam II-Hoshea	Israel
Isaiah	740 - 700	Uzziah-Hezekiah	Judah
Micah	740 - 687	Jotham-Hezekiah	Judah
Zephaniah	640 - 610	Josiah	Judah
Nahum	630 - 612	Josiah	Judah
Jeremiah	626 - 580	Josiah-The Exile	Judah
Habakkuk	600	Jehoiakim	Judah

Prophets from the exile and after:

Ezekiel   592 - 570

Obadiah   exile
Haggaai   520
Zechariah   520 - 518
Malachi   500 - 400

Parts of the Book of Isaiah are assigned to this period which is sometimes referred to as Deutero-Isaiah and Trito-Isaiah.

Elisha replaces Elijah or "my god is Yahweh" replaces "my god is salvation." Elisha is primarily known for his many miracles, but his task, as the Eerdmans' Bible Dictionary[1] puts it, "was actually three-fold: to heal, prophesy, and complete Elijah's assignments." As healer he cures Naaman, the commander of the Syrian army, who suffered from leprosy, by having him bathe three times in the Jordan River. As prophet he correctly predicts that the combined forces of Jehosaphat of Judah and Jehoram of Israel will defeat the Moabites in battle. To complete Elijah's duties he travels to Damascus to anoint Hazael as legitimate sovereign. But in the popular mind Elisha will always be associated with miracles. And just what is a miracle? The most famous discussion of miracles is by David Hume in his *Enquiry Concerning Human Understanding:*[2]

> A miracle is a violation of the laws of nature; and as a firm and unalterable experience has established these laws, the proof against a miracle, from the very nature of the fact, is as entire as any argument from experience can possibly be imagined. Why is it more than probable, that all men must die; that lead cannot, of itself, remain suspended in the air; that fire consumes wood, and is extinguished by water; unless it be, that these events are found agreeable to the laws of nature, and there is required a violation of these laws, or in other words, a miracle to prevent them? Nothing is esteemed a miracle, if it ever happen in the common course of nature. It is no miracle that a man, seemingly in good health, should die on a sudden: because such a kind of death, though more

---

[1] *The Eerdmans Bible Dictionary*, edited by Allen C. Myers, *et.al.*, and published by William B. Eerdmans Publishing Company, Grand Rapids, Michigan, is a first rate reference work. It contains entries on almost everything and everyone in the Bible.

[2] David Hume, *An Enquiry Concerning Human Understanding and Selections from A Treatise of Human Nature, Chicago: Open Court, 1912*. Section 10.

unusual than any other, has yet been frequently observed to happen. But it is a miracle, that a dead man should come to life; because that has never been observed, in any age or country. There must, therefore, be an uniform experience against every miraculous event, otherwise the event would not merit that appellation. And as a uniform experience amounts to a proof, there is here a direct and full proof, from the nature of the fact, against the existence of any miracle; nor can such a proof be destroyed, or the miracle rendered credible, but by an opposite proof, which is superior.

The plain consequence is (and it is a general maxim worthy of our attention), 'That no testimony is sufficient to establish a miracle, unless the testimony be of such a kind, that its falsehood would be more miraculous, than the fact, which it endeavours to establish: And even in that case there is a mutual destruction of arguments, and the superior only gives us an assurance suitable to that degree of force, which remains, after deducting the inferior.' When any one tells me, that he saw a dead man restored to life, I immediately consider with myself, whether it be more probable, that this person should either deceive or be deceived, or that the fact, which he relates, should really have happened. I weigh the one miracle against the other; and according to the superiority, which I discover, I pronounce my decision, and always reject the greater miracle. If the falsehood of his testimony would be more miraculous, than the event which he relates; then, and not till then, can he pretend to command my belief or opinion.

From this we get a working definition which also coincides with the way we use the word 'miracle': "a miracle is an event of an extraordinary kind brought about by a god and of religious significance."[3] Thus, for example, the claim in Joshua 10.13 that the sun stayed still for one day while the Israelites defeated the Amorites, would count as an extraordinary event since it violates Newtonian laws; the event is reported to have been brought about by Yahweh, and was another significant exhibition of Yahweh's power and his intervention into history on the part of his chosen people. Using Hume's criterion for testing this claim we would weigh the probability of the sun standing still versus the probability that the report is false. Surely such an event would have been

---

[3] Richard Swinburne, editor. *Miracles*, Macmillan Publishing Company, New York. Page 2.

reported by witnesses all over the world, for it would have been of great moment; but we have testimony of the event only from the Hebrew writer, who wants to tell a particular story about divine intervention. It seems more likely that the writer is proclaiming the miracle rather than describing it. Hume has four arguments designed to show that "there never was a miraculous event established" in Part II of his Section 10. Hume argues that "there is not to be found, in all history, any miracle attested by a sufficient number of men, of such unquestioned good sense, education, and learning, as to secure us against all delusions in themselves." Secondly, he notes that people love to gossip about the unusual and that religious people are not beyond using falsehood to support what they take to be basically true. His third point is that "it forms a strong presumption against all supernatural and miraculous relations, that they are observed chiefly to abound among ignorant and barbarous people." These three points turn on factual matters, and take miracles as serious claims about matters of fact. It may well be, however, that miracles are matters of the form of a story and not the facts of the matter. Miracles do not offer evidence for the existence of god; miracles presuppose the existence of god. Hume's fourth argument is logical in nature and is an important one to consider:

> I may add as a fourth reason, which diminishes the authority of prodigies, that there is no testimony for any, even those which have not been expressly detected, that is not opposed by an infinite number of witnesses; so that not only the miracle destroys the credit of testimony, but the testimony destroys itself. To make this the better understood, let us consider, that, in matters of religion, whatever is different is contrary; and that it is impossible the religions of ancient Rome, of Turkey, of Siam, and of China should, all of them, be established on any solid foundation. Every miracle, therefore, pretended to have been wrought in any of these religions (and all of them abound in miracles), as its direct scope is to establish the particular system to which it is attributed; so has it the same force, though more indirectly, to overthrow every other system. In destroying a rival system, it likewise destroys the credit of those miracles, on which that system was established; so that all the prodigies of different religions are to be regarded as contrary facts, and the evidences of these prodigies, whether weak or strong, as opposite to each other.

Multiple religions, each offering miracle as evidence for its truth, act to weaken miracle as evidence, to the extent that each religion is exclusive. One way out of this problem is to see that miracles are literary devices used to affirm or ground the claims of a particular *official line*. When a prophet, in a story, accurately tells the future, that is a sign of authenticity, a way of establishing the prophet as a trustworthy story teller. When one prophet is reported as repeating a previous prophet's miracle, as when Jesus feeds the five thousand with five loaves and two fishes, while earlier Elisha had fed one hundred with twenty barley loaves and some fresh ripe ears of corn, it is a way of indicating that Jesus is a new and more powerful Elisha.[4]

Consider other than biblical miracles. We have all heard of the person (maybe even a friend or relative) who is diagnosed as having cancer and is then given a prognosis of "less than a year to live." But the person recovers, and the doctor says that the cancer is gone. The person's life is imperiled; against expectation, the person is saved. Isn't that a miracle? It depends upon who is *reading the events*. From the medical point of view, such examples indicate that medical prediction, in many cases, is not particularly accurate. And this does not mean that the doctor was an incompetent or the cancer was never there. Part of the description of a particular case may well include remission and even cure with no "treatment" at all. Since the human body is a complex system and the state of our knowledge of the various kinds of cancers is incomplete, it is not at all a violation of natural law that this particular person has recovered. But now consider these same facts from the point of view of the patient. Imagine that after the diagnosis the patient goes to see her priest and together they pray. And several times a day she prays to her god for assistance. From her point of view a miracle has occurred. Her petition has been granted and no matter what others say she will continue to believe that a miracle has occurred and that her life is the only evidence required. The popular press is full of these sorts of stories of prayer-miracles. Another kind of example comes from near escapes from potentially deadly accidents. In a recent severe windstorm in British Columbia several trees were blown down in populated areas. House after house suffered damage from large Douglas Fir trees suddenly uprooted by the wind and thrown into the house. In one case a couple were in bed in their water bed thinking about getting up to prepare for the day. Since the roads were blocked and the ferry was not running it seemed

---

[4] 5,000/100 = 50; therefore Jesus is fifty times more powerful than Elisha.

probable that going to work late was not a bad idea. The man moved across the water bed to "cuddle" a bit before getting up. Crash! His side of the bed suddenly had an arm thick branch puncturing the very spot where he had just been. Miracle? Or coincidence? The significance of some coincidences as opposed to others (the cat was under the bed, say, and was impaled by the branch) comes about because of the relation between the coincidence and a set of human hopes, fears, and desires. The non-religious person would, as he jumped out of the deflating bed, thank his good luck for saving him at the cost of the cat. Coincidence-miracles depend upon the point of view of the persons involved. What the non-religious person calls luck is called the grace of God or a miracle of God by the religious person. When such a coincidence does occur, and when from a particular person's point of view that coincidence is significant, the tendency is to think of oneself as being special (Lady Luck smiles on *you*). Once again we find a flawed argument at work: If I am special then God will look after me by arranging for good things to happen to me. Good things happen to me; therefore, I am special. Such a coincidence can be taken by the religious person as a sign that god is at work in the universe and that god cares about persons. But, unfortunately for this reading, bad things happen to good people.

Hume is skeptical in part because it seems that miracles always happen long ago and far away. In those cases then we have to depend upon "eyewitness" testimony, and as we all know it is less than perfect. If we think of miracles as events that are conceptually impossible and empirically certain[5] then at least we get the idea of what would count as a miracle. It is conceptually impossible to "part the waters" of a sea, or to stop the sun for a period of time, or to make the sun go backwards. If one witnessed such an event one would have good evidence that it occurred, but if one reads about it one has not a miracle but a miracle-story. In order for us to believe the story we will have to believe the story teller, and one way of establishing the authority of the text is by privileging it, by naming it "scripture" instead of story.

Elisha's 'violation' miracles include making an iron axe float, making leprosy come and go on command, overhearing the King of Aram from a vast distance, causing persons to be blind and then restoring their sight, raising a child from the dead, and foretelling the future. All of these affirm that he is a

---

[5] See R. F. Holland, "The Miraculous," *American Philosophical Quarterly*, 1965, 2: 43-51.

'man of god'. The narrative relates the fortunes of the kings of the divided kingdom and above all provides a reading for why the chosen people are not flourishing in the promised land. Throughout this part of Kings we are reminded of the violation of the religious laws of Yahweh, particularly in the use of hill shrines for sacrifice. The struggle between Yahweh and Baal is reported here and it comes to a climax in 2 Kings 10 when Jehu orders a sacred ceremony for Baal to be held. "Jehu himself sent word throughout Israel, and all the ministers of Baal came; there was not a man left who did not come. They went into the temple of Baal and it was filled from end to end." Once he has all of the ministers of Baal in one place he orders them to be killed by the soldiers he has stationed outside. "So they slew them without quarter." The sacred pillar of the Baal and the temple which housed it are destroyed and made into a privy. "Thus Jehu stamped out the worship of Baal in Israel," and he is properly rewarded: "You have done what is right in my eyes," says the Lord, "...your sons to the fourth generation shall sit on the throne of Israel." (Do you remember that commandment: Thou shalt not kill?) Jehu reigned over Israel for twenty-eight years. Elisha continues to perform his magical rituals and during the reign of Jehoash he dies and is buried. But this is not the last we hear of him. Even in death this prophet is presented as having supernatural powers.

> Year by year Moabite raiders used to invade the land. Once some men were burying a dead man when they caught sight of the raiders. They threw the body into the grave of Elisha and made off; when the body touched the prophet's bones, the man came to life and rose to his feet. (2 Kings 13.21)

Elisha has been presented as a prophet capable of violation miracles, including, making iron float on water, a feeding miracle, a resurrection miracle, and the power to bring others back to life even after he has died. One way of asserting the special status of an Old Testament hero is to tell stories that show him as a miracle worker. The rest of 2 Kings relates the downfall of the southern and northern kingdoms until the time that the troops of Nebuchadnezzar besiege Jerusalem. After a prolonged siege he takes the city, defeats the king and his army, and burns the palace, the temple, and all the houses of the city. Jerusalem is destroyed. The chosen people are defeated and their most holy of sites is destroyed. How could this horrible destruction and defeat have happened? We are told, "All this happened to the Israelites because they had sinned against the Lord their God who brought them up from Egypt..." (2 Kings 17.7) Now begins the Babylonian Exile (587 - 539 B.C.E.).

This flourishing, chosen, and special people are completely defeated and taken in to captivity, where their king, instead of ruling the promised land will be a welfare case at the table of the Babylonian king, to be fed at the pleasure of Babylon. During this exile from the land it would have been easy for the Jews to become exiled from their religion as well. They had no formal text - no scripture to turn to for comfort and explanation. The stories of their past were an integral part of them but they were as scattered as were the people. In a strange land with its strange customs and stranger gods, they must have experienced an alienation worthy of twentieth century existential analysis. Cut off from their poetry, their priests, and their god, they would have felt utterly alone and abandoned. From the high point of the United Kingdom to the low point of the diaspora the fall has been great. The first fall (disobedience) had resulted in expulsion from the Garden of Eden; this fall also results in expulsion from the promised land and reasons for it are sought by the prophets. One can imagine the prophet/poets in exile searching their memories and whatever documents they possessed for the answers to the burning question: what happened? What happened to the promise made in the covenant? Why have we fallen so low? And they would have found the answer: disobedience. One imagines them working feverishly to record the story of the covenant and prescribing those actions required to purge the guilt and recover the promise. The 'Poetic Genius' of the prophets was historical in the sense that, with hindsight, it revealed a story which in turn revealed a growth and development of the human spirit, from childhood to adulthood, or, as Blake would later put it, from innocence to experience. One aspect of the story is its affirmation of the importance of prophets. Citing many examples that the destruction could have been avoided had the king and people listened to the prophets (2 Kings 17.13; 23; 20.16-18; 22.15-18; 24.2, 13) sent to them by God, the writers attempt to reestablish the authority of the prophets as mediators between God and the people. The new prophets must reinterpret the text to explain the destruction of Jerusalem and to build a future city for the chosen people.

After all, Amos, "one of the sheep-farmers of Tekoa," had prophesied in about 760 B.C.E. that the Lord would destroy the nation because of its disobedience.

"For you alone have I cared
among all the nations of the world;
therefore will I punish you
for all your iniquities.

And he had given a careful description of the problems that would
cause the wrath of the Lord:

You who loll on beds inlaid with ivory
and sprawl over your couches,
feasting on lambs from the flock
and fatted calves,
you who pluck the strings of the lute
and invent musical instruments like David,
you who drink wine by the bowlful
and lard yourselves with the richest of oils,
but are not grieved at the ruin of Joseph -
now, therefore,
you shall head the column of exiles;
that will be the end of sprawling and revelry.

Gluttony, drunkenness, lack of industry - these are all a part of the
disease, but the most serious and deadly sin of all is to be "not grieved at the
ruin of Joseph," which asserts one of the common themes of the Old
Testament: forget the past and die. Looking back on Amos from the period of
exile must have been an experience of discovery, for Amos had described the
illness and the result of the illness almost 200 years before. In a vision Amos
had seen a swarm of locusts devouring the land, had seen the Lord summoning
a "flame of fire to devour all of creation," and had seen the Lord with a plumb
line in his hand to measure the heart of the people. But he had also sounded a
promise for the future: "I will restore David's fallen house; I will repair its
gaping walls and restore its ruins."

Jonah is a favorite prophet because of the detail of his story. "Jonah"
has also been a battleground for fundamentalists and skeptics who debate
whether or not a man could live inside a fish or not. One side argues that living
inside a fish would be no problem, if the fish were large enough, and there
were air to breathe, and the man didn't get crushed on the way in. The other
side argues that the man would never get by the throat, would be digested if he
did get by, and if he were not digested or crushed he would be suffocated.

'Therefore, the Bible is true,' says the fundamentalist. 'No, therefore, the Bible is false,' says the skeptic. Both readings depend upon taking the story as composed of propositions which are either true or false. But this story is not description; it is prescription. And it is a powerful and necessary prescription for a serious "illness" of the Old Testament: intolerance. It is one of the first treatments offered for this devastating "illness" of the spirit, which shrivels and starves the human spirit by restricting acceptance of the different and blocking love of what is. Intolerance is like an alien and indigestible food in the stomach - constipating and unhealthy, and until it is eliminated health will be impossible.

It is ironic that The Book Jonah would become a battleground for arguments between literalists and debunkers, each filled with the intolerant and passionate intensity that a single correct reading provides. But wait a minute. Is this story about whether or not a man can live inside a fish? Consider this pattern: Joseph Campbell, in his book *The Hero with a Thousand Faces*, brings together hundreds of stories from many different cultures to argue that we all tell the same stories and that our heroes all have the same face. He extracts a pattern from hero stories that looks like this:

A. SEPARATION

  1. the call to adventure
  2. refusal of the call
  3. supernatural aid
  4. the crossing of the first threshold
  5. the belly of the whale

B. INITIATION
  1. the road of trials
  2. the meeting with the goddess
  3. woman as the temptress
  4. atonement with the father
  5. apotheosis
  6. the ultimate boon

C. RETURN

1. refusal of return
2. the magic flight
3. rescue from without
4. the crossing of the return threshold
5. master of the two worlds
6. freedom to live

> Whether the hero be ridiculous of sublime, Greek or barbarian, gentile or Jew, his journey varies little in essential plan. Popular tales represent the heroic action as physical; the higher religions show the deed to be moral; nevertheless, there will be found astonishingly little variation in the morphology of the adventure, the character roles involved, the victories gained.
> (page 38, Campbell)

If we use this map to chart the meaning of the Jonah story we do not find a realistic description of how things are, but rather a prescription of how things ought to be, presented in the genre of protest fiction. Jonah gets the call to go to Nineveh, but attempts to refuse it. The reluctant hero is such a part of our heritage that we tend to overlook the reluctance, but we still hold to the cultural myth that tells us that a leader (hero) should be reluctant, should not really want to lead us but should somehow be talked into the task. ("I don't want to run, but many have urged me to do so," or "Duty called me to this position of power; I was quite happy before the call just selling used cars.") Jonah is cut of the same verbal cloth as Moses, who is the paradigmatic reluctant hero; both try valiantly to escape their destiny, to hide from the call. Separation, initiation and return are all present in this story. Jonah refuses the call, but he can not escape his own life; he is initiated into the new by the bizarre experience of being swallowed up; and he returns or passes the threshold after calling out to God:

> I called to the Lord in my distress,
> and he answered me;
> out of the belly of Sheol I cried
> for help,
> and thou hast heard my cry.
> Thou didst cast me into the depths,
> far out at sea,

and the flood closed round me;
all thy waves, all thy billows, passed
over me.
I thought I was banished from thy sight
and should never see thy holy temple again.

After this experience Jonah is called a second time, "Go to the great city of Nineveh, go now and denounce it in the words I give you." Jonah obeys at once. Armed with his new found power he proceeds to Nineveh to chastise and punish the evildoers in the name of his god. Like Samuel and Elijah before him, Jonah is rigid in his intolerance of evil and is almost gleefully and righteously looking forward to the destruction of Nineveh. If Elisha could kill forty two boys for making fun of his bald head, then surely Jonah can witness the destruction of one hundred and twenty thousand sinners at the hand of an angry god. But the people repent and "God saw what they did, and how they abandoned their wicked ways, and he repented and did not bring upon them the disaster he had threatened."

Jonah is angry. This is what he had feared: he would make this trip to Nineveh to bring them destruction and death for their sinful ways and at the last minute God would get soft on him and show compassion. He still has not learned what his "trip" was about; he cannot *read* the experience he has just undergone. God provides him with one more experience by which to understand the meaning of his call. After providing Jonah with a gourd to shade and protect him from the weather God causes a worm to destroy the gourd. At the loss of this simple gourd, Jonah is mortally angered, and we read in King James, Jonah 4.9-11:

> 9. And God said to Jonah, Doest thou well to
> be angry for the gourd? And he said, I do well to
> be angry, even unto death.
> 10. Then said the Lord, Thou hast had pity on
> the gourd, for the which thou hast not laboured,
> neither madest it grow; which came up in a night,
> and perished in a night:
> 11. And should i not spare Nineveh, that
> great city, wherein are more than sixscore thousand
> persons that cannot discern between their
> right hand and their left hand; and also much
> cattle?

Nineveh is not destroyed. This god is changing, and for the first time we have a story which explicitly champions religious tolerance. Jonah's bigotry is rebuked by the religious tolerance of God. Jonah will bring back a boon for all of his community: Be tolerant of the new and the different, for we are responsible for our own suffering, our own destiny.

Ezekiel (may God strengthen) is priest and prophet who began his career in the last years of the Kingdom of Judah and ended it during the captivity in Babylon after the destruction of Jerusalem in 587 B.C.E. He is the prophet of ecstatic visions, of clairvoyance, of out of body experiences, catatonic states, and allegory. He is addressed as "Man" or "Son of Man" by the Lord who comes upon him and gives him his prophetic powers. The empowering experience, described in chapter 1, is in the form of an experience rich in visual splendour and symbol. By the river Kebar Ezekiel sees a storm cloud carried by the wind and bristling with flashes of fire and brilliant light. In the fire he sees four living creatures with human form and animal faces. Images of lions, eagles, oxen, wings and radiant fire exhibit the power and majesty of God in this complex visual metaphor. As Ezekiel looks at the living creatures he notices wheels on the ground beside each of the four creatures. "The wheels sparkled like topaz, and they were all alike: in form and working they were like a wheel inside a wheel, and when they moved in any of the four directions they never swerved in their course." (1.15) the rims of these wheels are "full of eyes all round." The imagery is unmistakable: all seeing eyes in fire, these are the eyes that will see into the past and into the future - powerful and omniscient. These are the eyes of a prophet, blinded by the normal but sensitive to the divine. Above the wheels and the creatures, above the vault over their heads, emerging from what looks like a furnace of molten brass is a human figure, radiant and powerful "like the appearance of the Lord." This imagery is the empowering scene for this prophet, who the Lord refers to as simply "Man," or literally "Son of Man." The Lord gives him a task to perform: "I am sending you to the Israelites, a nation of rebels who have rebelled against me." Imaged in fire and wind, this god will now complete the commission by having his prophet literally eat the words he is to speak. "Open your mouth and eat what I give you."

Ezekiel reports: "Then I saw a hand stretched out to me, holding a scroll. He unrolled it before me, and it was written all over on both sides with dirges and laments and words of woe. Then he said to me, 'Man, eat what is in front of you, eat this scroll; then go and speak to the Israelites.' So I opened my mouth and he gave me the scroll to eat. Then he said, 'Man, swallow this

scroll I give you, and fill yourself full. So I ate it, and it tasted sweet as honey."
(Ezek. 2.9 - 3.3) Ezekiel eats the *word* of his god and now contains the word,
or the *word* is made flesh in Ezekiel's act of eating it. He is now transported
by a spirit atop the wheels and with a rushing sound he is suddenly with the
exiles, where he stays for seven days and is dumbfounded. It is as if there is a
requirement for Ezekiel to digest the word, and to do that he must spend a
week without speech in order that he will be properly prepared to deliver the
word when it is required. The word of the divine has taken on the form of the
human. "Man, I have made you a watchman for the Israelites; you will take
messages from me and carry my warnings to them." Each of these messages
will be introduced by a standard formula: "these are the words of the Lord
God," a formula we will read some twenty times in the rest of the book.

Words, messages, prophesies, scrolls, speech and speechlessness,
tongues and tongues tied, listen, refuse to listen - all of these are the diction of
images of the book of destiny, the plot that the divine has chosen to reveal to a
living and human prophet. And this is an angry god, a god who brings a
whirlwind of revenge, destruction, desolation and death to a people who are
his chosen people: "An end is coming, the end is coming upon the four corners
of the earth. The end is now upon you; I will unleash my anger against you; I
will call you to account for your doings and bring your abominations upon your
own heads." (7.3) This anger will lead to the destruction of Israel and to the en-
slavement of her people. For rebelling against the Laws of the covenant, these
chosen but fallen people will be punished by their god who will bring a sword
against them and destroy the hill-shrines, altars, and idols, along with the cities
and the lands. "I will scatter your bones about your altars," the Lord says,
through Ezekiel, who sees six men with battle-axes who have come to destroy
all of the sinners. One of the six is a man dressed in linen who has a pen and
ink at his waist, and whose task is to put a mark on the foreheads of those who
are worthy of being spared. Only those with the mark will be spared; all others
will be killed without pity.

These visions of Ezekiel's spark with energy, are alive with imagination
and freshness. It is as if the poet's powers are increased in the company of
destruction and desolation. An angry god feeds the imagination with powerful
images of famine, pestilence, and destruction. There is a condemnation of
Jerusalem. The city is described as a wanton woman fornicating with everyone
and even paying the fornicators. A whirlwind of images are heaped up to be

thrown at the abominable Israelites who have sinned against Yahweh. New principles of justice are introduced through Ezekiel, for example, Yahweh tells him:

> You may ask, 'Why is the son not punished for his father's iniquity?' Because he has always done what is just and right and has been careful to obey all my laws, therefore he shall live. It is the soul that sins, and no other, that shall die; a son shall not share a father's guilt, nor a father his sons's.

And then a bit later Yahweh bitterly says, "'The Lord acts without principle,' say the Israelites. No, Israelites, it is you who act without principle, not I." But in defense of the Israelites one might well remember the earlier words of this god when he said "I punish the children for the sins of the fathers to the third and fourth generations of those who hate me." These two principles are logically incompatible. And a god who changes moral principles is hard to tell apart from one who is without principles. A long list of punishments to be levelled against the sinful Israelites leads to the next set of prophesies which are against foreign nations. Ammon, Sidon, Tyre, Egypt, Moab, Edom, Seir (the hill country of Edom) are all to be punished, in some cases because they rejoiced when they saw the destruction of Jerusalem and the dispersion of the people, in other cases so that the people will know that Yahweh is the Lord.

All of this imagery of destruction leads to another experience for Ezekiel: "The hand of the Lord came upon me, and he carried me down in a plain full of bones." There Ezekiel is made to go to and fro across the bones until he has been around them all. They cover the plain and are "very dry." Here then is the imaged end, the promise of a nation has ended in a valley of dry bones, lacking any life or flesh, spirit or vitality. Those Hebrews rescued from Egyptian slavery so long ago, those peoples who had been forged into a congregation in the desert, those chosen tribes who were to be as numerous as stars in the sky, as multitudinous as sand on the beach, are now seen in this vision as dead and dry, devoid of life.

But then Ezekiel is ordered to take one leaf of a wooden tablet and write on it, 'Judah and his associates of Israel.' And to take another and write on it, 'Joseph, the leaf of Ephraim and all his associates of Israel.' And to bring the two together to form a single tablet. And like the tablet in Ezekiel's hand the Lord will bring together the exiled Israelites and assemble them from their places and restore them to their own soil. The restoration of the united kingdom is imaged in writers' works - the restored kingdom is in the book, as it were. "The leaves on which you write shall be visible in your hand for all to see." And the leaves on which Yahweh writes, the leaves of history, will be visible for all to see also, in the renewed covenant and the rebuilt city of Jerusalem, in the midst of which will be the sanctuary of the Lord. The theocracy is to be restored and detailed directions are given for the construction of the temple. Ezekiel looks back at the sin of the Israelites, tells of the consequences of the sin, and then promises a future which will resurrect the best of the past. Ezekiel also looks forward to the beginnings of the Christian story in the New Testament. Its hero/prophet, Jesus, will also have the power to see more than any other can see, and will, like Ezekiel, be an incarnation of the *word* in the flesh. "The perimeter of the city shall be eighteen thousand cubits, and the city's name for ever after shall be Jehovah-shammah."[6]

---

[6] That is "the Lord is there." Other prophets have given Jerusalem other names as signs of future transformation. See Isaiah 1.26; 60.14; 62.2-4; Jer. 3.17; Zech.8.3.

CHAPTER 11: "WHO DO THEY SAY THAT I AM?"

Mark has a marvellous story about Jesus and a fig tree. He tells of a time when Jesus and the disciples are walking from Bethany to Jerusalem. Jesus feels hungry and "noticing in the distance a fig-tree in leaf, he went to see if he could find anything on it." Since it is not the season for figs, there are none on the tree. Jesus is angered by the lack of figs and curses the tree: "'May no one ever again eat fruit from you!' And his disciples were listening." The group proceeds to Jerusalem where Jesus goes into the temple and, still angry, drives out the money changers, upsets their tables, turns over the seats of the pigeon sellers, and cleans out all commercial activities in the temple. He then teaches the crowd about the proper use of the temple. Early the next morning Jesus and the disciples are walking back toward Bethany when they pass by the fig tree. Peter says, "Rabbi, look, the fig-tree which you cursed has withered," and indeed we are told that "the fig-tree had withered from the roots up." Still later, on the Mount of Olives, Jesus uses the fig tree in a lesson to his disciples about the Endtime which is coming. "'Learn a lesson from the fig-tree. When its tender shoots appear and are breaking into leaf, you know that summer is near. In the same way, when you see all this happening, you may know that the end is near, at the very door. I tell you this: the present generation will live to see it all.'"

First we see the fig tree in leaf. Then we see it withered and dead as a result of Jesus' curse. And then it is used by Jesus as an example in a parable about the Endtime. A hungry Jesus has killed a fig tree because it had no fruit in a season when it could not have fruit. What kind of story is this? What does it tell us about this god-man? Here is the entry in *The Interpreters'*

Bible:[1]

> It is well to begin any consideration of this story of the barren fig
> tree with the frank recognition that it is the *least attractive*
> of all the narratives about Jesus. Luke omits it entirely, possibly
> because he already has a parable of a barren fig tree (Luke 13.6-9).
> At any rate most scholars would applaud his judgment, *as shown
> by the omission*. There are two main objections to taking the
> story literally, as an exact record. The first is the *unfavorable
> light* in which it seems to put the judgment, or common sense, of
> Jesus; he could have had no rational expectation of finding figs out
> of season. The second is that the miracle is quite "out of character"
> with Jesus' mind and with other miracles....Mark takes the story as
> a proof of Jesus' power, but that "proof" was on a level devoid of
> moral and religious significance.
>
> For teaching and preaching the church has taken the story as a
> symbolic representation of the truth that life without fruit is
> worthless. ...The incident was taken by many in the early church as
> an acted parable of judgment on the religion of Israel because of its
> lack of ethical and spiritual fruit....(emphasis mine).

This kind of apology raises several interesting questions. Why should
we applaud Luke's judgment for omitting a story about Jesus? On the grounds
that the story casts Jesus in an "unfavorable light"? The implication here is that
any time we run into a story that casts the hero in an "unfavorable light" we are
justified in omitting the story. And just what is an "unfavorable light"?
Unfavorable from whose point of view? If what we are told by Mark is the
"least attractive" of all the stories about Jesus, then how can that fact be
justification for editing it out? These would be justifications only if we are
presenting propaganda, or in today's terminology, a media image. A deeper
epistemological question arises: if the gospels are the source of all that we
know about Jesus then on what other grounds can we make judgments about
his attractiveness or lack of it? How can we justifiably pay attention only to
those stories that match some preconceived idea of what an attractive hero
looks like? Whose gospel is being proclaimed in a statement like the one about

---

[1] *The Interpreters' Bible*, Abingdon Press, New York, Volume 7, p.828.

the church using the story for symbolic and didactic purposes? I will argue that misreading stories about Jesus is an industry. An industry that started with Paul. Mark gives us stories *about* Jesus and the message of Jesus. Paul gives us *his* message about Jesus.

Consider the fig tree from a literary point of view. Jesus teaches his disciples about Endtime: "'Learn a lesson from the fig-tree. When its tender shoots appear and are breaking into leaf, you know that summer is near. In the same way, when you see all this [a set of eschatological signs] happening, you may know that the end is near, at the very door.'" Just as leaves signal spring and summer, so do the signs of darkened sun and moon, falling stars and celestial explosions signal Endtime, when the mighty Son of Man will arrive in "great power and glory" and "gather his chosen." Jesus goes on to say, "I tell you this: the present generation will live to see it all. (Mark 13.30) Because Endtime is imminent he warns his disciples to 'Keep Awake.' The specific signs that Jesus says will be present right before Endtime also include these:

> When you hear the noise of battle near at hand and the news of battles far away, do not be alarmed. Such things are bound to happen; but the end is still to come. For nation will make war upon nation, kingdom upon kingdom; there will be earthquakes in many places; there will be famines. With these things the birth-pangs of the new age begin. (Mark 13.7-9)

Some of these warnings seem to relate to the destruction of Jerusalem in the first century of the common era, while some sound as if they warn of the end of history. Mark, of course, writes after the Second Temple destruction and would be in a position to know what was going to happen after the time period covered in the narrative. Prophesying after the fact is as good a "prediction" as one can get. In terms of valuable predictors these signs just will not do. They are too vague to pick out any particular time just because they pick out almost any time. What generation goes by without experiencing widespread wars, natural disasters, and famines? Taken as a literal prediction these words are just useless. But from a narrative point of view they function to warn us as readers of the impending doom of the final conflict in the life of the hero, Jesus. Such ominous signs are often found in works of art signalling a dramatic change in the fortunes of the hero. Shakespeare has celestial storms in *Julius Caesar* which work to heighten the tension in the play. Modern movies use thunder storms or lightening flashes whenever the bad guy is about to show up.

"Keep Awake." Be prepared. Endtime is approaching. Learn from the fig-tree - not only that you can tell what season it is by the growth of the tree, but also learn from that specific fig-tree, that one which one day in leaf, was the next day dead. One day it was alive; the next day it was dead. The moment of death for each one of us also is unknown. We know that we will die but we know not the hour or the day.

The anger that Jesus exhibits by withering the fig tree and chasing the money lenders out of the temple unites him with Old Testament prophets. They too exhibited anger, whether it was Samuel chopping up Agag or Elisha killing forty-two boys for ridiculing his bald head. Jesus is cut of the same narrative material as Samuel, Elijah, Elisha, and Ezekiel. He performs miracles: he raises the dead, he casts out devils, he heals, and he feeds multitudes with very little food. Like Ezekiel he is called the Son of Man. As Mark's narrative continues we see the climax of the cluster of images that have to do with the fig tree. Anger first exhibited when a fig tree did not have fruit on it for the hungry man-god to eat, will now be shown one more time in the scene at the place called Gethsemane. There Jesus asks Peter, James, and John to wait for him while he, overcome with "horror and dismay," goes on a way up the path to pray. "Stop here, and *stay awake*" [emphasis God's], he orders his disciples. Jesus goes on ahead and "threw himself on the ground" and asks for the hour to pass him by. He comes back to find his disciples asleep. In anger and disappointment he shouts, "Were you not able to stay awake for one hour?" And then orders, "Stay awake, all of you."

Yet a second time he goes off to pray and when he returns they are asleep again. When asked why they could not stay awake, "they did not know how to answer him."

The third time we sense a dramatic shift in tone. Upon his return Jesus says quietly, "Still sleeping? Still taking your ease? Enough. The hour has come." (Mark 14.41)

Anger and frustration shown in the fig tree story, the temple story, and in the Gethsemane story are finally washed away by the prayer and by the act of accepting his own death. "The hour has come." There is a quiet resolution in that sentence. Acceptance has replaced anger and now Jesus can complete his destiny. Until one has accepted one's own mortality, accepted death in a personal and lucid sense, one cannot live. Thus Jesus teaches us: there is life in death. Death, as the poet Wallace Stevens reminds us, "is the mother of beauty."

Most contemporary scholars agree that the gospels were not written by eyewitnesses of the ministry of Jesus. Some would argue that the reason for this is that Jesus never existed.[2] The internal evidence is confusing and the external evidence is sketchy. We simply do not know who wrote them and when we speak of "Matthew," "Mark," "Luke," and "John" we do so only for convenience (and because of tradition); the actual names of the evangelists are forever lost to us. The gospels were written in the period between 70 and 100, forty years or more after the crucifixion, and we believe that they originally circulated anonymously. The gospels of Matthew, Mark, and Luke are usually called the synoptic gospels from the Greek, *synoptikos - seeing the whole together*. The relationship among the synoptic gospels is a complex one and 19th century scholars learned much of the pattern of inter-relatedness from a careful reading and comparison of the texts. B. F. Wescott, for example, calculated the percentages of shared textual material and suggested that the narrative material is distributed as follows:

	Peculiar	Shared
Mark	7%	93%
Matthew	42%	58%
Luke	59%	41%
John	92%	8%

Comparing the synoptics on the same event can be revealing:

Then Jesus arrived at the Jordan from Galilee, and came to John to be baptized by him. John tried to dissuade him. 'Do you come to me?' he said; 'I need rather to be baptized by you.' Jesus replied, 'Let it be so for the present; we do well to conform in this way with all that god requires.' John then allowed him to come. After baptism Jesus came up out of the water at once, and at that moment heaven opened; he saw the Spirit of God descending like a

---

[2] See, e.g., the excellent debate between Gary Habermas and Antony Flew in *Did Jesus Rise From the Dead? - The Resurrection Debate*, edited by Terry L. Miethe, Harper and Row, San Francisco, 1987.

dove to alight upon him; and a voice from heaven was heard saying, 'This is my Son, my Beloved, on whom my favour rests.' (Matt. 3.13-17)

It happened at this time that Jesus came from Nazareth in Galilee and was baptized in the Jordan by John. At the moment when he came up out of the water, he saw the heavens torn open and the Spirit, like a dove, descending upon him. And a voice spoke from heaven: 'Thou art my Son, my Beloved; on thee my favour rests. (Mark 1.9-11)

During a general baptism of the people, when Jesus too had been baptized and was praying, heaven opened and the Holy Spirit descended on him in bodily form like a dove; and there came a voice from heaven, 'Thou art my Son, my beloved, on thee my favour rests.' (Luke 3. 21-22)

Looking at these passages closely we see that Matthew and Mark can agree against Luke, and Mark and Luke can agree against Matthew, but Matthew and Luke do not agree against Mark. In Matthew and Mark Jesus came from Galilee, but this is not mentioned in Luke. The voice from heaven says, 'Thou art my Son, my beloved, on thee my favour rests' in Mark and Luke, but 'This is my Son, my Beloved, on whom my favour rests' in Matthew. As far as the order of events in the narrative is concerned Matthew and Mark can agree against Luke and Luke and Mark against Matthew, but Matthew and Luke never agree against Mark. This pattern is observable throughout the gospels and leads to the hypothesis that the gospel of Mark was written first and that Matthew and Luke have both used it as a source. In addition sections of Matthew and Luke are so close verbally that they must be using a common source, but that source cannot be Mark since he does not have these sections. Compare for example:

When he saw many of the Pharisees and Sadducees coming for baptism he said to them: 'You vipers' brood! Who warned you to escape from the coming retribution? Then prove your repentance by the fruit it bears; and do not presume to say to yourselves, "We have Abraham for our father." I tell you that God can make children for Abraham out of these stones here. Already the axe is laid to the roots of the trees; and every tree that fails to produce good fruit is cut down and thrown on the fire. (Matt. 3.7-10)

Crowds of people came out to be baptized by him, and he said to them: 'You vipers' brood! Who warned you to escape from the coming retribution? Then prove your repentance by the fruit it bears; and do not begin saying to yourselves, "We have Abraham for our father." I tell you that God can make children for Abraham out of these stones here. Already the axe is laid to the roots of the trees; and every tree that fails to produce good fruit is cut down and thrown on the fire.' (Luke 3.7-9)

This common material is almost always "teaching material." The constant appearance of parallel passages in Matthew and Luke has led to the conclusion that they have a source in common in addition to the gospel of Mark, a source consisting of mostly "sayings" material. In addition they each have special material unique to each writer. The common sources for Matthew and Luke are thus believed to be Mark and some unknown manuscript called simply "Q".[3] Each of Matthew and Luke have special material that is unique to it. In addition each writer can make a unique contribution by the way he chooses to tell the story. One branch of biblical criticism (redaction criticism) suggests that we should emphasize the contribution made by the final writer. Look again at Mark 1.9-11 and Luke 3.21-22. In Luke's version all the emphasis is on the descent of the spirit on Jesus. His baptism has become one of the three circumstances (a general baptism, his baptism, the fact that he was praying) that set the stage for the descent of the spirit, whereas in Mark the baptism and the descent of the spirit are equally significant.

Or, again, notice that Mark and Matthew mention the thieves who were crucified with Jesus, but say nothing of one of them being saved and one being damned. Luke, however, tells us that one of the thieves asserts his belief at the final moment and is saved. This has become the story most of us remember. Luke's editorial emphasis has significantly changed the material presented in Mark and repeated in Matthew.

The Old Testament takes the Hebrews through the Red Sea into the wilderness and finally to the promised land, while the New Testament takes the individual from baptism into the wilderness to the resurrection. The New

---

[3] Q probably comes from "quelle" the German word for "source."

Testament attempts through its stories to universalize the nature of God while at the same time making the necessary covenant sign of baptism an individual and not a societal agreement. For the Old Testament Hebrews there was the wilderness and the promised land of milk and honey. For Paul and the first Christians there were hell and heaven as the two conditions promised for those not chosen and those chosen. The four gospels proclaim the constitutive rules of the new religion, each with a different emphasis, but all asserting the basic proposition of a man-god, crucifixion, and redemption, in some form or another. John provides us with a mystical interpretation of the new religion and emphasizes the fulfillment of the prophesies in the Old Testament by using or alluding to some twenty-five quotations from the early books. Mark is the most apocalyptic in his presentation of the last days insisting more than the others that all will occur within his generation. Matthew emphasizes the church as the living institution through which God is calling the peoples of the world to repentance and faith. For him Jesus is the final agent of mediation between the divine and the vulgar. Luke and Matthew provide us with birth narratives for Jesus while Mark has none. John was probably written by a committee. Luke is a compilation of material from many sources but probably written by one writer. Luke opens with the Zechariah and Elizabeth story which no one else reports. It is a parallel to the Elkanah and Hannah story that we read in Samuel. John will play Samuel to Jesus's Saul in the story told by Luke. The cleansing of the Temple which is the last straw for the leaders of Jerusalem and the next to last angry act of Jesus in Mark's story is placed at the beginning of Jesus's career in John. John's work comes out of a Hellenistic world view and unlike Mark John offers a reading which says that the judgment is not something that has already fallen, nor is it something that will come in the last days, but it is what occurs to an individual in the moment that individual makes the decision of faith in Jesus the Son of God. For John history has been internalized and judgment has been transformed to the present moment of "decision" of faith. John's Jesus says "I am the resurrection and I am life," and "I am the good shepherd," and "I am what I am." Mark's "who am I?" has become "I am...". John's Jesus is not really a historical figure at all, but "lives" in a context of eternity, while Mark's story is of a man on this earth. John's Jesus says "Now my soul is in turmoil, and what am I to say? 'Father, save me from this hour.' No, it was for this that I came to this hour. Father, glorify thy name." Mark's Jesus says, "Abba, Father, all things are possible to thee; take this cup away from me."

Matthew presents the story especially addressed to the Jews in an effort to prove that Jesus was the Messiah whom they had expected while Luke aims his text primarily at the Greeks and Romans, and John argues that Jesus was not only the human Messiah expected by the Jews but also the divine Son of God, the redeemer not only of the Jewish peoples but also of the fallen world. His doctrine of the Logos or Word is established in his prologue. John's reinterpretation and rearrangement of the events in the other stories is aimed at showing that the Word in the Old Testament is fulfilled in the Jesus as redeemer myth. He uses "scripture is fulfilled", "scripture says", and "in order that it might be fulfilled" as introductory phrases time after time.

One good reason to read Mark first is that there are good reasons to believe that Mark's gospel was written several years before Luke and Matthew wrote. Another good reason to read Mark first is that he creates a new literary form: the gospel. Like other new genres, the gospel both builds on existing forms and strikes out in new directions. Mark is obviously influenced by the apocalyptic writings of the first century B.C.E., writings which describe in symbolic language the coming of divine power to cleanse the earth of corruption and to restore the "kingdom" to the chosen people who had been faithful to the covenant. Mark makes it clear in several places that the imminent power of the divine is about to explode into history. In fact, it is hard to see how Christianity could have survived the generation for which Mark wrote without the interpretive work done by Paul and published in his letters. Mark's Jesus says clearly that all will come to pass within a short time. As Kee puts it, "the reality of Jesus Christ was to be sought in the church's preaching, not in the historian's reconstruction of who he was."[5] In other words, Christianity has from the beginning depended upon an *interpretation* of a story, a reading of a life.

Mark's story may be, as Kee says, "a propaganda writing produced by and for a community that made no cultural claims for itself and offered its writings as a direct appeal for adherents rather than as a way of attracting the attention of intellectuals or literati of the day."[6] But it is also a sophisticated and well crafted work. Although it does not present argument for its proclamations it does present the proclamations with the authority and credibility

---

[5] Kee, *op.cit.*, page 33.
[6] Kee, *op. cit.* page 138.

that comes from the literary devices employed. Mark's story *sounds* true. Read it aloud; you cannot miss the"back to the wall" truth-telling tone. It is there in the first line, "Here begins the gospel of Jesus...." It is there in the transitions: "It happened at this time", "After John had been arrested...", "Very early next morning...", "that evening after sunset...", "When after some days he returned...". It is there in the "facts": "John was dressed in a rough coat of camel's hair...and he fed on locusts and wild honey." "So they opened up the roof over the place where Jesus was, and when they had broken through they lowered the bed on which the paralyzed man was lying." The first gives us particulars that identify John and fix him forever in our literary history. The second draws upon an intimate knowledge of the beds and houses of that time and place. Mark also tells us that Jesus's sanity was questioned, that he was misunderstood, dismissed, and ridiculed. What better way to convince readers of his overall veracity than to be specific and concrete with his examples? If this is propaganda let it be understood as first rate propaganda. Mark is an artist. Look at the beginning and ending of his story: the first image is one of flocks of people coming to John at the Jordan to be baptized, and the last image is the empty tomb. He opens with hundreds of people looking to be "saved," searching for some meaning in their lives. And he ends with the promise signalled by the empty tomb. Could this image have within it the answer to the needs expressed by the flocks of people at the beginning? Mark gives us the hint, the mystery, and the fear: "They said nothing to anybody, for they were afraid." The perfect ending for his story. But, of course, someone has added verses 9-20, the resurrection stories, to ruin the artistry of Mark with the didacticism of the official line.

The struggle between Saul and Samuel, which was the struggle between king and prophet, is repeated in the suggested struggle between John and Jesus, but is resolved in the figure of the character Jesus. He is a merging of the kingly figure and the priestly figure. Jesus has the authority and charisma of David, the super natural powers of Samuel (who also returns from the dead), and the mission and focus of Elisha. He, like Moses, is a composite character who embodies the virtues of the leaders from priestly and monarchic traditions. Add to that the frustrations and anticipations of a people once more under the power of conquerors with different gods and the time for Endtime is ripe. The story is familiar to us: a people is under the oppressive power of a rich and powerful nation; their god is challenged by another divine figure who has earthly power, they desperately need a leader to take them out of their slavery, to deliver them from evil. But now it is the Romans, not the Egyptians, who have brought their god into Palestine in the form of Caesar. The Hebrews anxiously await the next chapter in the covenant story.

Mark's Jesus arrives as one of the multitude of people seeking baptism from John. The Red Sea, which separated the Hebrews from the Egyptians, is replaced by the River Jordan, and baptism becomes the sign of the new covenant. Water, to wash away the sins of the past, is the perfect image for conversion with its cleansing, life-sustaining, and purifying powers. While Saul was picked out of the crowd by being a head taller than everyone else, Jesus is picked out as special because he is ordinary. John recognizes him as special in the story, and the specialness is shown by the image of the descending dove and the voice which speaks to Jesus in a private word from the heavens: "Thou art my Son, my Beloved; on thee my favour rests." These signs serve the same narrative function as did the burning bush in the Moses story, the ladder in Jacob's dream, the fire in the Samson story, or the small still voice that Ezekiel hears: they identify and empower the hero. Known only to the prophet (and the reader) these signs indicate to the individual a connection with the Other and the beginning of a special quest. These private signs (the call) will now become public in the narrative form of miracles which are the authenticating images of the authority given to the hero. The result will be shown in the response of the immediate audience which serves as witness to the events, and who will attest, "Never before have we seen the like."

What is unique about this hero's story? He shares much with earlier heroes. he performs healing miracles, but so did Elisha. He can control natural forces, but so did Moses. He can change water to wine, but Elisha could change putrid water to potable water. Jesus feeds multitudes, but others have done that also. He comes back from the dead, but Samuel was called up from the dead earlier. He teaches in parables, but Nathan did that too. Jesus walks on water; Elisha made an iron axe float on water. The miracles performed by Jesus are of a kind with those performed by other prophets. He is the word incarnate, but so was Ezekiel. He will be raised to heaven, but so was Elijah. He is thought to be out of his mind, but Samuel was often in a state of rapture. What then is unique about Jesus? Mark tells us nothing of his birth, does not mention anything about a supernatural birth at all; and though Matthew and Luke do provide birth narratives, these too are familiar to us from the birth of Isaac to the birth of Samuel. Two of the most dramatic healing miracles in Mark are found in the giving of sight to the blind man from Bethsaida and later to blind Bartimaeus. In both cases these stories come at a time when

Jesus has been trying to explain something to his obtuse disciples. He asks them to recognize the truth in a story he tells them, to *read* his sayings as he intends them, and they fail miserably as readers. But how does one read the intention of the gods? That is the story of these stories. Jesus asks his disciples to recognize truth in his stories and they fail. After each failure a blind man is suddenly given sight and can see. "Do you still not understand? Are your minds closed? You have eyes; can you not see?" are questions Jesus asks his disciples in frustration when they are unable to understand what his mission is, what knowledge he has that they can not re-cognize. One's sympathy is with the students here. The lesson is not all that clear.

Is the "lesson" not clear because Jesus is not a good teacher? No, he is usually patient and repetitive, only rarely chastising his students with the lash of rhetorical questions: 'Are your minds closed?' 'Can you not see?' What teacher has not used these very questions of frustration? Shortly after restoring the sight of the blind man at Bethsaida Jesus asks his disciples "Who do men say that I am?" and after getting several answers - John the Baptist, Elijah, one of the prophets - he asks Peter, "Who do you say that I am?" Peter replies: "You are the Messiah." Peter's eyes are opened. He can see. The narrative reveals in its form a "truth" that it wants to proclaim: the true identity of the hero, who in most hero narratives is of humble birth, a king hidden as a commoner. All of the ocular imagery in the story functions to serve the idea of seeing the "truth" which is hidden behind or under some appearance or other and must be pierced by sight or in-sight in order to be understood. The hero must be recognized. Secrecy, one of Mark's main themes, must be pierced at some point in the story and the hero recognized for who he really is - the recognition scene announced by Peter is consummated in the transfiguration where Jesus appears on a mountain top with the spirits of Moses and Elijah. The voice, private at the river, is now public, "This is my Son, my Beloved; listen to him." Peter, James, and John, we are told, are witnesses to this scene of the confirmation of the hero by the divine. Those who might think that Jesus is Moses are shown to be wrong for there he is with Moses. Those who might think he is Elijah are shown to be wrong for there he is with Elijah. In typical Markan strategy the truth, hidden in secrecy, is revealed to a small audience, and in the telling of that story, revealed to us as readers. This literary strategy reveals also a perception about the nature of truth. It says truth is hidden behind appearances, sometimes revealed, objective, god-given, magical, and beyond unaided humans. Jesus, who like Ezekiel, embodies the Word or Logos, is the messenger of God's word, bringing glimpses of another level of reality to his disciples. There is a tension in Mark between this supernatural messenger and the developing man-character called Jesus. The interesting side of Mark's Jesus is his human side: changing, frustrated, seeking, loving, talking, teaching, human Jesus. It is here that we find his uniqueness; it is here that we "see" his lesson.

But, of course, this reading is not the *official line*. Believers have from the gospels on proclaimed that Jesus was the Christ, the son of God, sent to establish a new covenant with the people who will believe and be baptized. He is proclaimed to be a god. But that is not unique. Every Caesar was also so proclaimed. Osiris, Tammuz, Adonis, Dionysus, and Mithras all died for the sins of the people. They also had cults which grew around them which included ceremonies like baptism to symbolize rebirth, and communion to symbolize unity with the redeemer-god. They also talked of redemption and a pain free life in the future. One cult grew up around Attis and Cybele. Its followers celebrated a Day of Blood in the month of March each year. At that time they hanged Attis in effigy to a tree where he bled to death. Then they took his "body" into a burial place and for several days mourned his passing. At the end of the mourning period the proclamation was made that Attis had risen from the dead, and the people rejoiced and celebrated this victory over death. Redeemers and saviour-gods were not unique to the time. Jesus is unique; Christ is not. Dr. Crane puts it this way:

> Jesus taught that we should love our enemies; Christ walked on water. Jesus taught that we should not judge others, should forgive them; Christ turned water into wine. Jesus taught that the kingdom of God is within us; Christ raised Lazarus from the dead. Jesus taught that we should not lay up treasures for ourselves on earth; Christ fed the multitude with a few loaves and fishes. Jesus was a charismatic human being; Christ is a saviour, a messiah - an ancient idea. Created by humanity.[8]

There is a sense in which Jesus is a model for human beings to follow. He was a man of his time who held the assumptions and beliefs of his era. He is portrayed as a charismatic man who lived with intense purpose and drive, who had an existential thrust to his life, who cared deeply about human beings,

---

[8] "The Limitations of Christ," Dr. John Alexie Crane, from *Reflections on the Nature of Things*, Volume IV, Number 9, Jefferson Unitarian Church, Golden, Colorado.

and who wrestled with profound questions of ethics. The stories that grew up around him have affected the world for two thousand years and have touched the deepest parts of our humanity with their simplicity of image and their promise of "salvation".

Several years before the gospel stories were written down another hero appears on the scene to spread the gospel and to deal with the many questions of meaning asked by the early Christians. This "first Christian" is Paul. He provides us with the only written documents about Christianity for the period between 30 and 70 BCE. His letters provide a reading of the spiritual life and teachings of Jesus and are extremely important in establishing the doctrines of early Christianity. Like Moses before him, Paul is a hero who comes from the inner circle of the "enemy". While Moses was raised in Pharaoh's household only later to find his call in the desert experience with Yahweh, Paul is a Roman Jew who is working with alacrity to wipe out Christianity when he has his conversion experience on the road to Damascus.

> Meanwhile Saul was still breathing murderous threats against the disciples of the Lord. He went to the High Priest and applied for letters to the synagogues at Damascus authorizing him to arrest anyone he found, men or women, who followed the new way, and bring them to Jerusalem. While he was still on the road and nearing Damascus, suddenly a light flashed from the sky all around him. He fell to the ground and heard a voice saying, 'Saul, Saul, why do you persecute me?' 'Tell me. Lord,' he said, 'who you are.' The voice answered, 'I am Jesus, whom you are persecuting. But get up and go into the city, and you will be told what you have to do.' Meanwhile the men who were travelling with him stood speechless; they heard the voice but could see no one. Saul got up from the ground, but when he opened his eyes he could not see; so they led him by the hand and brought him into Damascus. He was blind for three days, and took no food or drink. (Acts 9.1-9)

Saul, the persecutor of Christians, will now become the "chosen instrument" to spread the story of Christianity to the nations and the kings and the people of Israel. Saul of Tarsus, converted to the very doctrine he had been attempting to stamp out, is now renamed Paul, baptized in the name of Christ, and sent out to spread the "good news" which he took on that day on the road to Damascus. And as we have seen so many times in these stories the change of direction in his life is signalled by a change in name. The conversion story is an important introduction for this hero and as we might expect it is told more than once. A bit later (Acts 22.6-10) Paul tells the story in first person:

> I was on the road to Damascus, when suddenly about midday a great light flashed from the sky all around me, and I fell to the ground. Then I heard a voice saying to me, "Saul, Saul, why do you persecute me?" I answered, "Tell me, Lord, who you are." "I am Jesus of Nazareth," he said, "whom you are persecuting." My companions saw the light, but did not hear the voice that spoke to me. "What shall I do, Lord?"

As we have seen so often before when reading about heroes in the biblical stories, the details in the two versions are different. In one the fellow travellers see the light but hear no voice, in the other they see nothing but hear the voice. The importance to the story of this experience, however, is clear: Paul is authenticated as a hero by a conversion experience with the divine force which speaks to him and gives him a task to perform in the midst of great danger. It is puzzling why the writer, presumably Luke, did not make the necessary changes to the text to provide consistency. One possible explanation is to speculate that the first person account was extant in a letter and thus could not be changed, while Luke at the same time could see the problem with the first person account. That is, in Paul's account if the light blinded him then why did it not blind the observers who witnessed the light? But whatever the case, part of the resolution of the problem comes from a realization that this is a story and that it follows certain patterns and images. Paul is blinded. How does that function in the story? He is blinded to the old ways, and after a period of time (three days) he is brought back whole, and with a new commitment to Christianity. One of the other fascinating "meanings" present in the conversion of Paul story is the example it establishes: if one who is persecuting Christians can be converted and saved then clearly anyone can be converted and saved. The form of the story carries the content of the doctrine of universality.

Paul is a Jew born in Tarsus, raised in Jerusalem, educated under the tutelage of Gamaliel, a Pharisee, and a Roman citizen. He died, according to tradition, in Rome under Nero in the early 60's. He never read the gospels, did not meet Jesus, and never once in his writings refers to Jesus's miraculous birth or to his miracles. Paul represents Jesus as the second Adam (Acts 5.12-19), concentrates on the spiritual side of the man-god, and argues for three important constitutive rules of the new religion: (1) monotheism, (2) universalism, and (3) grace. Paul is perhaps best considered as the first Christian missionary, if not the first Christian. He is interested in the spread of the new religion from Jerusalem to Judea, Samaria, Syria, Asia Minor, Macedonia, Greece, and finally all the way to Rome. While the Jewish Christians continued to believe that Jesus was the long promised Messiah, whose ministry, death, and resurrection signalled the beginning of the final age of history, Paul concentrated his efforts on converting pagans to the new religion. He emphasizes the resurrection of Jesus above all else, and his message is one of the imminence of the new age with the urgency for spreading the good news obviously increased by not knowing exactly when the return of the Lord will occur. For the Jewish Christian Jesus was a human selected by God to be the Messiah, while for Paul Jesus was divine from the beginning.

Paul's letters give a picture of a dedicated missionary who travels all over the middle east to proselytize for the new religion. But he does much more than proselytize, he also establishes rules for the religion as the need for them arises. Time after time he proclaims and stipulates what the new religion will be, often in answer to specific questions or problems raised by a specific congregation. He addresses the congregation in Corinth with a letter which appeals to them to stop their bickering and squabbling about who is the first among the missionaries:

> I appeal to you, my brothers, in the name of our Lord Jesus Christ: agree among yourselves, and avoid divisions; be firmly joined in unity of mind and thought. I have been told, my brothers, by Chloe's people that there are quarrels among you. What I mean is this: each of you is saying, 'I am Paul's man,' or 'I am for Appollos'; 'I follow Cephas', or 'I am Christ's.' Surely Christ has not been divided among you! (1 Cor. 1.10-13)

The human propensity for quarreling is manifest here. One man fights with another over which person baptized him, or over the ranking of the officials within the church. The residue of thousands of years of belief in the divisive doctrine of "chosenness" is impossible to erase. Although Paul is certainly a monotheistic universalist himself, the proclamation that all shall be welcome into the new religion is met with opposition and concern by the newly converted. The strong belief that one's tribe has been chosen by the "true" god for some manifest destiny rings out across the centuries, and it often rings out from a killing field where the proclamation is tested, where the gods of one's fathers must meet in combat to determine who is chosen. (Any solution to the deep conflicts in the Middle East today seems highly unlikely as long as the religious claims of all participants are based on the strongly held belief that each is the chosen representative of the only true god.) Paul's first letter, "The First Letter of Paul to the Thessalonians" allows us to draw certain conclusions about the problems that were arising in the congregations some twenty years after the ministry of Jesus. A big puzzle for all was what was to happen to Christians who die before the return of the Lord. How were they to become apart of the new covenant, the new order? It was a problem, one imagines, because the second-coming was not on schedule, was not as quick as expected. Paul assures the congregation in the letter that the Christian dead will rise and join the other Christians "up in the clouds." As we have seen in Mark there is a strong belief in the impending return of Jesus as divine ruler of the new kingdom. Another set of problems faced by Paul also have the second-coming as their source: if Jesus as Messiah/Redeemer is returning to the earth to redress injustice and bring about the new order, and if this occurrence is imminent, then why should anyone continue to pay attention to the matters of the world? Why, indeed, should one work or plan for the future in any way at all? Paul is uncertain about the time of the Parousia[9] saying only that "the Day of the Lord comes like a thief in the night." But he is certain about how one must conduct oneself while waiting for the second coming. "You must abstain from fornication," he says, and "you must learn to gain mastery over your body." In a second letter to the Thessalonians[10] Paul orders that "the man who will not work shall not eat," an injunction which suggests that many were not working but "idling their time away" while waiting for Godot.

Romans, as the headnote in the *New English Bible* says, "contains the fullest and most balanced statement of his [Paul's] theology." And what is the centre of this theology? In a word *grace*. It is by means of God's grace, Paul argues, that righteousness and eternal life enter in to the sinful world. "God's act of grace," he writes, "is out of all proportion to Adam's

---

[9] The future coming of Christ.

[10] There is some debate about whether Paul actually wrote 2 Thessalonians. The theme and style do not strike all scholars as similar enough to be a genuine Pauline letter. I think that the insistence of authenticity at the end of 2 Thessalonians, "The greeting is in my own hand, signed with my name, PAUL; this authenticates all my letters; this is how I write," suggests that the letter is a forgery. Why else insist on its authenticity?

wrongdoing." The wrongdoing of Adam brought sin and death, but the grace of God brought Jesus the Messiah who brings acquittal to all of humankind. Believe and you will be saved. Paul emphasizes the importance of love in the life of the Christian, and insists upon the doctrine of grace. He attempts to upset the idea of a chosen people, not by arguing, as I would,[11] that its consequences are disastrous, but by proclaiming a different point of view as true. "For God has no favourites," he writes, "so my gospel states." No circumcision is required; no special dietary rules are proscribed in this new religion. These are external marks and the true circumcision, Paul proclaims, "is of the heart." His new religion will embrace those Jews who will be baptized and will also reach out beyond the tribes to all the peoples who will listen and believe. Paul's story is one of a man driven by a religious call to spread the news to all of the peoples of the region in order to assure that they will be aware of the new dispensation from God. But Paul, like Mark, seems to believe that the Endtime is right around the corner, and that the return of the Lord to rule the world is imminent. That belief in the imminence of the second coming is the constant throughout Christian history. How Christianity continued to flourish past the first century CE is a puzzle to non-believers and a testimony to the power of the institution called the church and the irrationality of human beings as soon as they enter the arena of religion.

The Jesus of the synoptic gospels is comprised largely of "snapshots." We see him through the lenses of three different artists, each with his own set of intentions and his own sense of audience. We see him during about one hundred days of his life, performing miracles, healing, and teaching. We know almost nothing of him outside of the New Testament stories; we cannot say with any certainty that he even existed outside of those stories. What we read of him in the gospels is quite different from what Paul tells us through his letters. In a sense the Jesus of the church or churches is a Pauline fabrication: the living, feeling, shouting man of Mark's stories, who can destroy a fig tree, clean out a temple, and throw himself to the ground in despair, has become a spiritual and conceptual isolate in Paul's theological discourse. The Old

---

[11] The war raging in the Persian Gulf as I write can be seen as a clash between and among God's chosen peoples. Each people seems to believe that God has chosen them for some reason or other to be a special repository of God's intentions and plans. As we have seen time after time the stories of the bible show us what happens when someone is chosen for special treatment for absolutely no reason.

Testament begins with "In the beginning..." and the New Testament ends with "Amen. Come, Lord Jesus!" as a hopeful reply to the last voice in the narrative, that of the character, Jesus, who speaks "Yes, I am coming soon!"

From beginning to end we have lingered in these stories for some time; their power will continue to serve them, and you, well, in the ongoing human story.

Alter, Robert, *The Art of Biblical Narrative*, Basic Books Inc., New York, 1981, p. 32.

Auden, W. H., *The Dyer's Hand*, Random House, New York, 1962, p. 4.

Auerbach, Erich, *Mimesis*, Doubleday Anchor books, New York, 1957, p. 4.

Brams, Steven J., *Biblical Games: A Strategic Analysis of Stories in the Old Testament*, MIT Press, Cambridge, Mass., 1980, p. 36.

Bright, John, *A History of Israel*, 3rd edition, Westminster Press, Philadelphia, 1981, p. 120.

Campbell, Joseph, *The Masks of God: Primitive Mythology*, The MacMillan Company of Canada, 1968.

Crane, John A., "The Limitations of Christ," *Reflections on the Nature of Things*, volume iv, number 9, Jefferson Unitarian Church, Golden, Colorado.

Dever, William G., "Archaeology and the Bible," *Biblical Archaeology Review*, May/June 1990, p. 52ff.

Frost, Robert, *The Poetry of Robert Frost*, Holt, Rinehart, Winston, New York, 1969, p. 484-5.

Fry, Christopher, *The Firstborn,* Oxford University Press, London, 1952, p. 34.

Frye, Northrop, *The Great Code: The Bible and Literature*, Harcourt, Brace, Jovanovich, New york and London, 1982, p. 3.

Graff, Gerald, *Literature Against Itself*, University of Chicago Press, Chicago and London, 1979, p. 199.

Greenberg, Moshe, *The Hab / piru*, American Oriental Society, New Haven, 1955.

Gwilt, J. R., "Biblical ills and remedies," *Journal of the Royal Society of Medicine,* vol. 79, dec. 1986.

Hooke, S. H., *In the Beginning*, Clarendon Press, Oxford, 1947.

Hume, David, *An Enquiry Concerning Human Understanding,* Open Court, Chicago, 1912, section 12.

Holland, R. F., "The Miraculous," *American Philosophical Quarterly*, 1965, 2:43-51.

Kiekegaard, Soren, *Fear and Trembling and The Sickness Unto Death*, translated by Walter Lowrie, Princeton University Press, Princeton, p. 15.

Leach, Edmund, *Genesis as Myth and Other Essays*, Jonathan Cape, 1969, London, p. 5.

McConnell, Frank, editor, *The Bible and the Narrative Tradition*, Oxford University Press, 1986.

MacKenzie, R. A. F., *Faith and History in the Old Testament*, University of Minnesota Press, Minneapolis, 1963, p. 39-40.

Mendenhall, George E., *Law and Covenant in Israel and the Ancient Near East*, The Biblical Colloquium, Pittsburgh, 1955, p. 30.

Miethe, T. L., editor, *Did Jesus Rise from the Dead?*, Harper and Row, San Francisco, 1987.

Miller, J. Maxwell, *The Old Testament and the Historian*, Fortress Press, Philadelphia, 1973, p. 7.

Minton, A. J. and Shipka, T. A., editors, *Philosophy: Paradox and Discovery*, McGraw Hill, Inc., 1984.

Mollenkott, Virginia Ramey, *The Divine Feminine*, Crossroad Press, New York, 1981.

Murray, John Courtney, *The Problem of God*, Yale University Press, New Haven and London, 1964, p. 8-9.

Myers, Allen C., editor, *The Eerdmans Bible Dictionary*, William B. Eerdmans Publishing Company, Grand Rapids, Michigan.

Noth, Martin, *The History of Israel*, Harper and Row, New York, 1958, p. 415.

Penelhum, Terence, editor, *Faith*, MacMillan Publishing Company, New York, 1989, p. 5.

Swinburne, Richard, editor, *Miracles*, MacMillan Publishing Company, New York, 1990, p. 2.

Wellhausen, Julius, *Prologomena to the History of Israel*, [1878] reprint Gloucester, Mass., 1973, p. 262.

Weiser, Arthur, *The Old Testament: Its Formation and Development*, D. M. Borton, translator, Association Press, New York, 1971.

Weiss, Paul, "God, Job, and Evil," *Commentary*, vol. vi, 1948.

West, James King, *Introduction to the Old Testament*, the MacMillan Company, New York, 1971, p. 5.

Wisdom, John, "Gods," *Proceedings of the Aristotelian Society*, 1944-45.

Wordsworth, William, "A Slumber did my Spirit Seal," *The Norton Anthology of English Literature*, 3rd edition, W. W. Norton and Company, p. 142.

ABOUT THE AUTHOR

Robert D. (Bob) Lane is the Coordinator of Philosophy at Malaspina College in Nanaimo, B. C., Canada. There he teaches a course called Philosophy in Literature: The Bible, and another course in the Old and New Testaments as literary texts in the humanities. Lane was educated at the University of California in Santa Barbara where he studied English and Continental literature. After teaching in Coos Bay, Oregon, as an Assistant Professor of English, he moved to Canada in 1969 when Malaspina College first opened. There he taught introductory English, Survey of English Literature, and Creative Writing. He then studied philosophy at Simon Fraser University and continues to teach in the Philosophy Department. Influenced by Professor Douwe Stuurman, Lane has continued to teach and write in both literature and philosophy.

Born in Denver, Colorado, Lane was raised on a wheat farm in Eastern Colorado by his mother and step-father. At 16 he ran away from home and at 17 was in the United States Marine Corps for a four year hitch. After four years in the marines, served during the Korean war, Lane went to school on the G.I. Bill, starting as an engineering student at the University of Texas. But after hearing T. S. Eliot read his poetry at Southern Methodist University on a rainy night in April he moved to California and changed to a math and later English major.

Lane writes often for the magazine *Humanist in Canada* and is also known as a frequent book reviewer for several papers and magazines. His other interests include medical ethics and he has published in that field as well.

He has been a marine, a service station attendant, a farm hand, a grocery clerk, a personnel supervisor, a junior accountant, an electronics technician, a small press editor, a construction laborer, and an author and teacher. *Reading the Bible: Intention, Text, and Interpretation* is his first book.